Research Series on the Chinese Dream and China's Development Path

Drawing on a large body of empirical studies done over the last two decades, this Series provides its readers with in-depth analyses of the past and present and forecasts for the future course of China's development. It contains the latest research results made by members of the Chinese Academy of Social Sciences. This series is an invaluable companion to every researcher who is trying to gain a deeper understanding of the development model, path and experience unique to China. Thanks to the adoption of Socialism with Chinese characteristics, and the implementation of comprehensive reform and opening-up, China has made tremendous achievements in areas such as political reform, economic development, and social construction, and is making great strides towards the realization of the Chinese dream of national rejuvenation. In addition to presenting a detailed account of many of these achievements, the authors also discuss what lessons other countries can learn from China's experience.

More information about this series at http://www.springer.com/series/13571

Weiguang Wang · Yaming Liu
Editors

Annual Report on China's Response to Climate Change (2017)

Implementing The Paris Agreement

SSAP

Springer

Editors
Weiguang Wang
Chinese Academy of Social Sciences
Beijing, China

Yaming Liu
China Meteorological Administration
Beijing, China

Published with financial support of the Innovation Program of the Chinese Academy of Social Sciences.

ISSN 2363-6866 ISSN 2363-6874 (electronic)
Research Series on the Chinese Dream and China's Development Path
ISBN 978-981-13-9659-5 ISBN 978-981-13-9660-1 (eBook)
https://doi.org/10.1007/978-981-13-9660-1

Jointly published with Social Sciences Academic Press
The print edition is not for sale in China Mainland. Customers from China Mainland please order the print book from: Social Sciences Academic Press.

This Springer imprint is published by the registered company Springer Nature Singapore Pte Ltd.
The registered company address is: 152 Beach Road, #21-01/04 Gateway East, Singapore 189721, Singapore

Series Preface

Since China's reform and opening began in 1978, the country has come a long way on the path of Socialism with Chinese Characteristics, under the leadership of the Communist Party of China. Over 30 years of reform efforts and sustained spectacular economic growth have turned China into the world's second largest economy and wrought many profound changes in Chinese society. These historically significant developments have been garnering increasing attention from scholars, governments, and the general public alike around the world since the 1990s when the newest wave of China studies began to gather steam. Some of the hottest topics have included the so-called China miracle, Chinese phenomenon, Chinese experience, Chinese path, and the Chinese model. Homegrown researchers have soon followed suit. Already hugely productive, this vibrant field is putting out a large number of books each year, with Social Sciences Academic Press alone having published hundreds of titles on a wide range of subjects.

Because most of these books have been written and published in Chinese, however, readership has been limited outside China—even among many who study China—for whom English is still the lingua franca. This language barrier has been an impediment to efforts by academia, business communities, and policy-makers in other countries to form a thorough understanding of contemporary China, of what is distinct about China's past and present may mean not only for her future but also for the future of the world. The need to remove such an impediment is both real and urgent, and the *Research Series on the Chinese Dream and China's Development Path* is my answer to the call.

This series features some of the most notable achievements from the last 20 years by scholars in China in a variety of research topics related to reform and opening. They include both theoretical explorations and empirical studies and cover economy, society, politics, law, culture, and ecology, the six areas in which reform and opening policies have had the deepest impact and farthest reaching consequences for the country. Authors for the series have also tried to articulate their visions of the "Chinese Dream" and how the country can realize it in these fields and beyond.

All of the editors and authors for the *Research Series on the Chinese Dream and China's Development Path* are both longtime students of reform and opening and recognized authorities in their respective academic fields. Their credentials and expertise lend credibility to these books, each of which having been subject to a rigorous peer-review process for inclusion in the series. As part of the Reform and Development Program under the State Administration of Press, Publication, Radio, Film and Television of the People's Republic of China, the series is published by Springer, a Germany-based academic publisher of international repute, and distributed overseas. I am confident that it will help fill a lacuna in studies of China in the era of reform and opening.

Xie Shouguang

Contents

Chapter 1
Implementing the Paris Agreement: Forging Ahead Despite Challenges

Ying Chen and Qingchen Chao

Abstract This paper reviews the developments in and major events associated with global climate change and the international response in 2016 and 2017, briefly analyzes the challenges and opportunities we face when implementing the Paris Agreement, and urges signatories to continue to stay committed.

Keywords Climate change · Paris agreement · International climate governance · 2030 agenda for sustainable development · Belt and road initiative

The Climate Conference held in Paris at the end of 2015 attracted worldwide attention and the *Paris Agreement* ("*Agreement*" hereafter) adopted at the conference set a new milestone for international climate governance. As the *Agreement* entered into force as scheduled on November 4, 2016, less than a year after its adoption, a renewed sense of hope spread across the international community. The focus of international climate negotiations then shifted to technical details of its implementation. In the months that followed, however, instead of substantial progress among signatories toward achieving the targets set out in the *Agreement*, the world saw challenges associated with global climate change become increasingly

---

Ying Chen is Director of the Sustainable Development Office, Institute for Urban and Environmental Studies, Chinese Academy of Social Sciences, and research fellow. Chen's research interests include global environmental governance, environmental economics, and climate change policy. Qingchen Chao is Deputy Director of the National Climate Center, China Meteorological Administration, and research fellow. Chao specializes in climate change policy and air-sea interaction.

Y. Chen (✉)
Sustainable Development Office, Institute for Urban and Environmental Studies, Chinese Academy of Social Sciences, Xiamen, China
e-mail: cy_cass@163.com

Q. Chao
China Meteorological Administration, National Climate Center, Beijing, China
e-mail: chaoqc@cma.gov.cn

W. Wang (ed.), *Annual Report on China's Response to Climate Change (2017)*,
Research Series on the Chinese Dream and China's Development Path,
https://doi.org/10.1007/978-981-13-9660-1_1

severe. Efforts to build a less carbon-dependent economy and to implement the *Agreement* have been hampered by many obstacles. International climate governance has a bumpy road ahead.

1.1 Record-High Climate Change Indicators

In August 2017, the National Oceanic and Atmospheric Administration (NOAA) and the American Meteorological Society (AMS) released the *State of the Climate in 2016*. The annual report pointed out that as many major indicators of climate change, such as land and ocean temperatures, set new historical records, the need to address climate change had never been more urgent. In 2016, the global surface temperature was 0.45–0.56 °C higher than the average level of 1981–2010, going up for the third consecutive year to a new record high. Specifically, this figure is 0.01–0.12 °C higher than that of 2015 and 0.18–0.25 °C higher than that of 2014. Such a high temperature is the result of the combined influence of long-term global warming and a strong El Niño in the first half of the year.

Greenhouse gas (GHG) emissions rose to new highs. In 2016, the concentrations of major GHGs such as CO_2, CH_4 and N_2O in the atmosphere reached new highs. The annual average atmospheric CO_2 concentration reached 402.9 part per million (ppm), surpassing the 400 ppm mark for the first time in the 800,000 years with data available. The annual average atmospheric CO_2 concentration of 2016 was 3.5 ppm higher than that of 2015, which was the largest annual increase observed in the 58 years with data available.

The year 2016 saw more frequent extreme heat warnings. In 2016, high temperatures were frequently reported across the world. Unprecedented high temperatures were observed in both Mexico and India. The northern and eastern parts of the Indian peninsula were hit by a week-long heat wave in April 2016, with temperatures exceeding 111 °K (44 °C), killing 300 people.

Global lower tropospheric temperature exceeded the highest on record. In the region of the atmosphere just above the Earth's surface the global average tropospheric temperature reached new record high, so did the sea surface temperature. Since the 21st century (2000–2016), the growth of the sea surface temperature is much greater than the growth of +1.0 °C between 1950 and 2016.

The global upper ocean heat content was also close to the highest level on record. Globally, the upper ocean contained a bit less heat in 2016 when compared to the record set in 2015, but heat continued to accumulate within the top 700 m of the ocean. Oceans absorb more than 90% of Earth's excess heat as the globe warms up.

The global sea level rose to a new record high, marking the sixth consecutive year of sea level rise. In 2016, the global average sea level was about 82 mm higher than in 1993 when satellite altimeter record started. Over the past two decades, the global sea level has risen at an average rate of about 34 mm per year, with the highest rates of increase observed in the Western Pacific and the Indian Ocean.

Extremes were frequently observed in the global water cycle and precipitation. An increase in the water cycle caused by global warming, combined with strong El Niño, enhanced the variability of precipitation around the world. Meanwhile, warm currents caused by the El Niño in the equatorial Pacific also increased precipitation in some places. For example, repeated heavy flooding was observed in Argentina, Paraguay, and Uruguay. Wetter-than-usual conditions were also reported for Eastern Europe and central Asia. In the United States, the El Niño brought rainfall to California where drought had built up for several years.

The Arctic continued to warm and glaciers shrunk significantly. The average surface temperature of the Arctic was 2.0 °C higher than the average of 1981–2010 and the glaciers had been shrinking for 37 consecutive years. The mass of the Greenland Ice Sheet declined by 341 billion tons in 2016 and the ice cover near the North Pole remains thin and unable to reverse the general trend of melting.

1.2 Frequent Climate-Related Disasters Worldwide

As indicators of global climate change reached new record highs, extreme weather events and climate-related disasters have increased significantly around the world, causing serious losses.

Extreme weather events have increased significantly. According to the *State of the Climate in 2016*, a total of ninety three named tropical storms were formed near the equator in 2016, 13% higher than the 1981–2010 average. Three basins, i.e. the North Atlantic, and eastern and western North Pacific, experienced more tropical storm activities than normal, while the Australian basin had the least active season since 1970. Globally, four tropical cyclones reached the Saffir–Simpson category five intensity level. Climate anomalies were observed across the world. North America was battered by hurricanes, causing huge losses. On August 26, 2017, the Atlantic tropical cyclone Harvey slammed into Texas, causing dozens of deaths and severe flooding in many cities. Harvey is the strongest hurricane hitting the U.S. in twelve years. Less than half a month later, Hurricane Irma raked the Caribbean and landed on the southern coast of the U.S. In addition to causing casualties and property loss to the Caribbean and the southern part of the U.S., the two super-strong hurricanes formed in the Atlantic Ocean also had a huge impact on tourism and the international energy market. Their impact was global. According to a statement issued by the World Meteorological Organization (WMO), human behavior has an impact on the atmospheric water vapor content near the Earth's surface and global warming may lead to more frequent hurricanes.

1.3 Increasing Uncertainties in Global Climate Governance

After the Paris Agreement entered into force, many believed that disputes over the urgency to address the global climate challenge would temporarily calm down and that the international community would finally unite to implement the Agreement. However, they were soon doused with a harsh dose of reality. A series of policy changes made by the Trump administration after it took office and the reaction of the international community to such changes have increased uncertainties in global climate governance and brought grim challenges.

There has been a major shift in the U.S. climate policy. Since taking office in February 2017, Donald Trump has completely reversed the previous climate change efforts made by the Obama administration by announcing the U.S. exit from the Paris Agreement and eliminating the Clean Power Plan. Although it takes time for the U.S. to complete the legal process of quitting the Paris Agreement, the negative impact of the changes in the U.S. climate policy has been deeply felt across the world. However, it should also be noted that the global trend towards green and low-carbon development is irreversible. Given the complexity of the U.S. domestic political system and the choice of the market, the actual impact of the changes in the U.S. climate policy remains to be seen.

The G20 plays a more important role in global climate governance. The America First stance adopted by the U.S. is shocking and disappointing to the international community but the G20 Summit held in July 2017, despite differences, still brought some exciting news to the world with regard to climate change. At least all G20 members except the U.S. agreed on the *G20 Hamburg Climate and Energy Action Plan for Growth*, showing their commitment to the Paris Agreement.

The BRICS countries have also been active in global climate governance. In September 2017, leaders from BRICS countries issued the Xiamen Declaration at the BRICS Summit held in Xiamen, China, making the commitment "to further promoting green development and low-carbon economy in the context of sustainable development and poverty eradication, enhancing BRICS cooperation on climate change, and expanding green financing," and "calling upon all countries to fully implement the Paris Agreement adopted under the principles of the United Nations Framework Convention on Climate Change (UNFCCC) including the principles of common but differentiated responsibilities and respective capabilities."

1.4 New Opportunities for Global Climate Governance

The UNFCCC is a major platform for climate change negotiations, but the content of global climate governance, which is a broad-based concept, is not limited to UNFCCC. Other international governance processes, such as the 2030 Agenda for

Sustainable Development and the Belt and Road Initiative have created new opportunities for the implementation of the Paris Agreement.

The 2030 Agenda for Sustainable Development: The 2030 Agenda for Sustainable Development, adopted in 2015, and the Paris Agreement are mutually reinforcing, both of holding out common visions that will reshape the world by 2030. Addressing climate change is one of the Sustainable Development Goals (SDGs). Countries are urged to address climate change within the framework of sustainable development. The 2030 Agenda for Sustainable Development and the Paris Agreement are complementary and mutually reinforcing.

The Belt and Road Initiative: In May 2017, the Belt and Road Forum was held in Beijing, China. It deepened the international community's understanding of the Belt and Road Initiative and set off a new round of construction under the framework. The Paris Agreement and the Belt and Road Initiative have a lot in common. To start with, both of the two framework documents push for the transition to green and low-carbon development. Deepening international cooperation on climate change under the framework of the Belt and Road Initiative and advancing the implementation of the 2030 Agenda for Sustainable Development and the Paris Agreement are not only central to China's own Ecological Civilization strategy, but also in line with the interests of countries along the Belt and Road.

1.5 In Pursuit of Green Growth, China

1.5.1 Plays a Leading Role in Global Governance

The Chinese government attaches great importance to tackling climate change and building an "ecological civilization." Committed to pursuing innovative, coordinated, green, open and shared development, it has embarked on a new path of socialism with Chinese characteristics. Currently, China is seeking to achieve its Intended Nationally Determined Contributions (INDCs) by adjusting its economic structure, building a low-carbon energy system, developing green buildings and low-carbon transportation, establishing a national carbon emission trading market, ramping up environmental protection, and promoting the development of the circular economy. In 2016, China's CO_2 emissions per unit of GDP fell by about 43% from 2005, and non-fossil energy consumption accounted for 13.3% of the country's total primary energy consumption. The country has been strengthening environmental protection and transforming environmental benefits into economic benefits in accordance with the green development concept put forward by President Xi Jinping. Take the Saihanba Plantation Forest for example. The project has turned more than 1 million *mu* of barren gobi desert into an oasis by planting trees, effectively improving the environment of the area. In northern China, a coal-to-gas project has been launched in rural areas to reduce carbon emissions and improve air quality. In addition, China is steadily advancing its plan to launch a national carbon emissions trading market in 2017. Meanwhile, the Chinese government has set aside 100 million US dollars for South-South climate cooperation.

China will continue to advance the implementation of the Paris Agreement, work with other members of the international community to gradually step up efforts to address climate change, protect common interests of mankind, lead the international endeavor to address global climate change, actively contribute to global climate governance and push for a new type of international relations featuring win-win cooperation and global development.

1.6 Conclusion

Global climate governance has had a bumpy journey in the past two years. The Paris Agreement is a hard-won achievement and the path towards fulfilling its goals is long and tortuous with all kinds of risks, challenges and opportunities. We firmly believe that the global trend towards green and low-carbon development is irreversible. As a responsible big country, China will not only follow the trend, but also take more initiative and assume more international responsibilities to lead the way forward.

Chapter 2
Storm Resilience of Chinese Cities: Ranking and Analysis

Jianqing Zhai, Yan Zheng and Ying Li

Abstract In recent years, many cities in China have been hit frequently by storms and floods, leading to an increase in the attention of the academic circle and the general public to the resilience of cities. Based on the IPCC climate risk assessment framework, this paper creates a storm resilience index for cities with indicators such as storm disaster risk and city adaptability. It then ranks provincial capitals, municipalities, and pilot cities of the Sponge City Program and the Climate Resilient City Program in China by their storm resilience and divides these cities into the three categories of high-resilience, medium-resilience, and low-resilience cities. The resilience evaluation methods used here and the results thus obtained can be used by researchers and decision-makers to increase public attention to disaster risks faced by large and medium-sized cities in China during the urbanization process across the country.

Keywords Climate change · Storm · Resilient cities

Jianqing Zhai, associate research fellow at the National Climate Center of China, specializing in climate change impact assessment; Yan Zheng, associate research fellow at the Institute for Urban and Environmental Studies, Chinese Academy of Social Sciences, specializing in climate change economics; Ying Li, associate research fellow at the National Climate Center of China, specializing in climate change impact assessment.

J. Zhai (✉) · Y. Li
National Climate Center, China Meteorological Administration, Beijing, China
e-mail: zhaijq@cma.gov.cn

Y. Li
e-mail: sdkdfly@163.com

Y. Zheng
Institute for Urban and Environmental Studies, Chinese Academy of Social Sciences, Xiamen, China
e-mail: zhengy_cass@163.com

W. Wang (ed.), *Annual Report on China's Response to Climate Change (2017)*,
Research Series on the Chinese Dream and China's Development Path,
https://doi.org/10.1007/978-981-13-9660-1_2

2.1 Background

Urban areas are central to the international efforts to tackle climate change. The urbanization rate of China climbed from 18.1% in 1978, when the reform and opening up policy was launched, to 57.4% in 2016, and China's urban population increased from 1.7 billion to 7.9 billion in the meantime. It is estimated that by 2030, the urbanization rate of China will reach 70% and the total urban population will exceed 1 billion. The rapid expansion of cities, the highly concentrated populations, and the high intensity of economic activities all push up the exposure to natural disaster risks. In recent years, Chinese cities have seen an increase in the incidence of new and complex urban disasters such as smog, urban heat islands, typhoons, and urban waterlog. Direct economic losses caused by climate-related disasters in cities and the proportion of such losses in the country's total losses caused by natural disasters are both on the rise. According to China Meteorological Administration, climate change will increase the frequency and intensity of climate-related disasters such as high temperatures, droughts, floods and heavy rains in China and increase safety risks in urban areas.

In order to help cities tackle risks associated with climate change, the international community has proposed the concept of "resilient city." Resilient cities promote a sustainable, holistic and forward-looking urban planning approach based on the resilience theory. Since 2015, China has launched pilot projects for the Sponge City Program and the Climate Resilient City Program. Both aim to improve the resilience of cities, i.e. the ability of urban systems to cope with various internal and external risks (economic risks, disaster risks, etc.). Sponge cities are designed to withstand heavy rains and promote water recycling, while climate resilient cities are mainly designed to address disaster risks associated with climate change. The Sponge City Program seeks to replace traditional stormwater management systems with innovative green alternatives to build up the flood defense capability of coastal and inland cities. In contrast, the Climate Resilient City Program develop adaptation plans for urban systems based on the results of a scientific evaluation of climate risks to enhance city resilience to climate change in a forward-looking and holistic manner. It is an all-encompassing program covering a wide range of fields, including green building, disaster prevention and mitigation, ecosystems, and low-carbon technologies. The two pilot projects draw the attention of policy makers in China to disaster risks faced by cities and help cities improve their ability to tackle disasters associated with climate change.

However, China is a vast country and there are huge disparities between its cities in disaster risks and development stages. Therefore, problems faced by Chinese cities and countermeasures also vary widely across the country. In order to gain in-depth insights into the current development stages of Chinese cities and the risks faced by them, it is imperative that we evaluate the resilience of Chinese cities. According to the National Climate Center, China's top three climate-related disasters, ranked according to prevalence, frequency and economic loss caused, are storms/flooding, droughts, and typhoons (tropical cyclones). Therefore, storms/

flooding are selected as the main disaster risk in this study of the resilience of Chinese cities. This paper evaluates thirty municipalities and provincial capitals and more than forty pilot cities above the prefecture level under the Sponge City Program and the Climate Resilient City Program, ranks them by storm resilience and puts forth policy recommendations based on the rankings.

2.2 Indicators and Methodology

1. Evaluation Framework and Key Indicators

This paper adopts the IPCC climate risk assessment framework, which consists of the following three indicators: ① Hazard, i.e., the risk of occurrence of climate-related disasters, such as the frequency and intensity of extreme weather/climate events; ② Exposure, i.e., population, infrastructure, and social wealth exposed to a hazard; ③ Vulnerability, i.e., the degree to which a system is affected by or responsive to exposure to a hazard. Disaster risk can be expressed by a function of hazard, exposure and vulnerability, as follows:

$$\text{Risk (R)} = \text{f}\{\text{Hazard (H); Exposure (E); Vulnerability (V)}\} \tag{2.1}$$

Based on the above conceptual framework and relevant expert advice, we selected indicators following the principle of being scientific and simple and defined "resilience" as the opposite of risk, putting the emphasis on the planning and design for the purpose of improving adaptability and reducing disaster vulnerability. Based on this definition, the resilience index of cities is constructed as follows:

$$\text{City Storm Resilience Index} = \text{Adaptability Index/Storm Hazard} \tag{2.2}$$

The WMO defines a climate normal as the average value of a meteorological element over thirty years. We examined the changes in the storm risk index over a period of about fifty years. The storm risk index is determined by two factors: (1) the average storm days per year from 1971 to 2016; and (2) the annual change in storm days. The annual average storm days (daily precipitation $\geq$ 50 mm) and the annual change in storm days of more than eighty weather stations representative of the evaluated cities during 1971–2016 were calculated. Arithmetic means were computed from normalized numbers [see formula (2.3)]. The evaluated cities were then ranked by the storm hazard rating.

$$\text{Storm Risk Index} = \text{AVG(Average Annual Storm Days} + \text{Annual Change in the Storm Days)} \tag{2.3}$$

City resilience or adaptability, as a multi-dimensional concept, can be defined from different perspectives. From the perspective of the ability to adapt, economic condition is the basis for climate change adaptation of a country or city and has a significant impact on environmental input, public awareness, governance capacity, etc. In addition to traditional flood control and drainage infrastructure, "green infrastructure" such as forests and wetlands leverage the functions and services of ecosystems to mitigate the effects of heat waves, floods and droughts. Built on evaluations conducted by experts, we constructed the adaptability index of cities as follows:

$$\text{Adaptability Index} = \text{AVG (Per CapitaGDP} + \text{Drainage Network Density in Built-up Area} + \text{Green Coverage Rate in Built-up Area)}$$

The adaptability index is the arithmetic mean of the three indicators of per capita GDP, drainage network density in built-up areas, and green coverage rate in built-up areas. The storm resilience index is also normalized using the min-max standardization method:

$$X = \frac{x - min}{\max - min} \tag{2.4}$$

where max is the maximum value of the sample data and min is the minimum value of the sample data.

2. Threshold Values of Storm Resilience

Based on relevant theories and previous studies, we set the threshold values of the storm risk index and the adaptability index, which are used to determine the level of resilience of the evaluated cities to storms.

High storm risk is defined at or above the 80th percentile of the storm risk index.[1] There are fourteen high-risk cities in the sample cities, which are, ranked by risk from top to bottom, Zhuhai, Shenzhen, Dongguan, Guangzhou, Haikou, Sanya, Hebi, Chongqing, Wuhan, Nanchang, Xiamen, Pingxiang, Jiujiang, and Nanning. It should be pointed out that this study uses the definition of storm in the Chinese standard document *Grade of Precipitation (GB/T28592-2020)*, which defines storms as rain events equal to or greater than 50 mm in twenty four hours. In view of the vast territory of China and the wide regional disparities in precipitation, there are certain inadequacies in calculating storm risk by using a unified national storm definition. In addition, we only use data from representative stations, so the representation of larger cities may also be insufficient.

The above threshold values of storm resilience were determined based on the empirical data of domestic and foreign cities. To determine the threshold values of the three adaptability indicators, we took the following conditions into

[1]The percentile is a value such that at least p percent of the observations are less than or equal to this value and at least (100-p) percent of the observations are greater than or equal to this value.

consideration: per capita GDP reflects the overall economic condition of a country or region, and upper middle-income economies have a per capita GDP of 8,000 US dollars or more; the density of the drainage network is about nine km per km^2 in Chinese cities and 15–30 km per km^2 in developed countries such as the United States and Japan; China's garden city construction standard requires that the green coverage rate in built-up areas be greater than 45%. Therefore, high resilience is defined in this paper as an event where a city's per capita GDP is equal to or above 8,000 US dollars (about 53,000 yuan), drainage network density is no less than 9 km per km^2, and green coverage rate of built-up areas is 45% or higher.

The storm resilience of a city is graded based on the following standards: (1) high resilience: all three adaptability indicators of the city are at or above the threshold values; (2) medium resilience: only two adaptability indicators of the city are at or above the threshold values; (3) low resilience: only one adaptability indicator of the city is at or above the threshold value. Cities in each category (i.e., high-resilience, medium-resilience, and low-resilience cities) were then ranked by the ratio of adaptability index to storm risk index. The higher the ratio, the higher the storm resilience index and the ranking.

2.3 Conclusions

Based on the above, we will rank all the cities evaluated, divide them into the three groups: high-resilience, medium-resilience, and low-resilience. The results are given below:

1. Ranking and analysis of twenty nine municipalities and provincial capitals in China

As can be seen from Table 2.1, four cities (Beijing, Hefei, Guiyang, and Nanjing, ranked from top to bottom) have high storm resilience with all three adaptability indicators at or above the threshold values. Cities ranked 5th–13th are medium-resilience cities, while those ranked 14th–29th are low-resilience cities. In terms of storm risk, the four high-resilience cities do not face high risks; three medium-resilience cities (Guangzhou, Wuhan, and Nanchang) are at a high risk of storms and two low-resilience cities (Haikou and Chongqing) are at a high risk of storms.

2. Ranking and analysis of forty four pilot cities above prefecture level in China

As can be seen from Table 2.2, there are six high-resilience cities among all pilot cities of the Sponge City Program and the Climate Resilient City Program. All the three adaptability indicators of these six pilot cities are at or above the threshold values. The cities ranked 7th–14th are medium-resilience cities, while those ranked 15th to 44th are low-resilience cities.

Table 2.1 Ranking of municipalities and provincial capitals in China by storm resilience

Province	City	Ranking	Resilience
–	Beijing	1	High
Anhui	Hefei	2	High
Guizhou	Guiyang	3	High
Jiangsu	Nanjing	4	High
–	Tianjin	5	Medium
Jilin	Changchun	6	Medium
Liaoning	Shenyang	7	Medium
Shaanxi	Xi'an	8	Medium
Zhejiang	Hangzhou	9	Medium
–	Shanghai	10	Medium
Hubei	Wuhan	11	Medium
Guangdong	Guangzhou	12	Medium
Jiangxi	Nanchang	13	Medium
Inner Mongolia	Hohhot	14	Low
Hebei	Shijiazhuang	15	Low
Shanxi	Taiyuan	16	Low
Tibet	Lhasa	17	Low
Xinjiang	Urumqi	18	Low
Qinghai	Xining	19	Low
Ningxia	Yinchuan	20	Low
Henan	Zhengzhou	21	Low
Shandong	Jinan	22	Low
Yunnan	Kunming	23	Low
Fujian	Fuzhou	24	Low
Hunan	Changsha	25	Low
Hainan	Haikou	26	Low
Heilongjiang	Harbin	27	Low
Gansu	Lanzhou	28	Low
–	Chongqing	29	Low

Note Data for some cities, such as Chengdu, Sichuan, are not available

Among the pilot cities of the two programs, twelve are at high risk of storms. Obviously, these cities are aware of their own disaster risks and hope to improve their adaptability by participating in the pilot projects. Among them, Shenzhen and Zhuhai are among the top 10% of all storm-prone pilot cities, and their adaptability is also among the best. They are typical high-risk and high-resilience cities. Their experience in the pilot projects has significant implications for other cities. We recommend they step up their efforts to increase resilience. Shanghai, Wuhan, Xiamen, and Sanya are medium-resilience cities with high risk and medium adaptability. These cities should leverage the pilot projects to identify and shore up their weak points and increase investment in climate adaptability infrastructure.

Table 2.2 Ranking of Sponge cities and climate resilient cities in China by storm resilience

Province	City	Ranking	Resilience
–	Beijing	1	High
Shandong	Qingdao	2	High
Anhui	Hefei	3	High
Guizhou	Guiyang (Gui'an New District)	4	High
Guangdong	Shenzhen	5	High
Guangdong	Zhuhai	6	High
Tianjin	Tianjin	7	Medium
Liaoning	Dalian	8	Medium
Zhejiang	Ningbo	9	Medium
Jiangsu	Zhenjiang	10	Medium
–	Shanghai	11	Medium
Hubei	Wuhan	12	Medium
Fujian	Xiamen	13	Medium
Hainan	Sanya	14	Medium
Liaoning	Chaoyang	15	Low
Inner Mongolia	Hohhot	16	Low
Qinghai	Xining (Huangzhong County)	17	Low
Yunnan	Yuxi	18	Low
Henan	Zhengzhou	19	Low
Zhejiang	Jiaxing	20	Low
Zhejiang	Lishui	21	Low
Shandong	Jinan	22	Low
Hunan	Yueyang	23	Low
Jiangxi	Jiujiang	24	Low
Sichuan	Guangyuan	25	Low
Fujian	Fuzhou	26	Low
Guizhou	Liupanshui	27	Low
Hainan	Haikou	28	Low
Anhui	Huaibei	29	Low
Gansu	Lanzhou	30	Low
Jilin	Baicheng	31	Low
Gansu	Baiyin	32	Low
Shaanxi	Xianyang (Xixian New District)	33	Low
Hubei	Shiyan	34	Low
Shaanxi	Shangluo	35	Low
Henan	Anyang	36	Low
Guizhou	Bijie (Hezhang County)	37	Low
Hunan	Changde	38	Low
Guangxi	Baise	39	Low
Jiangxi	Pingxiang	40	Low

(continued)

Table 2.2 (continued)

Province	City	Ranking	Resilience
–	Chongqing (Bishan District and Tongnan District)	41	Low
Guangxi	Nanning	42	Low
Gansu	Qingyang (Xifeng District)	43	Low
Henan	Hebi	44	Low

Note There are 28 pilot cities under the Climate Resilient City Program and 30 under the Sponge City Program with an overlap of eight

Jiujiang, Haikou, Pingxiang, Chongqing, Nanning, and Hebi are prone to storms but have the lowest adaptability values. As high-risk and low-resilience cities, they should leverage the pilot projects to strengthen their ability to tackle storms.

The above analysis can only roughly reflect the common problems in China's big cities and pilot cities. Due to the limitations of methodology, indicators and threshold values, the above analysis should only be deemed as a positive attempt to evaluate the storm resilience of Chinese cities. Further efforts will be required to reduce the uncertainty and increase the validity and comparability of the evaluation results. For example, storms are defined in this paper as rain events that accumulate to 50 mm or more in 24 h. However, in practice, many northern cities define storms as rain events that accumulate to a level of 20–30 mm. Therefore, the level of storm resilience in many northern cities are overplayed in the storm resilience rankings in this paper which also do not reflect the wide disparities of cities in terms of geographic location, population size and climate type. There are still much room for improvement.

2.4 Suggestions for Building Resilient Cities

Based on the above, this paper offers a new perspective on the resilience of cities and proposes to evaluate the resilience of cities in terms of both disaster risks and adaptability. The higher a city's adaptability to disaster risks, the stronger its resilience. The purpose of this study is not to evaluate and rank the cities in China, but to urge decision-makers in China's big cities and pilot cities to pay more attention to the cities' resilience to storms, enhance urban climate risk awareness, incorporate disaster risk assessment into urban planning, and strive to build resilient cities. To this end, we put forward the following policy recommendations:

1. The Climate Resilient City Program and the Sponge City Program should be implemented in good coordination. The two programs intersect in several fields and steering departments. They can be mutually reinforcing. For example, the National Development and Reform Commission can draw on the experience of

the Ministry of Housing and Urban-Rural Development in running the Sponge City Program to strengthen technical guidance for and assessment of climate resilient cities, while the Sponge City Program can emulate sponge cities to attach greater importance to the adaptability of cities and incorporate the assessment and prevention of long-term climate change risks into holistic urban planning and design. At the city level, eight cities serve as pilot cities for both programs, namely Wuhan (Hubei), Jinan (Shandong), Dalian (Liaoning), Changde (Hunan), Chongqing, Xixian New District (Shaanxi), Qingyang (Gansu), and Xining (Qinghai). These pilot cities should strengthen the linkage between the two programs and improve coordination.

2. The Chinese government should increase support for the development of resilient cities in the central and western regions. In the next thirty years, cities in the central and western parts of the country will absorb nearly 100 million rural population. Due to climate change, in recent years, small-probability heavy rainfall events have been frequently observed in some arid and semi-arid cities in West China. The heat island and rain island effects caused by urbanization have also increased the probability of heavy rains in inland cities. The government should increase support to areas at high risk of climate disasters, including the West and the upper reaches of the Yangtze River, and help cities in these areas to strengthen infrastructure building and capacity building so that they can cope better with climate-related disasters.
3. Theoretical and practical research on the resilience of cities should be strengthened. First of all, in order to offer guidance to pilot cities, it is necessary to design key indicators and thresholds for the evaluation of the resilience of different types of cities regarding their risks to different types of disasters. Secondly, more theoretic research should be conducted on resilient cities and their risk mechanisms. For example, cities in the eastern and central regions are at high risk of disasters mainly due to the high exposure of population and property, while the vulnerability of cities in the western part of the country is caused largely by underdevelopment as well as the constraints of resources and environment. Thirdly, China should do more research on the impact of long-term climate change on cities, and urge large cities and pilot cities to adopt forward-looking and systematic risk planning approaches.

Chapter 3
Scientific Assessments of Climate Change in the Post-Paris Era

Lei Huang, Qingchen Chao, Yongxiang Zhang and Ting Hu

Abstract The *Paris Agreement* reached in December 2015 has created new institutional arrangements for post-2020 global climate change governance, but the implementation details of the agreement are yet to be ironed out. The post-Paris developments in scientific assessments of global climate change has also aroused widespread international concern. In September 2017, the United Nations Intergovernmental Panel on Climate Change (IPCC) finalized the outline of the *Sixth Assessment Report* (AR6), which will reshape future international talks and national actions on climate change. This paper provides details about the background and progress of AR6 and future direction of the IPCC, analyzes the trend of scientific assessments of climate change in the post-Paris era and its links to international institutional arrangements addressing climate change, and puts forwards recommendations as to how China could play a more positive role in the IPCC scientific assessment.

Keywords Paris agreement · IPCC · Climate change assessment

Lei Huang, Deputy Director and research associate at the National Climate Center, China Meteorological Administration (CMA), specializes in climate change. Qingchen Chao is Deputy Director and research fellow at the National Climate Center. Chao's research interests include climate change policy and air-sea interaction. Yongxiang Zhang is a research associate at the National Climate Center. Zhang's research interests include historical climatology and climate change impacts and policies. Ting Hu, research associate at the National Climate Center, specializes in climate change.

L. Huang (✉) · Q. Chao · Y. Zhang · T. Hu
China Meteorological Administration, National Climate Center, Beijing, China
e-mail: huanglei@cma.gov.cn

Q. Chao
e-mail: chaoqc@cma.gov.cn

Y. Zhang
e-mail: zhangyx@cma.gov.cn

T. Hu
e-mail: huting@cma.gov.cn

W. Wang (ed.), *Annual Report on China's Response to Climate Change (2017)*,
Research Series on the Chinese Dream and China's Development Path,
https://doi.org/10.1007/978-981-13-9660-1_3

The United Nations Intergovernmental Panel on Climate Change (IPCC) has issued five scientific assessment reports on climate change since 1990. These reports present scientific findings in a well-organized manner to guide the international response to climate change. Representing the international scientific community's current knowledge of climate change and its impacts and responses, they are highly policy-oriented and have received wide international attention. The *Paris Agreement* ("*Agreement*" hereafter) reached in December 2015 has made new institutional arrangements for post-2020 global climate change governance, but the implementation details of the *Agreement* are yet to be ironed out. The post-Paris developments in scientific assessments of global climate change has also aroused widespread international concern. In October 2016, March 2017, and September 2017, the IPCC agreed the outlines of the three special reports and three working group reports in the sixth assessment cycle (AR6). These assessment reports will definitely affect future international talks and national actions on climate change. This paper provides details about the background and progress of AR6 and future direction of the IPCC, analyzes the trend of scientific assessments of climate change in the post-Paris era and its links to international institutional arrangements addressing climate change, and puts forwards recommendations as to how China could play a more positive role in the IPCC scientific assessment.

3.1 Background to AR6

The IPCC Fifth Assessment Report (AR5), released over the course of 2013 and 2014, gained international recognition and played an important role in the international community's response to climate change. The IPCC has become an example of how scientific knowledge can influence public policy.

With lessons learned and experiences gained over the past twenty five years in mind, the IPCC launched a series of discussions on the future of the IPCC in early 2013, and on this basis, considered whether its organizational structure and functions needed to be modified or improved. These discussions involve among others future trends, product forms, organizational structure, and work arrangements for the next step.

Discussions about the future of the IPCC centered on whether the IPCC should consider adjustments and changes to the number and mandate of the Working Groups and Task Forces (including the possible creation of a new Working Group or Task Force), and the composition and size of the IPCC Bureau (including any specific role associated with certain positions), how to make arrangements for AR6 (including the commencement date, the writing cycle, product form), how to enhance active participation on all fronts, especially participation of developing countries. After a series of discussions and talks over the course of 2013 and 2014, the IPCC reached an agreement on future work arrangements and decided on the future product forms, organizational structure and ways to enhance participation of developing countries in early 2015.

The IPCC decided that it will continue to prepare, every 5–7 years comprehensive assessment reports, including regional aspects, together with the three-stage government/expert review process, supplemented by Special Reports; in determining its future reports and their timing, the IPCC will take into account the work of the United Nations Framework Convention on Climate Change (UNFCCC); the Special Reports, the Synthesis Report (SYR) and cross-cutting issues should be planned as early as possible and the increasing importance of enhanced cross-Working Group cooperation should be emphasized; the three working group reports should be released within about one year but no more than eighteen months; it will continue to prepare *Methodology Reports on National Greenhouse Gas Inventories* and other methodology reports or good practice guidance reports, further explore ways to enhance collaboration with other relevant international and scientific organizations, facilitate and enhance further the use of up to date digital technology for sharing and disseminating information, enhance the readability of IPCC products, and better reflect non-English language literature in IPCC reports.

With regards to the organizational structure of the IPCC, the IPCC decided that it will retain the current structure and mandate of the three Working Groups and the Task Force on National Greenhouse Gas Inventories (TFI) and consider adjustments of the size, structure and composition of the Bureau. The IPCC decided to add three positions to the new Bureau for the AR6 cycle and to distribute these additional positions equally among the three working groups. It also decided that the term of office of the new Bureau shall start in October 2015 and end in 2022 at the latest.

With respect to the administrative matters of the IPCC, the administrative arrangements for the IPCC Secretariat remain as agreed in the Memorandum of Understanding between the World Meteorological Organization (WMO) and the United Nations Environment Program (UNEP) on the establishment of the IPCC. The IPCC will establish Technical Support Units (TSUs) to support the preparations of IPCC products and activities during the AR6 cycle. The Secretariat and all TSUs are required to put in place workplace policies and practices that promote diversity, fairness, collaboration and inclusiveness. This should involve recruiting professional staff internationally and selection, performance appraisal and contract extension of TSU staff will be done jointly by both relevant Co-Chairs.

With regard to the participation of developing countries, the IPCC decided to adopt a number of measures to enhance the engagement of developing countries with the IPCC, including, among others, further encouraging Co-Chairs and other Bureau members to engage experts from developing countries in TSUs and author teams, increasing the number of IPCC activities in developing countries, arranging training sessions for government representatives of developing countries.

In October 2015, the IPCC elected the new Bureau for the AR6 cycle. North Korean scientist Hoesung Lee was elected as the new Chair and the three Vice-Chairs were from the United States, Brazil and Mali. Mr. Panmao Zhai, researcher from Chinese Academy of Meteorological Sciences serves as Co-chair of Working Group I (WGI), and together with the French scientist Valérie Masson-Delmotte, is tasked with preparing the AR6 WGI report The Co-Chairs of

WGII are from South Africa and Germany, WGIII from India and the United Kingdom, and TFI from Peru and Japan.

The IPCC assessment reports are important scientific basis for international negotiations on climate change and have played a central role in the negotiation process of the UNFCCC. AR6 will continue to provide the international community with up-to-date assessment results of the science basis, impact, adaptation and mitigation of climate change, aiming to address practical hurdles in global sustainable development and advance the implementation of the UN Sustainable Development Goals (SDGs). The AR6 report will not only be used to inform international climate change policies and actions, but also serve as an important source of knowledge on climate change for the general public.

3.2 Global Warming of 1.5 °C and Other Special Reports

Over the course of 2013 and 2014, the IPCC released the AR5 report, including three WG reports—*The Physical Science Basis*, *Impacts, Adaptation, and Vulnerability*, and *Mitigation of Climate Change*—and a Synthesis Report. The AR5 provides well-organized scientific conclusions to guide the international response to climate change. It had an important impact on the Paris talks on climate change. In December 2015, the United Nations Climate Change Conference (COP 21) in Paris adopted the *Paris Agreement*, which provides for the new institutional arrangements for global climate governance beyond 2020. As a landmark climate agreement, the *Agreement* has played a key role in guiding the development of the global climate governance model.

The COP21 also invited the IPCC to provide a special report in 2018 on the impacts of global warming of 1.5 °C above pre-industrial levels and related global greenhouse gas emission pathways. In April 2016, the IPCC discussed the number and themes of Special Reports during the AR6 cycle. Prior to the discussion, the IPCC received thirty one Special Report theme proposals in nine categories. Given the Special Report cycle, the organizing process and past experience, the IPCC Bureau suggested that the number of Special Reports should not exceed three, and the theme of the *Special Report on Global Warming of 1.5 °C* has been basically determined by the relevant resolution of the COP21. Considering the opinions of all stakeholders and the constraints of time, manpower, resources and reporting quality, the IPCC decided to produce three Special Reports in the AR6 cycle, in which *Global Warming of 1.5 °C* is scheduled to be released in the second half of 2018, and the other two Special Reports will be released in the second half of 2019.

In October 2016, the IPCC approved the title and outline of *Global Warming of 1.5 °C* (SR1.5) [1]. The full name of SR1.5 consists of a main title ("*Global Warming of 1.5 °C*") and a subtitle ("*an IPCC special report on the impacts of global warming of 1.5 °C above pre-industrial levels and related global greenhouse gas emission pathways, in the context of strengthening the global response to the threat of climate change, sustainable development, and efforts to eradicate poverty*"). SR 1.5 will consist of five chapters, the titles of which are "Framing and Context", "Mitigation pathways compatible with 1.5 °C in the context of sustainable development", "Impacts of 1.5 °C global warming on natural and human systems", "Strengthening and implementing the global response to the threat of climate change", and "Sustainable development, poverty eradication, and reducing inequalities". In addition, the special report also includes Front Matter, Summary for Policy Makers, Boxes (up to 20 pages) and FAQs (10 pages).

The length of the entire special report, including Summary for Policy Makers (up to 10 pages, including headline statements, tables, figures), is expected to be around 225 pages. According to the timetable approved by the IPCC, SR1.5 will be reviewed and officially released at the 48th Session of the IPCC in October 2018 in time for the facilitative dialogue at the 24th Conference of the Parties (COP24) to be held at the end of 2018.

In February 2017, the IPCC completed the selection of experts to prepare SR1.5. 86 experts from 39 countries will participate the development of the report. 51% of the experts come from developing countries and economies in transition, and 38% are women. Four Chinese scientists are selected. So far, the IPCC has held two SR1.5 Lead Author Meetings, and the preparation of the report is proceeding as planned.

In March 2017, the IPCC approved the outlines of the other two Special Reports. The *Special Report on the Ocean and Cryosphere in a Changing Climate* [2] consists of a summary for policy makers, a technical summary, six chapters, case studies, FAQs and a cross-chapter box about low-lying islands and coasts, with a total length of approximately 280 pages. The six chapters are "Framing and Context of the Report", "High Mountain Areas", "Polar Regions, Sea Level Rise and Implications for Low Lying Islands, Coasts and Communities", "Changing Ocean, Marine Ecosystems, and Dependent Communities", and "Extremes, Abrupt Changes and Managing Risks". *Climate Change and Land: An IPCC special report on climate change, desertification, land degradation, sustainable land management, food security, and greenhouse gas fluxes in terrestrial ecosystems* [3] consists of a summary for policy makers, a technical summary and seven chapters, with a total length of approximately 330 pages. The seven chapters are "Framing and Context", "Land-Climate Interactions", "Desertification", "Land Degradation", "Food Security", "Interlinkages between desertification, land degradation, food security and GHG fluxes: Synergies, Trade-offs and Integrated Response Options", and "Risk management and decision making in relation to sustainable development".

3.3 Frameworks of the Three IPCC AR6 Working Group Reports

According to the *Paris Agreement* which depends on voluntary mitigation contributions by the parties, countries will submit new or updated Nationally Determined Contributions (NDCs) every five years from the year 2020. Starting in 2023, and every five years thereafter, the UNFCCC will conduct a Global Stocktake (GST) to take stock of collective climate action and identify the need for enhanced action and international cooperation. The first GST in 2023 will become a key input into international climate negotiations. Whether countries need to ratchet up climate action according to the results of the GST will become the focus of negotiations. According to the IPCC's strategic plan, the three WG reports of AR6 will be released before 2023 in time to inform the first GST. Overall, there are two concerns concerning the linkages between the IPCC climate change assessment and the GST: first, whether the IPCC assessment cycle needs to be consistent with the global inventory cycle, and second, whether the scope of the IPCC assessment should contain the elements of the GST. Since the AR6 cycle has been determined, the IPCC should consider the linkage of its assessment cycle with the GST cycle starting from the AR7 cycle. The IPCC Secretariat has proposed three possible assessment cycles: once every five years to align to the GST cycle, or once every ten years (i.e., every two GST cycles) or to retain the six- or seven-year cycle. The IPCC Secretariat believes that the adjustment of the assessment cycle means an increase in workload and are more inclined to retain the original assessment frequency. In September 2017, the IPCC engaged in a brief discussion on the alignment of the IPCC and the GST cycle. However, due to time constraints, the discussion failed to produce results and the IPCC decided to set up a special task force to deal with this issue and postpone its decision until 2018.

In May 2017, the IPCC held a scoping meeting for the three WG reports of AR6. The meeting proposed the outlines of the three WG reports and themes for the Synthesis Report. In September 2017, the IPCC finalized the outline of the three WG reports. The linkage between the scopes of AR6 and the GST was the focus of the outline revision. The contents of the WGIII contribution to AR6 are most closely related to the GST. Countries such as the United States and Saudi Arabia maintained that the negotiations on the implementation details of the *Paris Agreement*, including the specifics of the GST, are still in progress; the IPCC assessment should be scientific in nature and any political content should be carefully scrutinized. Some EU countries held the view that the linkage to the global inventory is the highlight of the WGIII report, and AR6 should maintain reference to the GST. In addition, with respect to investment and finance, some countries proposed adding reference to financial flows to developing countries in the "Climate Finance and Financial Flow" chapter to meet the financial needs of the GST.

The finalized outlines of the AR6 WG reports involve some elements of GST such as mitigation, finance and technology transfer and clarify the need to provide funds and capacity building to developing countries, but do not underscore the implementation of NDGs by developing countries. The approved outline of the WGIII contribution to AR6 consists of seventeen chapters [4], covering introduction and framing, emissions trends and drivers, mitigation pathways compatible with long-term goals, mitigation and development pathways in the near- to mid-term, demand, services and social aspects of mitigation, energy systems, agriculture, forestry and other land-use (AFOLU), urban systems and other settlements, buildings, transport, industry, cross-sectoral perspectives, national and sub-national policies and institutions, international cooperation, investment and finance, innovation, technology development and transfer, and accelerating the transition in the context of sustainable development. The WGIII contribution to AR6 is scheduled to be released in July 2021.

The outline of the WGI contribution to AR6 [5] is centered on scientific advances in climate change, with special attention to its linkages with AR5, WGII and WGIII reports and three Special Reports to ensure continuity and coherence, and support comprehensive assessment of mitigation targets, the linkages with sustainable development and other top global concerns. Based on the outline, AR6 WGI report will be more streamlined and logically well-organized than the WGI contribution to AR5. The outline of the WGI contribution to AR6 contains twelve chapters, covering framing, context and methods, changing state of the climate system, human influence on the climate system, future global climate: scenario-based projections and near-term information, global carbon and other biogeochemical cycles and feedbacks, short-lived climate forcers (SLCFs), the Earth's energy budget, climate feedbacks, and climate sensitivity, water cycle changes, ocean, cryosphere and sea level change, linking global to regional climate change, weather and climate extreme events in a changing climate, and climate change information for regional impact and for risk assessment. The outline of WGI contribution contains the geoengineering aspect, but there is no direct reference to geoengineering. The geoengineering solutions is divided into two parts: greenhouse gas removal (GGR) and solar radiation management (SRM), because while GHG removal is a policy response included in the *Paris Agreement*, solar radiation management is not. The AR6 WGI report is scheduled to be released in April 2021.

The outline of the WGII contribution to AR6 contains eighteen chapters [6], including "Point of departure and key concepts" (Chap. 1) and three sections. Section 3.1 addresses risks, adaptation and sustainability for systems impacts by climate change and is comprised of seven chapters, covering terrestrial and freshwater ecosystems and their services, ocean and coastal ecosystems and their services, water, food, fibre, and other ecosystem products, cities, settlements and key infrastructure, health, wellbeing and the changing structure of communities, and poverty, livelihoods and sustainable development. Section 3.2 addresses regions and has seven chapters: Africa, Asia, Australia, Central and South America, Europe, North America, and Small Islands. Section 3.2 also includes seven cross-chapter papers, covering biodiversity hotspots, cities and settlements by the sea, deserts, semi-arid areas, and desertification, Mediterranean region, mountains, polar regions, and tropical forests. Section 3.3 addresses sustainable development pathways: integrating adaptation and mitigation, and includes three chapters, covering key risks across sectors and regions, decision-making options for managing risk, and climate resilient development pathways.

The loss and damage issue covered in the WGII report is closely related to the compensation for the adverse effects of climate change under the UNFCCC framework. Some countries do not wish the report contain an explicit reference to loss and damage and other sensitive words used in the UNFCCC negotiations. Small islands and developing countries held the view that the UNFCCC has established the Warsaw International Mechanism for Loss and Damage Associated with Climate Change Impacts and the *Paris Agreement* has also authorizes the IPCC to provide information on this subject, but the concept of "residual risk" used in previous IPCC reports is too narrow and fails to reflect the full meaning of loss and damage. Thus, they called for direct reference to loss and damage in AR6. Developed countries such as the United States and the United Kingdom maintained that, although the UNFCCC and the *Paris Agreement* authorize the IPCC to provide information on loss and damage, they does not specify the terminology specifically used by the IPCC in the scientific context, and that, since "loss and damage" is a political term under the UNFCCC, the IPCC cannot conduct an assessment to address a vague concept without a clear scientific definition. After several rounds of discussions, the IPCC defined "loss and damage" in Chapter One of the WGII as "scientific, technical and socioeconomic aspects of current and future residual impacts of climate change, including residual damage, irreversible loss, and economic and non-economic losses caused by slow onset and extreme events" and decided to avoid the direct reference to loss and damage. The AR6 WGII report will be released in October 2021.

The AR6 Synthesis Report (SYR) will focus on cross-cutting issues. The eight cross-cutting themes identified at the scope meeting in May 2017 are regions, scenarios, risks, cities, global stocktake, geoengineering, adaptation and mitigation, and approaches and processes for WG integration. The IPCC will hold a dedicated SYR scoping meeting in 2019 to finalize the outline of the SYR. The final SYR which will be released in the first half of 2022.

3.4 Reflections and Suggestions

The IPCC AR5 has played a central role in advancing the climate negotiations resulting in the *Paris Agreement*. The AR6 cycle in the post-Paris era is more closely linked to the facilitative dialogue and the global stocktake under the UNFCCC framework. The findings of AR6 will provide a science basis for global action on climate change, including mitigation, adaptation, finance, technology, and capacity building. AR6 will adopt more solution-focused approaches. In the meantime, it also underscores the uncertainty assessment to help improve communication regarding what is known and unknown about key dimensions of the climate issue. AR6 puts more emphasis on interdisciplinary and cross-WG integration, and case studies. In addition, IPCC is also actively encouraging researchers from developing countries including China to participate in AR6 and pays more attention to the demands of developing countries. In order to amplify China's influence and voice in the field of international climate change scientific assessment, it is necessary to build research capacity concerning issues at the core of climate change science, step up the cultivation of scientific talents, produce more scientific findings concerning the impact of global warming of 1.5 °C, climate change detection and attribution, climate system modeling, near- and long-term projections of climate change, and short-lived greenhouse gases, and narrow China's gap with global leaders in the research capacity concerning key climate issues. The nomination of authors for the three WG reports of AR6 is currently underway. Chinese scientists should actively participate in AR6 through various channels to present the research findings of the Chinese scientific community as far as possible and support China's full participation in global climate governance.

Acknowledgements This study is funded by the China Clean Development Mechanism Fund (Project No. 2014097) and the ninth sub-project of A Study of Major Issues related to Climate Change in the Post-Paris Era (2016), which is a research project set up under the auspices of the Ministry of Science and Technology of China.

References

1. Sixth Assessment Report (AR6) Products, Outlines of the Special Report on 1.5 °C. IPCC. Retrieved 2016, from http://www.ipcc.ch/meetings/session44/l2_adopted_outline_sr15.pdf.
2. Decision: Sixth Assessment Report (AR6) Products-Decision and Outline of the Special Report on Climate Change and Oceans and the Cryosphere. IPCC. Retrieved 2017, from http://www.ipcc.ch/meetings/session45/Decision_Outline_SR_Oceans.pdf.
3. Decision: Sixth Assessment Report (AR6) Products Decision and Outline of the Special Report on Climate Change, Desertification, Land Degradation, Sustainable Land Management, Food Security, and Greenhouse Gas Fluxes in Terrestrial Ecosystems. IPCC. Retrieved 2017, from http://www.ipcc.ch/meetings/session45/Decision_Outline_SR_LandUse.pdf.
4. Decision: Chapter Outline of the Working Group I Contribution to the IPCC Sixth Assessment Report (AR6). IPCC. Retrieved 2017, from http://www.IPCC.ch/meetings/session46/AR6_WGIII_outlines_P46.pdf.
5. Decision: Chapter Outline of the Working Group I Contribution to the IPCC Sixth Assessment Report (AR6). IPCC. Retrieved 2017, from http://www.ipcc.ch/meetings/session46/AR6_WGI_outlines_P46.pdf.
6. Decision: Chapter Outline of the Working Group I Contribution to the IPCC Sixth Assessment Report (AR6). IPCC. Retrieved 2017, from http://www.ipcc.ch/meetings/session46/AR6_WGII_outlines_P46.pdf.

Chapter 4
Climate Change Policies of the Trump Administration and China's Response

Haibin Zhang

Abstract Trump's domestic and foreign climate change policies have basically taken shape. He is using a wide array of presidential executive powers to gradually and systematically weaken or roll back Obama-era domestic and foreign policies on climate change. Trump's disregard of climate change is reflected in his announcement of withdrawing the U.S. from the *Paris Agreement*. The Trump administration's position on climate change is influenced by the U.S. domestic political factors and Trump's personal political views, rather than the claimed burdens imposed by the *Paris Agreement* on the United States. This blatant indifference on the part of the U.S. has significant implications for China and China-U.S. relations. After the U.S. withdrawal from the *Paris Agreement,* China faces mounting pressure from the international community to assume a leadership position on climate change. In response to Trump's stance on climate change, China should raise its nationally determined contribution (NDC) targets, rebuild the collective leadership system in global climate action by replacing the Group of Two (G2) with the Climate 5 (C5), and urge the United States to maintain its engagement in global climate action.

Keywords Trump · Climate change policy · Global governance

On January 20, 2017, Donald Trump was sworn in as 45th president of the United States. His famously ignorant comments about climate change during the election and the series of actions taken by him after assuming office to roll back climate change policies of previous administrations roused wide international concern. The

---

Haibin Zhang, professor and doctoral advisor at the School of International Studies, Peking University, and director of the Center for International Organization Studies, Peking University. Zhang's research interests include global environmental and climate governance and international organizations.

H. Zhang (✉)
School of International Studies, Peking University, Beijing, China
e-mail: zhanghb@pku.edu.cn

W. Wang (ed.), *Annual Report on China's Response to Climate Change (2017)*,
Research Series on the Chinese Dream and China's Development Path,
https://doi.org/10.1007/978-981-13-9660-1_4

Trump administration's position on climate change has become one of the biggest uncertainties in international climate negotiations and global climate governance since the *Paris Agreement* went into effect in 2016. How far will Trump depart from the Obama administration's climate change policy? What's behind the Trump administration's disregard of climate change? What impacts will Trump's disregard of climate change have on China and China-U.S. relations? How will China respond? These issues are important and deserve serious consideration. This paper seeks to take an in-depth look into these issues.

4.1 Climate Change Policies of the Trump Administration

Since taking office, Trump has made big changes to Obama-era domestic and foreign climate change policies.

1. Domestic climate change policies of the Trump administration

Since being sworn in, Trump has taken steps to undo progress in tackling climate change domestically.

First, the Trump administration has worked to control the dissemination of climate change information and openly questioned climate change. Trump immediately revised the White House official website following his assumption of office on January 20, 2017, and removed all climate change related pages that were built under the Obama administration. These pages, stuffed with copious reports and facts about climate change and its impact, used to be an important source of information on this subject for the public in the United States and other countries. The burial of these pages is undoubtedly a step backward on public climate change awareness. Trump also ordered the U.S. Environmental Protection Agency (EPA) to delete climate change references on its website. His climate change rhetoric in interviews and on Twitter has consistently reflect his belief that climate change has little to do with human action.

Second, he has filled key positions of his administration with climate change skeptics. Scott Pruitt, the current chief of the EPA and the former Attorney General of Oklahoma, is a well-known climate change skeptic. His campaign team was exposed in 2014 to accept hefty political donations from the fossil energy industry, and he himself joined lawsuits against Obama's *Clean Power Plan*.

After taking office, he has repeatedly denied human action is a primary contributor to climate change in public. Rick Perry, Secretary of Energy and the former governor of Texas, has also publicly aired his climate change skepticism. Secretary of State Rex Tillerson, the former CEO of ExxonMobil, has close ties to the U.S. fossil fuel industry. Trump's former chief adviser, Steve Bannon, is also a staunch skeptic of climate change and favored pulling the United States out from the *Paris Agreement* [1].

Third, on the front of institutional set-up, Trump took a hatchet to the EPA, demanding the EPA cut 3,200 positions, accounting for about 20% of the agency's current workforce. He also ordered the disbandment the Interagency Working Group on Social Cost of Greenhouse Gases (IWG) convened by the Council of Economic Advisers and the Office of Management and Budget.

Fourth, the Trump administration has cut climate change funding drastically. On March 16, 2017, the White House released Trump's first annual budget outline, which proposed deep cuts to public and foreign aid programs. The EPA's budget shrunk by 31% from about $8.3 billion to $5.7 billion. It was the largest cut among all federal departments and agencies. The budget also proposed to slash $3.1 billion or about 18% from the U.S. Department of Energy's research programs [2]. The Office of Energy Efficiency and Renewable Energy, which is responsible for promoting solar power, faced a 69% cut. The Office of Fossil Energy, which focuses on the research of carbon capture and storage technologies, faced a 54% cut. The Office of Nuclear Energy, which is seeking to extend the life of the United States' existing nuclear reactors, was hit by a 31% cut. Funding for basic climate change research has also shrunk dramatically. NASA's four climate science programs totaling $100 million were axed.

Fifth, Trump is moving in the opposite direction from Obama on energy and climate, as reflected in the *U.S. First Energy Plan* released immediately following his assumption of office as well as the annual budget outline and the *Presidential Executive Order on Promoting Energy Independence and Economic Growth* issued in March 2017. First, Trump calls for American energy independence. The Trump administration has taken steps to promote the development of domestic U.S. energy, remove regulations that fetter the operation of the energy industry, lower energy prices, reduce oil imports, continue the shale gas revolution, and revive the controversial Keystone XL and Dakota Access pipelines, which were blocked by the Obama administration.

On June 29, 2017, Trump announced a series of energy initiatives, including revisiting the current U.S. nuclear energy policy and supporting the construction of U.S. coal plants overseas. The Trump administration pledged to increase investment to ensure the share of nuclear power in the electric power sector. The Trump administration also said it would invest $120 million in the Yucca Mountain Nuclear Waste Repository in Nevada. The nuclear waste site was axed by Obama [3].

Second, the Trump administration seeks to drive economic and job growth by promoting the development of the energy sector. Trump is on a mission to rebuild roads, schools, bridges, and other public projects with money from the energy sector, promote the application of clean coal technologies, and revitalize the coal industry to drive job growth. According to the policy, the Trump administration will raise more than $36 billion in federal revenue by selling off energy resources and infrastructure and stepping up the development of oil and gas resources over the next 10 years; it will also provide federal funding to oil and gas drilling and the sale of oil and gas drilling leases will generate $1.8 billion in federal revenue by 2027. In the meantime, it also proposed diverting 37% of the federal revenues from oil and gas drilling in the Gulf of Mexico to Louisiana, Texas, Mississippi and Alabama [4].

Third, to avoid "inappropriately burdening the U.S. economy", Trump has scrapped the *Climate Action Plan*, a landmark policy of his predecessor; ordered the *Clean Power Plan* issued under the Obama Administration be reviewed, revised or rescinded; called for the establishment of an inter-agency working group to reassess the social costs of carbon emissions; directed the White House Council on Environmental Quality to rescind its guidance document regarding the consideration of climate change impacts in environmental reviews performed under the *National Environmental Policy Act* (NEPA); dismantled four climate change-related executive orders and presidential memoranda signed by Obama, including one that addressed climate change and national security.

2. The Trump Administration's stance in international talks on climate change

The Trump administration's stance on climate change on the international stage is reflected in the following actions:

First, it ceded the global leadership of the United States on climate change. The Obama-era *Climate Action Plan* and *Clean Power Plan* repeatedly position the United States as a global climate leader. Since Trump took office, the federal government has stopped using this rhetoric.

Second, the Trump administration has drastically slashed international climate assistance. Trump proposed discontinuing funding for any international climate change, climate change research and partnership programs of the EPA and directed the State Department stop funding the Global Climate Change Initiative and the UN's climate process, including the Green Climate Fund.

Third, it has blocked international talks and processes on climate change within G7, G20 and other multilateral frameworks outside the *United Nations Framework Convention on Climate Change* (UNFCCC). During the G20 Finance Ministers and Central Bank Governors Meeting in March 2017, the United States and Saudi Arabia opposed financing the fight against climate change. At the meeting of G7 Energy Ministers in April 2017, due to opposition from the United States, G7 countries failed to reach a common stance on climate and clean energy. Trump was also blamed by other G7 leaders for failure to reach a climate change agreement at the G7 summit that ended on May 27, 2017.

Fourth, despite strong opposition at home and abroad, Trump announced on June 1, 2017 that the United States would withdraw from the *Paris Agreement* and that, as of the day, the United States would cease the implementation of the agreement and the "draconian financial and economic burdens" the agreement imposes on the U.S., including discontinuing financing programs under the agreement. Following his win in the election, Trump wavered on his previously stated position, saying he has an "open mind" about the agreement [5], and repeatedly put off a decision on whether to quit the accord. Despite being on the fence briefly, Trump eventually chose to back out of the agreement. In his exit statement, four keywords are worth pondering. First, economy. Trump claimed that compliance with the agreement has subject the U.S. economy to harsh restrictions.

Second, fairness. Trump believes that the agreement is very unfair because it punishes the United States while imposing no meaningful obligations on the world's leading polluters. Third, environmental impact. Trump stressed that even if the agreement were implemented in full, it would only produce a 0.2°C reduction in global temperature by the year 2100 and thus the exit of the United States would have little impact on global warming. Fourth, sovereignty. Trump accused the agreement of posing serious obstacles for the United States to tap its energy reserves and intruded on the United States' sovereignty.

On August 4, 2017, the U.S. State Department issued a statement saying that the United States had submitted an official letter on the same day to the United Nations on its move to exit the *Paris Agreement*. A report on the Wall Street Journal on September 17, 2017 attracted wide international attention. The report quoted a senior EU energy official saying the Trump administration stated on September 16 that the United States would not pull out from the *Paris Agreement* and re-establish a new international mechanism to address climate change but they would try to review the terms on which they could be engaged under this agreement. However, the White House later dismissed the claim, stating that there had been no change in the position of the United States on the agreement.

As can be seen above, Trump's domestic and foreign climate change policies have basically taken shape. He is using a wide array of presidential executive powers to gradually and systematically weaken or roll back Obama-era domestic and foreign policies on climate change. Trump's disregard of climate change is reflected in his announcement of withdrawing the U.S. from the *Paris Agreement*. However, it should be noted that, under the U.S. system of separation of powers, the powers concerning the U.S. climate change policy are divided and vested in the Congress, the executive branch, and the Supreme Court. Furthermore, rising climate change awareness and concern within the borders of the United States will pose a serious challenge for the Trump administration. In short, there is a gap between what the Trump administration wants to do in the area of climate change and what it can actually accomplish. There is massive uncertainty regarding how Trump's climate change policy will shape the future.

4.2 Causes of the Trump Administration's Disregard of Climate Change

For most people, speeding up the transition to a green and low-carbon development path is a major and irreversible global development trend. Therefore, it is natural for people to question why the Trump administration moves in the opposite direction of this trend by adopting a climate change denial policy. There are five reasons behind Trump's disregard of climate change.

First, the Trump administration has close ties with fossil fuel interests. Interest group politics is one of the most prominent dimensions of American politics. The

Trump administration and Republicans at large have inextricable connections to interests groups in the fossil fuel industry. For example, it is reported that many officials of the Trump administration, including Trump himself, Vice President Mike Pence and EPA Administrator Scott Pruitt, have close ties to Koch Industries, a large petrochemical company.

Withdrawal from the *Paris Agreement* will release the United States from emissions restrictions under the agreement and benefit the Koch Industries, which has made hefty campaign contributions to the Republican and Trump's campaign team [6]. On May 25, 2017, when Trump was sitting on the fence, twenty-two top GOP senators sent a letter to Trump, urging him to make good on his campaign promise and pull out of the *Paris Agreement*. According to a survey, the twenty-two senators received more than 10 million US dollars in campaign donations from coal, oil and gas companies from 2012 to 2016 [7].

Second, the U.S. politics and society are severely polarized, characterized by strong out-group animosity [8]. The Charlottesville riot on August 21, 2017 is just the latest incident that testifies to alarming racial tensions and social divisions in the United States. As a Republican, Trump naturally leans toward the position of the Republican Party on political issues because no matter whether Trump modifies his climate change policy, his political base will not change much. In the meantime, eyeing the next presidential election, Trump needs to make good on his campaign promises so that his own constituency will continue to support him in the next presidential race.

Third, Trump has always been a climate change skeptic, and refused to acknowledge the cornerstone of global climate governance—the "common but differentiated responsibilities" principle. Although the conclusion that climate change is occurring and is caused largely by human is the basic consensus on climate change in the U.S. scientific community, Trump has never officially acknowledged this conclusion. In his statement announcing the withdrawal of the United States from the *Paris Agreement*, Trump claimed that the agreement is unfair to the United States and compared China and India's mitigation obligations with the United States', taking no notice of the common but differentiated responsibility principle. It will be difficult to change Trump's stubborn and unyielding position on climate change and international affairs.

Fourth, "America First" is the overriding theme of Trump's foreign policy, which departs significantly from his predecessor's foreign policy. Obama believes that the *Paris Agreement* enhances America's climate security, speeds up the transition of the country to a low-carbon economy, promotes the renewable energy industry, strengthens American competitiveness, and creates jobs [9], whereas Trump believes that the agreement weakens the U.S. conventional energy industry, creates job losses and hurts the U.S. economy [10]. Obama stressed that the *Paris Agreement* helps the United States maintain its global leadership while Trump insists that the agreement undermines U.S. sovereignty. As a climate skeptic, Trump puts overwhelming weight on mitigation's economic costs and belittles its ecological and economic benefits, which is consistent with his nationalistic and isolationist America First world view.

Fifth, Trump's move to destroy Obama's legacy is driven by his animosity towards Obama [11]. The acrimony between Trump and Obama started during the 2016 presidential election and has deteriorated since then. New York University historian Naftali said that it is not uncommon for the incumbent president to have a bad relationship with the former president, but an animosity as deep and clear as the one between Trump and Obama is rare in American history [11]. Since taking office, Trump has been dead-set on dismantling everything Obama has done.

The U.S. accession to the *Paris Agreement* is the crown jewel of Obama's legacy, [12] which naturally makes it the primary target of Trump.

In short, the Trump administration's position on climate change is influenced by the U.S. domestic political factors and Trump's personal political views, rather than the claimed abuse and burdens imposed by the *Paris Agreement* on the United States.

4.3 Impacts of the Trump Administration's Climate Change Policies on China

The Trump administration's move to roll back Obama-era climate change policies has profound impacts on China and China-U.S. relations.

First, it will exacerbate ecological vulnerability and climate risk in China.

China is one of the countries that are most susceptible to the adverse effects of climate change. The United States plays a pivotal role in global climate governance. The U.S.' pessimistic climate change policy and withdrawal from the *Paris Agreement* will cause a setback for global efforts to combat climate change—it will make the consequences of global warming more disastrous, and as a result, China's ecological vulnerability and climate risk will increase markedly.

Second, it will increase emissions reduction burden and cost of China.

Since the United States has pulled out from the *Paris Agreement*, it is unlikely that the country will achieve its nationally determined contribution (NDC) targets. The absence of the U.S. in global action on climate change means China and other countries need to set up their efforts in emissions reduction to ensure the goal of limiting warming to below 2 °C above pre-industrial levels will be achieved. The multi-sector, multi-regional, dynamic global computable general equilibrium (CGE) model predicts that:

(1) In the scenario of the NDC targets,[1] if the U.S. reduces its emissions by 20, 13, and 0% below the 2005 levels by 2025, China will face a 0.8–1.1% decrease in the CO_2 emissions range in the year 2030. In the scenario of the 2 °C targets, if the U.S. only reduces its emissions by 20, 13, and 0% below the 2005 levels by

[1]NDC targets are the emissions reduction targets promised by the parties to the *Paris Agreement* in their nationally determined contributions and there is a certain gap between the NDC targets and the 2 °C targets.

2025, China will face a 1.5–1.7% decrease in the CO_2 emissions range in the year 2030.

(2) In the scenario of the NDC targets, if the U.S. only reduces its emissions by 20, 13, and 0% below the 2005 levels by 2025, the carbon price will rise by \$1.1–4.6 per ton in China. In the scenario of the 2 °C target, if the U.S. only reduces its emissions by 20, 13, and 0% below the 2005 levels by 2025, the carbon price will rise by \$4.4–14.6 per ton in China.

(3) In the scenario of the NDC targets, if the U.S. only reduces its emissions by 20, 13, and 0% below the 2005 levels by 2025, China will suffer an additional GDP loss of \$4.75–9.77 billion (per capita GDP loss of \$3.6–14.8). In the scenario of the 2 °C targets, if the U.S. only reduces its emissions by 20, 13, and 0% below the 2005 levels by 2025, China will suffer an additional GDP loss of \$22–71.1 billion (per capita GDP loss of \$16.4–53.1) [13].

Third, the importance of climate cooperation to the China-U.S. relationship has considerably diminished.

Under the Obama administration, China-U.S. cooperation on climate change was one of the major issues shaping the evolution of the relations between the two countries and plays an important role in enhancing mutual trust of the two sides. But the issue of climate change did not come up at either the Xi-Tillerson meeting on 19 March, 2017, or the Xi–Trump meeting at Mar-a-Lago in April 2017. This divergence between the Obama and Trump Administrations suggests that climate change is no longer central to China-U.S. relations.

Fourth, it will further consolidate China's dominant position in the field of renewable energy development.

In 2006, China and the United States were almost at the same level in terms of renewable energy development. The renewable energy power generation capacity in China and the United States was 148,446 MW and 107,917 MW, respectively. Since then, China has gradually taken the lead. By 2016, the renewable energy power generation capacity of China and the United States was 545,206 MW and 214,766 MW respectively [14]. It can be predicted that the withdrawal of the United States from the *Paris Agreement* will further increase China's leading position in the field of renewable energy development to the United States. Some American scholars have been deeply worried about this trend [15].

Fifth, China faces mounting international pressure to redefine its role in global climate governance.

China may be pushed to the global climate leadership position due to the absence the U.S. leadership. America's sudden renouncement of climate leadership departs strikingly from its joint efforts with China underlying the *Paris Agreement*, leading the world to pin its hopes on China. Many American scholars believe that Trump's climate change policy opens opportunities for China to displace the U.S. as a leader on climate change. But leadership means responsibility, and global leadership means global responsibility. There is a growing voice in the international community to urge China to fill the leadership void. China sees itself as a developing country and believes in that contributions should be commensurate with capabilities. It has rejected the idea of redefining its role to a global leader on climate change. As such, it remains a tricky diplomatic challenge for China to respond to the call to step up to fill the leadership vacuum left behind by Washington.

4.4 China's Response: Replacing G2 with C5

It has become obvious that the Trump administration's position on climate change is one of the biggest uncertainties in international climate negotiations and global climate governance. With the absence of the U.S., there is an enormous uncertainty surrounding the future of the *Paris Agreement* and global climate governance. Where is global climate governance heading and what role should China play have become major issues which may reshape the global climate governance system. In this context, China is now facing unprecedented historical opportunities and strategic risks. If China rises to the challenge, its influence in international fora will grow substantially. If not, China may miss the precious window of opportunity or even be hurt both economically and geopolitically.

President Xi has explicitly stated China's position on the *Paris Agreement* was in his speech entitled "Work Together to Build a Community of Shared Future for Mankind at the UN Office of Geneva in January 2017:" The *Paris Agreement* is a milestone in the history of climate governance.

We must ensure this endeavor is not derailed. All parties should work together to implement the *Paris Agreement*. "China will continue to take action to address climate change and assume 100% of its obligations." At present, the central task of global climate action is to rebuild the leadership of global climate governance. There are three possible strategies for China.

Strategy A: China should be committed to its NDC targets but should not make additional mitigation commitments. This strategy is less risky and less costly. However, if China fails to step up at the right time, it may miss a precious opportunity to raise its international influence. Overall, this is a more conservative solution.

Strategy B: China should go all out to fill the leadership void left by the US exit. Some pundits at home and abroad believe that now is the best time for China to redefine its role as a leader on climate change and China should seize the opportunity because it is fully equipped to assume the global climate leadership position. The advantage of this strategy is that it may shorten the time for China to move to the center stage of global governance, and raise its international influence to an unprecedented level. However, it overestimates China's capabilities and underestimates the complexity of global climate governance. It may disrupt China's development pace and increase the risk of strategic overstretch. Overall, this strategy depicts a more radical solution.

Strategy C: In addition to domestic climate action, China should also respond to the expectations of the international community in a positive way by promoting a collective leadership system for global climate governance. The advantage of this option is that it balances the benefits and risks of leading global climate action. It not only provides an opportunity for China to demonstrate its commitment to the global effort to fight climate change but also prevents China from over-stretching its resources. The downside is that it fails to fully tap China's potential as a major global power. Overall, this strategy depicts a progressive approach.

We believe it would be wise for China to adopt Strategy C. Domestically, China should not make additional mitigation commitments besides its NDC commitments, but it should reach the high ends of its current NDC targets, that is, to peak CO_2 emissions before 2030 and to lower the carbon intensity of per unit of GDP by 65% below 2005 levels before the year of 2030. Internationally, China should propose replacing the G2 mechanism with C5.

The Group of Two (G2) is made up by China and U.S. The two countries played a central role in advancing the Paris talks. With the withdrawal of the U.S. from the *Paris Agreement*, the G2 partnership has come to an end. Some Western media have suggested that a new G2 consisting of China and the EU should be formed to assume global leadership. However, this is a highly unlikely scenario. On the EU part, the greenhouse gas emissions (GHG) of the EU are declining. Furthermore, it remains mired in a host of crises and challenges, including the refugee crisis, the debt crisis, the financial crisis, the threat of terrorism and Brexit. The Brexit and its ongoing negotiations, in particular, will eat away the EU's attention to climate change and weaken the EU's position as a global leader. China, despite being a rising power, is still a developing country and lacks experience in agenda setting, global governance, and climate research. The potential China-EU partnership is further complicated by disagreements over the approach to climate governance. Therefore, the proposed new G2 cannot take on the mantle of leadership for global climate action.

In contrast, the C5 partnership is a better alternative. C5 is the abbreviation of "Climate 5", consisting of China, the EU, India, Brazil and South Africa. C5 is necessary because:

First, it can fill the void left by Washington. As mentioned above, the U.S. withdrawal has complex implications for the *Paris Agreement* and global climate governance. It requires collaboration among other major global players, including the UK, France, and Italy on the part of Western countries, as well as India, Brazil, and South Africa as representatives of developing countries, to fill the U.S. void. India in particular as a major emitter should have a bigger voice in future climate talks.

Second, C5 can facilitate cooperation between developed and developing countries to build a global united front against climate change. This partnership features diversity, with India, Brazil, and South Africa representing their respective continents. These countries are also powerful regional leaders in international affairs, contending for new Permanent Member status in the UN Security Council reform. Their engagement will facilitate North–South climate cooperation by fostering unity among countries of the Global South.

Third, the C5 partnership can help reduce the disproportionately high expectation that the international community holds for China since the withdrawal of Washington. This expectation is clearly beyond China's capabilities. Shared leadership will work better than single-nation leadership whether it's from the perspective of China or the international community.

We suggest that China initiate a C5 partnership ministerial conference in due course.

Last but not least, it should be noted that the U.S. is not to be left out.

History shows that no global climate mechanism can work effectively with the U.S. The U.S. has caused substantial loss to other members, including China, by pulling out from the *Paris Agreement*, and it is in every country's interest to bring the U.S. back. Therefore, it is in the interest of all parties to continue to exert pressure on the United States to withdraw from the *Paris Agreement* and find ways to bring the United States back. For now, China may keep the U.S. engaged in three ways. It can change the discourse, focusing more on energy efficiency and energy security and less on climate change within the G20 framework. It can pragmatically push for China-U.S. cooperation on nuclear energy, natural gas, and clean coal. And finally, it can also promote China-U.S. cooperation at the sub-national levels of provinces, states, and cities.

Acknowledgements This study is conducted under the auspices of the National Natural Science Foundation of China (NSFC)'s *2017 Emergency Program—Implications of the United States' Withdrawal from the Paris Agreement on Global Climate Governance and China's Response.*

References

1. Wang, D., & Xiang, Y. Steve Bannon: Trump is a soft-hearted businessman, while Kim Jong-un remain as rational and tough as ever. Caixin.com. Retrieved September 13, 2017, from http://international.caixin.com/2017-09-13/101144435.html.
2. FY2018 Congressional Budget Request, Budget in Brief. US Department of Energy. Retrieved May 2017, from https://energy.gov/sites/prod/files/2017/05/f34/FY2018BudgetinBrief_0.pdf.
3. Light, L. (2017). After Trump's Paris exit, what about nuclear? *CBS News*. Retrieved June 5, 2017, from http://www.cbsnews.com/news/trump-paris-exit-nuclear-power/.
4. Plumer, B., & Davenport, C. Trump budget proposes deep cuts in energy innovation programs. *The New York Times*. Retrieved May 23, 2017, from https://www.nytimes.com/2017/05/23/climate/trump-budget-energy.html.
5. Milman, O. (2016). Paris Climate deal: Trump says he now has an 'Open Mind' about accord. *The Guardian*. Retrieved November 22, 2016, from, https://www.theguardian.com/us-news/2016/nov/22/donald-trump-paris-climate-deal-change-open-mind.
6. Mayer, J. In the withdrawal from the Paris climate agreement, the Koch Brothers' campaign becomes overt. *The New Yorker*. Retrieved June 5, 2017, from http://www.newyorker.com/news/news-desk/in-the-withdrawal-from-the-paris-climate-agreement-the-koch-brothers-campaign-becomes-overt.

7. McCarthy, T., & Gambino, L. The Republicans who urged Trump to pull out of Paris deal are big oil darlings. *The Guardian*. Retrieved June 1, 2017, from https://www.theguardian.com/us-news/2017/jun/01/republican-senators-paris-climate-deal-energy-donations.
8. Haidt, J., & Abrams, S. *The top 10 reasons American politics are so broken*. Washington Post. Retrieved January 7, 2015, from https://www.washingtonpost.com/news/wonk/wp/2015/01/07/the-top-10-reasons-american-politics-are-worse-than-ever/.
9. Obama, B. (2017). The irreversible momentum of clean energy. *Science, 355*(2017), 6284.
10. Statement by president Trump on the Paris climate accord. *The White House*. Retrieved June 28, 2017, from https://www.whitehouse.gov/the-press-office/2017/06/01/statement-president-trump-paris-climate-accord.
11. Liptak, K., & Jones, A. With latest jabs, Trump—Obama relationship reaches historic nastiness. *CNN News*. Retrieved 28, June 2017, from http://edition.cnn.com/2017/06/28/politics/trump-obama-relationship/index.html.
12. President Obama's farewell address: Full video and text. *The New York Times*. Retrieved 10, 2017, from https://www.nytimes.com/2017/01/10/us/politics/obama-farewell-address–speech.html.
13. Dai, H., Zhang, H., & Wang, W. (2017). The impacts of U.S. withdrawal from *Paris Agreement* on the carbon emission space and mitigation cost of China, EU and Japan under constraints of global carbon emission space. *Advances in Climate Change Research, 5*.
14. Renewable Capacity Statistics 2017. (2017). International Renewable Energy Agency.
15. Sivaram, V., & Saha, S. Power outage: Cutting funding for energy innovation would be a grave mistake. *Foreign Affairs*. Retrieved May 22, 2017, from https://www.foreignaffairs.com/articles/united–states/2017-05-17/power-outage?cid=int-rec&pgtype=art.

Chapter 5
China's Role in Global Climate Governance and Causal Analysis

Yan Bo

Abstract As one of the world's biggest emitter of greenhouse gases, China is a key player in global climate governance and has a huge amount of influence on the development of the global climate governance mechanisms. Since 2011, China has played a central role in global climate governance, which is inseparable from China's growing willingness and improved ability to cooperate with other countries.

Keywords Global climate governance mechanism · China's role · Willingness to cooperate · Ability to cooperate

For purposes of this study, the global climate governance mechanism is defined as a set of intergovernmental institutional arrangements made through the UN climate talks to regulate greenhouse gas emissions from relevant actors. The global climate governance mechanism has evolved dynamically over the past 20 years. A series of multilateral climate agreements have been signed and resolutions been made, the most central of which are the *United Nations Framework Convention on Climate Change*, the *Kyoto Protocol* and the *Paris Agreement*. Among them, the Paris Agreement, which came into force in 2016, is based on the principle of "common but differentiated responsibilities and respective capabilities." As a milestone in global climate governance, it has established a basic institutional framework for post-2020 global climate governance.

Nearly 200 countries have participated in the global climate governance mechanism, and China is one of the earliest participants. Although views on

---

Yan Bo is a professor and doctoral advisor at the School of International Relations and Public Affairs at Fudan University. Bo's research interests include environment and international relations, international organizations, and global governance.

Y. Bo (✉)
School of International Relations and Public Affairs, Fudan University, Shanghai, China
e-mail: boyan@fudan.edu.cn

W. Wang (ed.), *Annual Report on China's Response to Climate Change (2017)*,
Research Series on the Chinese Dream and China's Development Path,
https://doi.org/10.1007/978-981-13-9660-1_5

China's role in the international climate governance mechanism vary widely, there is a broad consensus that China is a key player in global climate governance and its role in the international climate governance mechanism is becoming increasingly important. So, what role does China play in the development of the global climate governance mechanism? What factors influence China's participation in global climate governance? These are the issues we will discuss in this paper.

5.1 China's Role in Global Climate Governance

As one of the world's biggest emitter of greenhouse gases, China is a key player in global climate governance and has a huge amount of influence on the development of the global climate governance mechanisms.

Needless to say, China's increasing greenhouse gas (GHG) emissions highlight its image as a huge emitter of greenhouse gases. According to China's official statistics, the total amount of GHG emissions in China (excluding emissions from land use change and forestry) in 1994 was about 4.057 billion tons of CO_2 equivalent, of which CO_2 emissions accounted for 75.8%. This figure rose to about 7.467 billion tons of CO_2 equivalent in 2005, of which CO_2 emissions accounted for 80.0%. In 2012, it further rose to 11.896 billion tons of CO_2 equivalent, of which CO_2 emissions accounted for 83.2% [1]. As can be seen from the above data, since 1994, especially since 2005, China's GHG emissions have has been growing rapidly, and the proportion of CO_2 in GHG has been ticking upward.

According to data from some foreign institutions, in 2015, China emitted 10.4 billion tons of CO_2, accounting for 29% of the total global CO_2 emissions. The United States and the EU accounted for 15% and 10%, respectively. China's annual GHG emissions have exceeded the total emissions of the United States and the EU combined. As for the cumulative emissions from 1870 to 2015, the United States accounted for 26%, the EU 23%, and China 13%.

Although China's contribution to the global cumulative emissions is still lower than the United States and the EU, it is catching up. In 2015, the global per capita CO_2 emissions stood at 4.9 tons; the per capita CO_2 emissions of China, the United States and the EU were 7.5 tons, 16.8 tons and 7.0 tons, respectively. China's per capita CO_2 emissions have exceeded the EU [2].

Because China is a huge emitter, the international community will benefit greatly from the reduction of GHG emissions in China. For example, the global GHG emissions leveled off in 2015 mainly due to the slowdown of China's annual emission growth [3]. It is foreseeable that China will make a substantial contribution to the reduction of global GHG emissions if its GHG emissions reach the peak or decline as scheduled.

China also has a huge amount of influence on the evolution of the global climate governance mechanisms. China was among the earliest countries participating in the global climate governance mechanism which was established in the early 1990s and played an important role in the establishment of the principle of "common but differentiated responsibilities and respective capabilities." However, at that time, China was more regarded as an important member of the developing country camp, and its influence were relatively limited. Views on China's position in the Kyoto talk and the post-Kyoto process vary widely. Some scholars believe that China is a cautious and cooperative participant in international climate talks despite its refusal to assume any reduction obligations [4]. Some scholars believe that China's role has changed from a passive actor to a cautious and conservative participant and then to an active participant [5]. Some Western scholars and media used to cast China in a negative light and describe China's position in global climate talks as "conservative", "defensive", and "stubbornly uncooperative".

Although China made a great effort to bring about an agreement at the 2009 UN Climate Summit in Copenhagen, the agreement was dismissed by many countries as a failure attributed to China because of its refusal to agree to binding targets to reduce its GHG emissions by 2050. Given China and other emerging countries' economic growth, climbing GHG emissions, and rising international influence, their refusal to agree to global long-term emission reduction targets put forward by developed countries was once considered by Western scholars as an attempt to increase influence in global climate governance.

China played a more central and constructive role in the 2011 international climate talks in Durban. It worked hard to safeguard the interests of developing countries and adopted a more flexible and pragmatic negotiation strategy to seek common ground between developed and developing countries. During the 2015 Paris Climate Conference, China proposed that the distinction between developed and developing countries should be reflected in the terms related to, among others, mitigation, adaptation, finance, technology development and transfer, and transparency of action and countries should take actions and assume obligations according to their national conditions. Xie Zhenhua said, China played a crucial role in securing an historic climate agreement in Paris [6] and its proposals have been reflected in the *Paris Agreement*. At the G20 State Leaders Hangzhou Summit, UN Secretary-General Ban Ki-moon spoke highly of President Xi Jinping's role in securing the *Paris Agreement*. China's contribution to the Paris Agreement is a typical example of China's deep involvement in global governance.

Shortly after the *Paris Agreement* entered into force, Donald Trump was sworn in as the president of the United States and took a hatchet to the climate policies of his predecessor. By contrast, Chinese President Xi Jinping said at the World Economic Forum in Davos in January 2017, "The Paris Agreement is a hard-won achievement which is in line with the underlying trend of global development. All signatories should stick to it instead of walking away from it because this is a responsibility we must assume for future generations." This statement has enhanced the confidence of the international community in the further implementation of the Paris Agreement and set the tone for China's stance in global climate action. The international community's expectation of China's leadership on climate is rising.

On March 4, 2017, the Christian Science Monitor published an article entitled "China's coal consumption drops again, boosting its leadership on climate change." According to the article, China has emerged as a world leader in addressing climate change. Some Western scholars believe that China is prepared to fill the void created by the Trump Administration's withdrawal from a crucial multilateral process. For China, this is not only an economic opportunity but also a diplomatic opportunity.

After Trump officially announced the withdrawal of the United States from the Paris Agreement on June 1, 2017, China indicated that it would continue to fulfill its obligations under the climate change accord. As China dramatically expands clean energy investment and creates millions of jobs in the clean energy sector, the international community's expectation for China's leadership on climate is rising. Although there is still debate over whether China should and could take leadership on climate in the post-Paris era, there is no question that China's role in global climate governance has more crucial and central in the post-Paris era.

5.2 Factors Influencing China's Role in Global Climate Governance

China's ability to assume a more central role in global climate governance can be largely attributed to China's growing willingness and improved capability to cooperate with other countries on climate.

1. Growing willingness to cooperate

China was moderately willing to participate in global climate governance in the early 1990s. Since 2011, it has become highly willing to cooperate with other countries in this sphere. China's cooperativeness is based on its sense of responsibility for global governance and for promoting the common and sustainable development of mankind.

China's activity on the international stage related to the reform of the global climate governance mechanism is guided by its global governance philosophies, which are uniquely Chinese. Chinese President Xi Jinping pointed out that the transformation of the global governance system is inseparable from the guidance of sophisticated ideas. At the opening ceremony of the Climate Change Conference in Paris on November 30, 2015, he delivered an important speech entitled "Work Together to Build a Win-Win, Equitable and Balanced Governance Mechanism on Climate Change", proposing that the member states should work to promote "common development," "create a future of the rule of law, fairness and justice," and "accept harmony without uniformity, allowing individual countries to seek their own solutions that best suit their respective national conditions."

This global climate governance ideology has distinctive Chinese characteristics [7]. Guided by the above ideology, China is committed to promoting an inclusive, fair and reasonable global climate governance system and pressing ahead multilateral climate change processes.

In the meantime, the term "ecological civilization" coined by the Chinese government also reflects China's willingness to take climate action domestically and on the international stage. On November 8, 2012, the 18th National Congress of the Communist Party of China proposed that the Chinese government should promote the concept of ecological civilization, respect nature, conform to nature, and protect nature, place ecological civilization construction in a prominent position, and integrate it into economic construction, political construction, cultural construction, social construction on all fronts and throughout the entire process [8]. *The Report to the 18th National Congress of the Communist Party of China* also mentioned that China should "work with the international community to actively respond to global climate change on the basis of equity and in accordance with the principle of common but differentiated responsibilities and respective capabilities" [9]. Apparently, tackling climate change has become an integral part of ecological civilization.

The 18th National Congress of the Communist Party of China set out the general requirements for the construction of ecological civilization. The third, fourth and fifth plenary sessions of the 18th CPC Central Committee specify the following tasks: the reform of ecological civilization system, rule of law and green development. On April 25, 2015, the *Opinions of the Central Committee of the Communist Party of China and the State Council on the Accelerating the Development of Ecological Civilization* was promulgated, pointing out that China should follow a green, cyclical, and low-carbon development path. It proposes that China should actively participate in global climate talks and promote the establishment of a fair and reasonable global climate governance mechanism on the basis of equity and in accordance with the principle of common but differentiated responsibilities and respective capabilities. This shows that tackling climate change has become an inherent part of China's sustainable development strategy.

In short, China has consistent domestic and foreign climate change policy. On the international stage, China emphasizes cooperation and common development in global climate governance and participates in global climate talks in a responsible and constructive manner. Domestically, it is committed to constructing an ecological civilization and integrating climate action in its sustainable development strategy.

2. Increased capability to cooperate

China's capability to cooperate with other countries on climate has improved significantly since 2011. First, the development of climate science in China as well as its wider participation in the IPCC work has given China a stronger voice in international climate negotiations. China has invested heavily in climate change research, established the National Expert Committee on Climate Change, and published two *National Climate Assessment Reports* to help Chinese policymakers make informed decisions regarding actions to fight climate change [10]. In addition, China has always participated in the preparation of the IPCC assessment reports. Chinese scientists made a greater-than-ever-before contribution to the fifth assessment report. The Chinese delegation participated in the review of the summary for policy makers of the IPCC Fifth Assessment Report was composed of Zheng Guoguang, director of the China Meteorological Administration (CMA), and Shen Xiaonong, deputy director of CMA, and experts from different government departments and agencies. The number of Chinese authors involved in the writing of the IPCC Assessment Report has also increased significantly. The number of Chinese authors involved in the first, second, third, fourth and fifth assessment reports of IPCC was nine, eleven, nineteen, twenty eight and forty three, respectively. Chinese authors were involved in the writing of every chapter of the WGI report of the IPCC Fifth Assessment Report [11].

In the meantime, the basic science research on climate change has also developed rapidly in China. For example, the China Meteorological Administration has been seeking to develop new climate projection technologies. It completed the IPCC Coupled Model Intercomparison Project Phase 5 (CMIP5) and provided model results for the IPCC Fifth Assessment Report [12].

Second, China has shifted to a more sustainable economic development model, which fundamentally improves China's capability to participate in global climate governance.

This shift is essential for China's climate governance. In 2013, the convening of the Third Plenary Session of the 18th CPC Central Committee marked a dramatic change in China's economic policy [13]. In 2014, President Xi Jinping put forward the "New Normal" concept. He also pointed out that the five dimensions of development, i.e., innovation, coordination, green, openness, and sharing, proposed at the Fifth Plenary Session of the 18th Central Committee of the CPC are solutions to current problems faced by China's economy and the global economy [14].

Before the Climate Change Conference in Paris, the positive effects of China's new economic growth model have already been shown. China's GDP growth rates in 2014 and 2015 were 7.3% and 6.9%, respectively. In 2015, China's service sector maintained rapid growth, reporting an 8.3% increase in the value added year on year [15]. The installed capacity of non-fossil energy as percentage of China's total installed power capacity increased from 27% in 2010 to 34% in 2015. China's total installed power capacity reached 1.51 billion kilowatts, an increase of 540 million kilowatts over 2010; the consumption of non-fossil energy as percentage of China's total energy consumption reached 12:0% (exceeding the target value 11.2%), an increase of 2.6 percentage points over 2010. During 2011–2015, China's energy consumption per 10,000 yuan of GDP decreased by 18.2%; coal consumption of thermal power plants decreased from 333 grams of standard coal per kilowatt hour in 2010 to 315 grams of standard coal per kilowatt hour in 2015 [16]. The transformation of China's economic growth model has given China more room for manoeuvre on global climate actions. After China's economic growth enters the new normal, low-carbon development is no longer considered a constraint. Chinese policymakers believe low-carbon development offer a strategic opportunity for China to cope with domestic environmental problems, build capacities in the field of low carbon technology and rid China of the notorious major emitter image [17].

Furthermore, China has made great strides in domestic climate governance. It has adjusted its domestic climate policies and strengthened capacity building to address climate change.

China's domestic climate governance capacity has improved significantly since 2011 due to the following actions. First, China has created a nationwide climate governance system under which the National Leading Group on Climate Change takes on the leadership role, the National Development and Reform Commission is responsible for centralized management of climate-related matters, the relevant government agencies and departments at both central and local levels have been assigned specific tasks and all sectors of society are encouraged to participate in climate action. Every province, municipality and autonomous region has set up a leading group on climate change, led by the head of the local government. Some cities have established offices to fight climate change or promote low-carbon development [18]. Second, the Chinese government has attached great importance to improving the top-level design, and developed important strategies to tackle climate change. In September 2014, the National Development and Reform Commission issued the *National Plan to Fight Climate Change (2014–2020).* Most provinces, municipalities and autonomous regions have issued their own special plans to address climate change and incorporated climate change tackling in their economic development plans. Since 2014, the National Development and Reform Commission has issued a series of climate-related policy documents and reports, including *China's Low-Carbon Development Strategy, and China's Low-Carbon Development Strategy—Master Report*. These documents and reports have played an important role in promoting low-carbon development in China and supporting China's participation in international climate talks. Third, the legislative bodies of China have been working to improve relevant laws, regulations and standards. The revised *Law of the People's Republic of China on Prevention and Control of Atmospheric Pollution* was passed at the 16th session of the Standing Committee of the 12th National People's Congress on August 29, 2015. Provincial-level legislative bodies in China have also been working hard to improve climate-related legislation, paving the way for central-level legislation in this field. Fourth, China has made a great effort to improve its basic statistical system and strengthen capacity building in this area. China has set up the National Leading Group on Climate Change, composed of twenty three government agencies and departments, including the National Development and Reform Commission and the National Bureau of Statistics, and established clear accountability for the implementation of the system [19]. Fifth, China has been working to improve its own capacity to mitigate climate change impacts within the country. The Chinese government has issued the *Twelfth Five-Year Plan for Controlling Greenhouse Gas Emissions*, which decomposed the reduction targets to provincial-level targets and established evaluation and accountability systems for the implementation of the targets. In April 2013, the National Development and Reform Commission organized the first trial evaluation of the implementation of GHG emission reduction targets across 31 provinces, municipalities and autonomous regions in 2012, and strengthened the monitoring, management and coordination of nationwide efforts to control GHG emissions [20]. In addition, in order to achieve reduction targets, China has launched a cap and trade pilot project and established a voluntary carbon credit trading mechanism [21].

Since 2011, China has made great strides in domestic climate change governance. By 2014, China's CO2 emissions per unit of GDP decreased by 6.2% year on year, a decrease of 15.8% over 2010; [22] the target of reducing emissions by 17% set by the *Twelfth Five-Year Plan* had been achieved; non-fossil energy accounted for 11.2% of China total energy consumption, an increase of 4.4 percentage points over 2005; forest stock increased by 2.188 billion m^3 over 2005, far exceeding the promised 1.5 billion m^3 [23].

Last but not least, China's capability to participate in the UN multilateral climate talks and mechanisms other than the UNFCCC has improved. China now pays more attention to bilateral and small multilateral consultations, exchanges and cooperation, and its influence on global climate change governance is increasing.

Since 2011, China has been participating in the global climate governance mechanism based on the UNFCCC in a more constructive manner, seeking to strengthen communication with all stakeholders and facilitate progress in international climate negotiations [24]. China has actively participated in the climate negotiations held in Durban, Doha, Warsaw, Lima and Paris, shown support for the host countries, pushing for open and in-depth dialogs [25]. China has also actively participated in multilateral talks beyond the UNFCCC, including the Petersberg Climate Dialogue, the Major Economies Forum on Energy and Climate Change, and climate negotiations held by the International Civil Aviation Organization (ICAO) and the International Maritime Organization (IMO). China has also participated in climate-related discussions held by international organizations beyond the UNFCCC, including the Global Alliance for Clean Cookstoves, the Climate and Clean Air Coalition, APEC, UNCTAD, and the World Trade Organization [26].

5.3 Conclusions

Since 2011, China has been adopting complementary domestic and foreign climate policies. China's current foreign climate policy is quite different from that in the 20th century. The Chinese government's deepened understanding of climate change and the introduction of the ecological civilization concept have paved the way for China's active role in global climate governance. China has seen remarkable progress in climate science at home. In the meantime, the Chinese government is under increasing pressure to clean up the air, which makes it more willing to participate in global climate action. China's capability to participate in global climate governance has also significantly improved. The advancement in the science of climate change, the shift of the economy to a more sustainable growth path, improved climate policy and the comprehensive climate diplomacy strategy has made China's NDC targets more credible and laid the foundation for China's climate action on the international stage. In the meantime, the global climate governance mechanism is becoming more realistic and flexible and the role of developing countries in global climate governance is rising. This change is conducive for the implementation of China's plans to tackle climate change, control air pollution, and promote green and low-carbon transformation.

In the post-Paris era, China will continue to play a key role in the evolution of the global climate governance mechanism not because of China's deliberate pursuit of leadership in this area, but because its capability to strengthen domestic climate governance and participate in global climate action has improved and it is now more willing to take on more international responsibility, address domestic environmental issues and build an ecological civilization. Now that the Chinese government has more science-based understanding of the climate change problem, it is a firm advocate of international cooperation beyond national self-interest, and innovative national and international development models. This is why China is in the vanguard of global climate action. The foreign climate policies of developed countries aim to reshape the production and consumption pattern of other countries whereas China's foreign climate policy is more about changing itself and setting an example for the rest of the world.

References

1. The First Biennial Climate Change Report of the People's Republic of China. China Climate Change Info-Net. Retrieved December 2016, http://www.ccchina.gov.cn/archiver/ccchinacn/UpFile/Files/Default/20170124155928346053.pdf.
2. Global Carbon Budget 2016. Global Carbon Project. Retrieved 2016, from http://wwwglobalcarbonproject.org/about/index.htm.
3. Xie, Z. Global carbon emissions leveled off in 2015 mainly due to the slowdown of China's annual emission growth. China Economic Net. Retrieved March 7, 2016 from http://www.ce.cn/xwzx/gnsz/gdxw/201603/07/t20160307_9330123.shtml.
4. Zhang, H. (2007). China and international climate talks. *The Journal of International Studies, 2007*(1), 21–36.
5. Yan, S., & Xiao, L. (2010). The evolution of China's position in international climate talks. *Journal of Contemporary Asia-Pacific Studies, 2010*(1), 80–90.
6. Xu, F., & Liu, Y. China played a crucial role in securing the Paris Agreement. CNR. Retrieved December 13, 2015, from http://news.cnr.cn/dj/20151213/t20151213_520776754.shtml.
7. Liu, Z. (2016). China's contribution to global climate governance. *Qiushi, 2016*(7), 56–58.
8. National Development and Reform Commission. (2013). *Annual Report on China's Policies and Actions to Address Climate Change*.
9. Report to the 18th National Congress of the Communist Party of China by Hu Jintao. Xinhua. Retrieved November 17, 2012, from http://news.xinhuanet.com/18cpcnc/2012–11/17/c_113711665.htm.
10. Zheng Guoguang stressed that talcking climate change is an inherent part of ecological civilization. Official website of China's central government network. Retrieved July 29, 2013, from http://www.gov.cn/gzdt/2013-07/29/content_2457561.htm.
11. Wang, S. (2014). Making China's Voice Be Heard by the World: China's Contribution to the IPCC Fifth Assessment Report. China Meteorological News, May 20, 2014, 3rd edition.

12. National Development and Reform Commission. (2012). *Annual Report on China's Policies and Actions to Address Climate Change*. Nov 2012.
13. Decision of the Central Committee of the Communist Party of China on Some Major Issues Concerning Comprehensively Deepening the Reforms, adopted at the Third Plenary Session of the 18th Central Committee of the Communist Party of China on November 12, 2013.
14. Xi Jinping elaborated the concept of new normal for the first time. Xinhua. Retrieved November 9, 2014, from http://news.xinhuanet.com/world/2014-11/09/c_1113175964.htm.
15. Service Sector Leads China's Economy in 2015. Official website of China's central government network. Retrieved March 10, 2016, from http://www.gov.cn/xinwen/2016-03/10/content_5051710.htm.
16. Communiqué on the Environmental Condition in China (2015). Official website of the Ministry of Environmental Protection of China. Retrieved June 20, 2016, from http://www.zhb.gov.cn/gkml/hbb/qt/201606/t20160602_353138.htm.
17. Hilton, I., & Kerr, O. (2017). The Paris agreement: China's 'new normal' role in international climate negotiations. *Climate Policy*, *17*(1), 48–58.
18. National Development and Reform Commission. (2013). *Annual Report on China's Policies and Actions to Address Climate Change*.
19. National Development and Reform Commission. (2015). *Annual Report on China's Policies and Actions to Address Climate Change*. Nov 2015.
20. National Development and Reform Commission. (2014). *Annual Report on China's Policies and Actions to Address Climate Change*. Nov 2014.
21. National Development and Reform Commission. (2012). Annual Report on China's Policies and Actions to Address Climate Change (2015). Nov 2015 National Development and Reform Commission. Annual Report on China's Policies and Actions to Address Climate Change (2012). Nov 2012.
22. China's CO_2 emissions per unit of GDP decreased by 6.1% year on year as of 2014. Official website of China's central government network. Retrieved November 19, 2015 from http://www.gov.cn/2015-11/19/content_2968261.htm.
23. National Development and Reform Commission. (2015). *Annual Report on China's Policies and Actions to Address Climate Change*. Nov 2015.
24. National Development and Reform Commission. (2012). *Annual Report on China's Policies and Actions to Address Climate Change*. Nov 2012.
25. National Development and Reform Commission. (2014). *Annual Report on China's Policies and Actions to Address Climate Change*. Nov 2014.
26. National Development and Reform Commission. (2014). Annual Report on China's Policies and Actions to Address Climate Change (2014). Nov 2014; National Development and Reform Commission. (2015). Annual Report on China's Policies and Actions to Address Climate Change (2015). Nov 2015; National Development and Reform Commission. (2016). Annual Report on China's Policies and Actions to Address Climate Change (2016). Nov 2016.

Chapter 6
Flood Risk and Flood Management Policies in China

Xiaotao Cheng

Abstract The scale and pace of China's urbanization over the past two decades is without precedent. The fast urbanization, combined with the impact of global warming, is reshaping the characteristics of flood risk and flooding preparedness needs. The flood control and drainage infrastructure in China's cities fails to catch up with the pace of urbanization. As a result, flooding has become a common problem in cities across the country. In the meantime, in rural China, due to labor shortages caused by the large-scale movement of workers, mostly young workers, from rural areas to cities, dikes in rural areas are poorly maintained and flood relief efforts during the flood season are weakened, thus increasing flood risk and damage. Chinese farmers can be easily caught in vicious cycle of flood and debt. Furthermore, the country's existing social assistance and disaster relief systems are not mature enough to help flood victims rebuild their lives. Based on the results of data analysis and the investigation of typical cases, this paper discusses the evolution of the characteristics of flood risk in China, and suggests that the Chinese policymakers should fully grasp the realities, reestablish harmony with nature, improve flood risk management and emergency response, and step up basic science research and capacity building in this sphere.

Keywords Flood · Risk management · Emergency response · Coping strategies

Xiaotao Cheng is a senior engineer at the Professor level and member of the China National Commission for Disaster Reduction (NCDR). Cheng's research interests include flood prevention and control.

X. Cheng (✉)
China National Commission for Disaster Reduction, Beijing, China
e-mail: chengxt@iwhr.com

W. Wang (ed.), *Annual Report on China's Response to Climate Change (2017)*,
Research Series on the Chinese Dream and China's Development Path,
https://doi.org/10.1007/978-981-13-9660-1_6

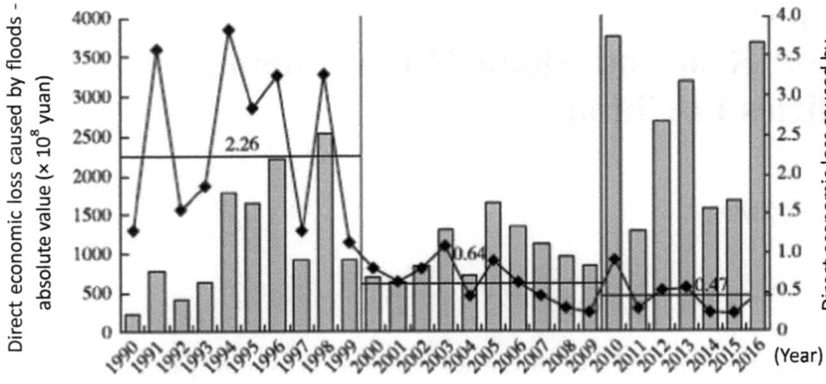

Fig. 6.1 Direct economic loss caused by floods in China during 1990–2016 (absolute value and as percentage of GDP)

6.1 Overview

1. Direct economic loss caused by floods in China since 1990

Figure 6.1 shows the temporal changes in the direct economic loss caused by floods in China since 1990.[1] In the 1990s, high precipitation, combined with reduced central and local government spending on flood prevention control, led to a sharp hike in the direct economic loss caused by floods in China. The direct economic loss caused by floods as percentage of GDP climbed to 1–4%, and the average economic loss over the decade was 2.26%, one or two orders of magnitude larger than in developed countries such as the U.S. and Japan.

To prevent any repetition of the disastrous floods in 1998, the Chinese government doubled the investment in flood control. The central government's spending on water management infrastructure in 1998–2002 was 2.36 times that of 1949–1997; investment in 2006–2010 was 1.93 times that of 2000–2005 [1]; investment in 2011–2015 was 2.9 times [2] that of 2006–2010.

After the beginning of the 21st century, flood control projects of major rivers in China has been fully completed. A number of flagship projects such as the Three Gorges, Xiaolangdi, the Nierji Dam and Linhuaigang have been put into operation. Flood prevention and control plans for reservoirs and small and medium-sized rivers across the country have been put in place. The national four-tiered flood and drought control and emergency response system has been gradually improved. The country's overall flood forecast and response capabilities have been significant enhanced, leading to a decline in damage caused by floods. The average economic loss as percentage of GDP over the first decade of the 21st century dropped to

[1]The data on direct economic loss caused by floods come from the *Report on Floods and Droughts in China*, and GDP data are from the National Bureau of Statistics of China.

0.62%. In the meantime, the number of deaths caused by floods has also decreased significantly. In the 1950s, the number of lives lost due to floods per year in China exceeded 8,500. This figure dropped to more than 4,000 in 1960–1990 and declined further to approximately 1,000 in the 21st century.[2]

However, recent years have seen a rise in the direct economic loss caused by floods in China. Although no floods on big river systems were reported during 2010–2016, China reported an annual flood-caused economic loss higher than that of 1998 in four out of the seven years. Despite this, the direct economic loss caused by floods as percentage of GDP dropped to 0.47, attributable to the rapid growth of GDP. Water is a key resource in sustainable development. The development of water management infrastructure has contributed to the decrease of the direct economic loss caused by floods as percentage of GDP, but China's flood prevention and control system is still facing enormous pressure.

2. Impact of rapid urbanization on the evolution of flood risk

The rapid growth of the economic loss caused by floods in recent years is closely related to the unprecedented pace of urbanization after the beginning of the 21st century and the increase in heavy precipitation events caused by global warming.

As cities grow in population and resources, the risks they face are also growing. Since 2006, more than 100 cities in China were inundated each year mostly by heavy rains. China still maintained the basic characteristics of an agrarian society when it started to implement the reform and opening-up strategy. At the time, the farming, forestry, animal husbandry and fishery sectors were the largest victims of floods. However, since 2010, cities have become the largest victims of floods.

International experience shows that, when more than 30% of the population of a country/region are urbanized, the pace of development of the country/region may accelerate. The percentage of China's total population living in urban areas exceeded 30% in 1998. In the same year, the central government of China began to gradually removed foreign trade restrictions on private companies in an attempt to pull the country out of the recession following the 1997 Asian financial crisis; ended the practice of allocating housing units and launched a "commercial housing" scheme which is the major reason why the real estate industry has become the primary driving force of economic growth in China in the past two decades; issued government bonds and increased government investment in infrastructure [3]. These policies and measures have led to accelerated urbanization in the country. The percentage of China's total population living in urban areas increased by about 12% from 1978 to 1998 and about 26% from 1998 to 2016. Since the beginning of the 21st century, the urban population of permanent residents in China has increased by 334 million, exceeding the total population of the United States. In 2000, there were only forty cities with a population of over one million in China, and by 2015 there were more than 140.

[2]The data on deaths caused by floods come from the *Report on Floods and Droughts in China*.

It should be noted that Chinese cities are growing in an extensive manner. China's land system has created convenient conditions for local governments to make money from selling land, leading to fast growth in construction land in urban areas. From 1981 to 2014, China's urban population increased 3.7 times, while construction land in China's urban areas increased 7.4 times. The enormous pressure from extensive urbanization on the environment and threats to water security far exceed in other countries.

The fast urbanization, combined with the impact of global warming, is reshaping the characteristics of flood risk (victims, cause, damage structure, etc.) and flooding preparedness needs in China. Property susceptible to flood damage expands from farmland and fish ponds to buildings and cars. Cities are becoming increasingly dependent on water supply, power supply, oil supply, gas supply, transportation, telecommunication, and other systems. If these systems are affected by floods, the supply chains of companies will be interrupted, causing indirect losses outside of the flooded area. In cities, floods not only damage underground shopping malls, parking lots, warehouses and subway systems but also affect high-rise buildings. In rural China, due to labor shortages caused by the large-scale movement of young workers from rural areas to cities, dikes in rural areas are poorly maintained and flood relief efforts during the flood season are weakened. In the meantime, the number of large farms in China are increase and these farms can be easily caught in vicious cycle of flood and debt. It is very difficult for the owners of these farms rebuild their lives after floods. Furthermore, people are now more demanding of water security. The flood prevention and control system is not only about reducing losses but also about risk mitigation and sharing. When a flood occurs, people not only wish to return to their normal life as soon as possible but also call for environment improvement. China is facing a historically unprecedented combine of challenges in water security.

In the meantime, during 2014–2016, we experienced an unprecedented streak of three consecutive record hot years; the probability of an extreme weather event and uncertainty in event attribution are increasing, which also makes weather forecast more difficult and put current flood defense infrastructure under enormous pressure.

6.2 Evolution of Flood Risk in the Context of Rapid Urbanization

6.2.1 Risk Characteristics: Case Studies

A. Wuhan, 2016

1. Characteristics of floods

In 2016, Wuhan had several big rainfall events. The most severe three rainfall events occurred on June 1, June 19 and June 30–July 6, inundating swaths of the city. The rainfall stretching from June 30 through July 6 was the worst. In three

Fig. 6.2 Nanhu Yayuan residential compound, Wuhan following the flood

days out of the seven-day stretch, the precipitation reached 50–100 mm/day (heavy rain), and the rain pattern was unfavorable. On the last day, the precipitation reached more than 200 mm/day and the accumulated rainfall reached 560.5 mm which was the highest weekly precipitation ever recorded in Wuhan. The second highest weekly precipitation record was 538.5 mm, reported in 1998. On July 7, the highest water level in the Wuhan section of the Yangtze River was 28.37 m, which was the fifth highest water level in this section ever.

On June 1 and 19, the rainfall in some areas of Wuhan exceeded 100 mm/day, causing twenty seven and fifty four observation points respectively in the city to be inundated. The most disastrous flood occurred in July 5–6. Heavy rainfall (above 200 mm/day) lashed the city, drowning nearly 190 observation points and affecting 757,000 people in twelve districts of the city. After the disaster relief team working around the clock for 24 h, the water levels at 162 observation points on trunk and secondary roads in the downtown area dropped by 90%, but the areas (about 9 km^2 in total) surrounding the Nanhu Lake and the Tangxun Lake remained inundated (inundation depth: 0.2–1.5 m), affecting more than 100 residential compounds and approximately 61,000 residents. The Nanhu Yayuan Residential Compound, located near the Nanhu Lake, was soaked in water for ten days. Although the first floor of these lakeside buildings was elevated to a flood protection elevation (see Fig. 6.2), the power supply system was damaged by the flood. To high-rising buildings, power outage also means loss of water supply. More than 8,600 residents trapped in the buildings were left without refrigeration, air conditioning, or running water and needed to be evacuated as soon as possible, putting extra pressure on the local disaster relief team.

Wuhan, stretching 8,494 km^2, is a wet southern city. It is where the Yangtze River meets the Hanjiang River. The city is home to 166 lakes and 277 reservoirs.

The total surface area of water bodies in the city reaches 2,117.6 km^2, accounting for one fourth of the total area of the city. The most part of the city is lying at an altitude of 20–24 m above sea while the average flood warning alert level of the Wuhan section of the Yangtze River is 24 m. To prevent flooding, Wuhan has demarcated a flood hazard zone in each of the three towns within its jurisdiction. When the water level reaches the drought alter water level of the Yangtze River (15–17 m), and the water in the flood hazard zones can be discharged without human intervention. In the flood season, the rainfall in the flood hazard zones needs to be diverted to lakes or discharged by pumping stations. In recent years, drainage infrastructure in Wuhan has improved significantly. During 2011–2015, the total pumping capacity of the pumping stations in the city increased by 30% over that in the 2006–2010 period. However, due to rapid urbanization and poor design of the flood control discharge system, the overall discharge capacity of the city is still insufficient. In June 2011, Wuhan was lashed by the strongest rainstorm since 1998. The catchphrase "watching the sea in the city" was created in Wuhan in the same year. In 2013, Wuhan launched a three-year plan to improve the flood control discharge system in the downtown area. Wuhan City was among the first group of cities selected in 2015 to participate in the Sponge City Pilot Program. In 2016, it was still frequently inundated and the government was lambasted by citizens on the Internet for its incompetence.

2. Problems and challenges

In 2016, Wuhan was inundated three times. Citizens began to ask the following questions:

(1) In 2013, Wuhan unveiled a 13 billion yuan plan to improve the flood control discharge system in the downtown area within three years. Now that three years have passed, why does Wuhan City still frequently drown in heavy rain? The Water Affairs Bureau of Wuhan City has responded to this question. According to the bureau, it developed a three-year plan in the first half of 2013 to improve the drainage system in the downtown area in a step-by-step manner. The plan consisted of 211 projects and the total estimated investment was 12.985 billion yuan. The goal was to improve the drainage capacity of the downtown area and ensure that the municipal services of the downtown area would not be affected by any rainfall event that is below 200 mm/day or 50 mm/h [4]. However, as of the end of June 2016, only 42.4% of the planned projects had been completed. Due to the difficulties of land acquisition, governmental red tape, and amendments of national engineering standards, a number of key drainage projects, especially large pumping stations and lakeside and riverside discharge channels the construction of which can only be carried out in non-flood seasons, fell behind schedule. Revamping the flood control discharge system of a city is a complex and arduous task which cannot be easily solved in the short-term by investing a massive amount of money.
(2) When did the Three Gorges Dam continue to release water when Wuhan was flooded? What role does the Three Gorges Dam play in flood control in the

middle and lower reaches of the Yangtze River? In fact, on July 1, 2016, the Three Gorges Dam in the upper reaches of the Yangtze River reported a peak flow of 50,000 m^3/s, and the flow rate of the Yangtze River after passing the Three Gorges Dam was 31,100 m^3/s. To reduce flood control pressure in the middle and lower reaches, the flow rate was further reduced to 25,000 m^3/s on July 6 and 20,000 m^3/s on July 7. On July 7, the peak water level at Hankou Station reached 28.37 m, which was more than 1 m lower than in 1954 (29.73 m) and 1998 (29.43 m). Obviously, the flooding in Wuhan was caused by local heavy rain and could not be solely solved by the Three Gorges Dam.

(3) Is the sharp drop in the surface area of the lakes in Wuhan City among the biggest culprits for the flooding in the city? Has the drop been effectively curbed? The total area of Wuhan is 8,494 km^2 and the area of built-up area in 2014 stood at 878.8 km^2, four times larger than in 1982 (173 km^2). The total surface area of lakes in Wuhan decreased from 1,222.4 km^2 in the early 1970s to 915.3 km^2 in 2015, mainly due to agricultural reclamation in the earlier days and land fill for the urban expansion purpose in the past two decades.

In fact, following *Measures for Protecting Natural Mountains and Lakes in Wuhan City* in 1999, Wuhan released *Lake Protection Regulations* in 2002 and *Implementation Rules for the Regulations* in 2005. In 2012, Wuhan became the first city in the country to set up a special government agency, the Lake Management Bureau, to integrate lake protection and water-related law enforcement, and developed a protection plan covering 40 lakes in the downtown areas. With a sound legal and regulatory framework in place for lake management, by 2015 the city had demarcated the boundaries of all its 166 lakes, the lakeside greenbelts and the buffer zones for lake protection. Remote sensing data show that land reclamation in Wuhan has been largely curbed in recent years, though the sizes of the lakes across the city, in the urban areas and suburban areas are all shrinking (see Fig. 6.3) [5]. However, it is near to impossible to restore the approx. 300 km^2 surface area of lakes that has already disappeared. In the past, the flood control systems in some areas focused primarily on the storage function. Now, due to the drop in the surface area of lakes, they need to place equal emphasis on the storage and discharge functions. In 2016, Wuhan launched a series of flood protection pumping station construction and revamp projects, including Jiangnan Pumping Station, Sixin Pumping Station and Houhu Pumping Station. Before the flood season in 2017, the total discharge capacity increased from 970 m^3/s to nearly 1,500 m^3/s with an annual increase of over 50%.

(4) Pollution of Huangxiao River

Huang Xiao River is an important part of the drainage system in Hankou, Wuhan. It is 9.6 km long and has a surface area of 48.53 km^2. It serves about 1.1 million local residents.

By the mid-twentieth century, the Hankou District had doubled in size, and the surface area of lakes in the Huangxiao River Basin declined from 20 km^2 to less than 3 km^2. By the 1980s, Huangxiao River had been severely polluted. Two heavy

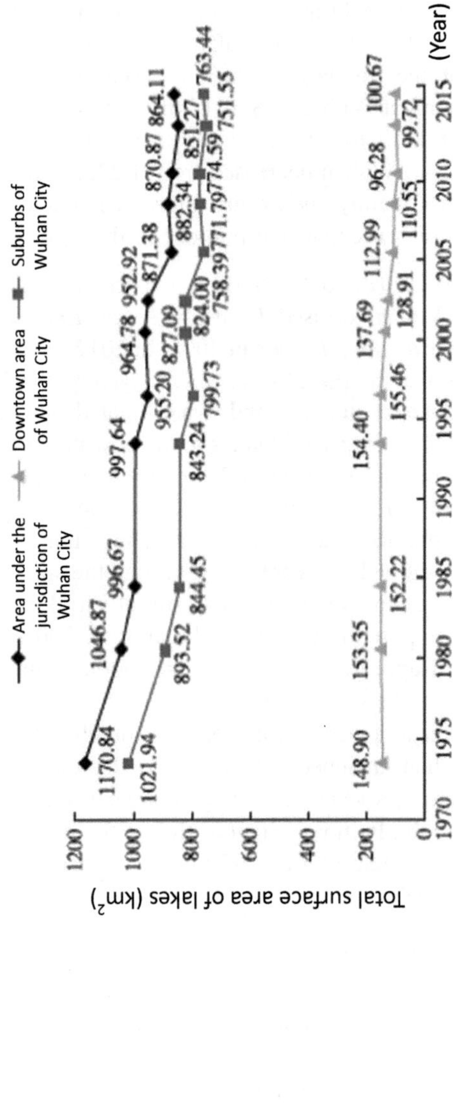

Fig. 6.3 Fluctuations of the surface area of lakes in suburbs, the downtown area and the area under the jurisdiction of Wuhan City, 1973–2015

rain events in 1982 and 1983 caused sewage overflows and collapse of buildings in the Hankou District. To avoid a repeat of such a disaster, the government of Wuhan has been working to improve the flood control system of the Huangxiao River. After eight years of hard work, the city has built 4.3 km underground box culverts and 5.3 km open channels, significantly increasing the discharge capacity of the Huangxia River. However, the total volume of sewage discharged into the Huangxiao River is about 300,000–400,000 tons/day, and the rate of rainwater flowing into the river is 97–130 m^3/s, but the discharge capacity of the Huangxia River is only 250,000 tons. The massive influx of sewage and rainwater into the open channels cannot be discharged in a timely manner and generates foul odors over time. Despite the dredging and shoreline remediation projects in 2007 and 2010, the Huangxiao River is still blanketed by the foul stench of sewage. The pollutants discharged into the river has far exceeded its self-cleaning capacity. It requires the concerted, sustained efforts on all fronts to clean up the Huangxiao River.

B. Anhui, 2016

1. Characteristics of floods

(1) Record high precipitation. From June 18 to July 5, 2016, the average rainfall in the Anhui section of the Yangtze River Basin was 551 mm. The maximum 3-day and 7-day precipitation was the highest ever recorded in this region (Fig. 6.4) and the maximum 15-day precipitation was second only to the highest record in 1969. Such a rainfall event has a one in fifty chance of occurring in a year.[3]

(2) High water levels in the Waijiang branch of the Yangtze River, with a particular section being the major contributor to the flooding. ① The water level reported at the Datong Station was 1.21–3.34 m higher than normal, and that at the Anqing Station was 2.79–5.13 m higher than normal. The lakes along the Yangtze River had been filled to the brim since April and thus could not perform the flood control storage function. ② The water level of the section of the Yangtze River stretching from the Huikou Station where the Yangtze River enters Anhui Province to the Datong Station was 0.8–1.5 m lower than that in 1998. The water level observed at the Maanshan Station where the Yangtze River leaves Anhui Province reaches the highest water level ever recorded at the site (which was recorded in 1999), indicating that the section from the Datong Station to the Maanshan Station was the main contributor to the flooding. ③ Thirty-four rivers in the Yangtze River Basin exceeded the warning level and thirteen rivers, including Zhanghe River, Xihe River and Yong'an River, reported historically unprecedented high water levels. Water levels in all lakes along the Yangtze River rose above the warning level. Among them, Baidang Lake, Fengsha Lake, Caizi Lake, and Shengjin Lake

[3]Reflection on the floods starting on May 18 in Anhui Province. Anhui Hydrology Bureau, July 31, 2016.

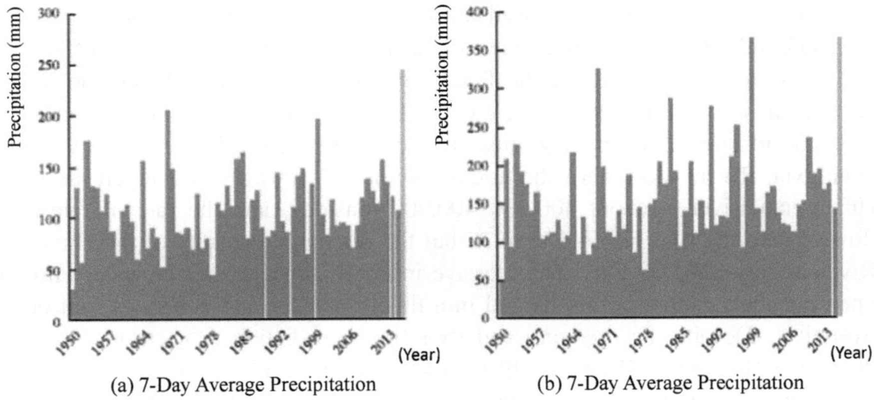

Fig. 6.4 3-day and 7-day average precipitation of the section of the Yangtze River Watershed in Anhui Province over the Years

exceeded their highest levels ever recorded. The flood volume in 2016 in the Yangtze River Basin was second only to that in 1954.

(3) Many small and medium-sized rivers and lakes reported water levels above flood stage. To prevent any repetition of the disastrous floods in 1998, the Chinese government has strengthened the embankments along the Yangtze River and the flood control embankments within cities. In 2016, no risk of severe flooding was reported in the flood season, and the flood risk of thirty-eight reservoirs which reported water levels above the alert levels was controlled in a timely and effective manner. However, the overall flood control measures for small and medium-sized rivers were still insufficient. Water levels at 1,831 riverside and lakeside polders rose above the alert levels. One hundred and twenty-nine polders covering an area of more than 1,000 mu were flooded, of which twelve covered an area more than 10,000 mu. The floods lasted from days to months. The number of flooded polders stretching over 10,000 mu was in the neighborhood of that in 1999 (see Table 6.1).[4]

2. Problems and challenges [6]

(1) The flood control systems have not been adapted to the changing society in a timely and effective manner. ① Due to the massive rural to urban migration, mainly of young people, the flood control, rescue and relief manpower in rural areas is severely insufficient. Flood control and relief work mainly relies on troops, armed police, government officials and militia. ② As a result of the land transfer policy, 40–90% of land in polders in the province is managed by large family farms in an intensive manner. The floods had destroyed crops, drowned animals, and damaged infrastructure and equipment, pushing farmers deeper into a cycle of debt that they couldn't escape. ③ Poor rural collectives

[4]Prepared by the author based on data from the flood and drought control office of Anhui Province.

Table 6.1 Polders flooded and at risk of being flooded in the Anhui section of the Yangtze River Basin in 2016 and 1999

	Number of polders at risk of being flooded		Number of flooded polders		Damaged cropland ($\times 10^4$ mu)
	Total number	Major embankments	Over 1,000 mu	Over 10,000 mu	
2016	1,831	24	129	12	1,210
1999	8,662	257	180	14	3,693
Number for the year 2016 divided by the number for the year 1999 (%)	21.1	9.3	71.7	85.7	32.8

don't have enough money to maintain flood prevention and relief teams, materials and equipment.

(2) There are still many problems in Anhui Province's flood protection and control system. ① There is a lack of up-front planning for flood risk management of small and medium-sized rivers and a lot of nonconforming embankments in the province. The majority of the flooded polders lie along the banks of small and medium-sized rivers and lakes. ② Following the 1998 floods, Anhui Province had put in place a program to return farmland to lakes and resettle residents living in polders. However, in order to maintain social stability, the government failed to follow through on the program.

In the meantime, some polders were connected and more polders were built, affecting flood control channels and reducing the storage volume of the lakes. ③ The existing flood discharge capacity in polders and some urban and rural areas remain insufficient. The flood control discharge systems in some newly built urban areas or development zones are still designed in accordance with older standards for rural areas. Some urban areas and low-lying areas in rural areas are vulnerable to flooding. ④ Active flow divergence is an effective approach but difficult to implement. The location, flow rate, and timing of divergence can be controlled and the loss caused by active divergence is also small. However, even when the embankments collapsed, the floodwater still was not diverged to appropriate areas, including some polders which had completed the resident resettlement program. ⑤ The critical water level, flood defense level and flood alert level have not been updated in a timely manner. ⑥ It is difficult for local government to decide whether to abandon certain embankments that are at risk of burst. If the government decides to shore up an embankment but the embankment eventually failed to hold up against the floodwater, the loss may be greater than if the embankment were abandoned; even if the government decides to give up the embankment, evacuate residents and diverge the floodwater to the low-lying area protected by the embankment, there are still compensation and accountability issues.

(3) There are many problems which reduce the effectiveness of flood control measures in Anhui Province. ① Constructing, revamping, upgrading, operating and maintaining flood risk monitoring, early warning and other flood prevention and control projects requires a lot of money. Local government coffers are usually not big enough to timely solve pressing problems in local flood control systems. ② Compensation and insurance mechanisms are still weak. Although it has been widely accepted by residents in flood-prone areas that it is necessary to diverge water to the areas they live when the flooding is difficult to contain, the lack of a reasonable compensation policy makes the fact hard to swallow. ③ At present, the key to improving the management of small and medium-sized rivers is to update the flood control standards of key sections and strengthen the overall planning. The relevant government agencies and departments should be encouraged to participate in flood control and link rural development, land remediation, resettlement, town development, land cultivation, transfer of rural house sites and other government work to flood control.

6.3 Suggestion for Policymakers: Adopting an Integrated Approach to Risk Reduction

(1) Understanding water control needs in different stages of economic and social development

The characteristics of flood risk vary widely across China due to different natural and geographical conditions. Water control systems must be designed with local realities in mind. Even in the same region, water management issues and needs are also different at different stages of economic and social development. Water management principles, approach and technical methods should be kept up to date.

After entering the 21st century, there has been a growing urgency on the global scale to strengthen the management of flood and drought risks [7]. Concerned about the new challenges brought about by global warming, economic globalization and population aging, developed countries are actively responding to the potential risks brought about by climate change and attempting to solve the increasingly complex water problems which pose a serious obstacle to sustainable development by promoting integrated basin management and risk management, keeping water management principles and methods up to date, facilitating information sharing and public participation, and establishing and maintaining a balanced and effective water security system.

The Chinese economy continues to grow at a fast pace. The increasing severe water scarcity problem, deteriorating water environments, and growing loss caused by floods rather than potential risks in the future are the main concern of the developing country. China's water security goal is not to simply curb the growth of loss caused by floods and droughts. It also aims to smartly use water projects to support the rapid and coordinated economic and social development. To this end, the Chinese government should improve its flood and drought risk management strategies, create well-functioning systems and mechanisms and strengthen capacity building.

In fact, China's permanent urban residents reached 57.4% of its total population in 2016. However, the urbanization pace varies widely across the country. The urban population in China's coastal areas have exceeded 60% of the total population in these areas. By contrast, the urban population in the country's central and western regions have just reached or are still less than 50% of their total populations. China is still finding its way towards an equilibrium state. The flood prevention and control infrastructure in the country is still lagging behind. It is important to understand the implications of "maintaining existing balance" and "establishing a new balance" on water management. It should be noted that, when it comes to water management approaches and principles, the latest is not always the best. It would be much wiser to adopt approaches and principles that best fit the current development stage.

Table 6.2 compares the definition of rivers, spatial extension of rivers, and function of rivers, river management approaches and systems in the following stages: ① the initial development stage, and the industrialization stage; ② the pollution control stage; and ③ the integrated management and sustainable use stage [8].

As shown in Table 6.2, the water control measures in the first two stages are mainly centralized and large-scale engineering measures. Decentralized, small, and green infrastructure begin to play a more important role in the third stage. Most regions in China are still in the pollution control stage, and some western regions are still in the initial development stage or the industrialization stage. Only some eastern regions have entered the integrated management and sustainable use stage. Therefore, currently, a combination of large grey infrastructure and small green infrastructure are the most suitable river management approach for China.

2. Promoting integrated water management models which place emphasis on human relationships with water

In the new era, water projects should pay more attention to human relationships with water. Flood control systems should be reasonably planned, designed in accordance with up-to-date standards, kept in good working order and deployed scientifically. In addition to increasing flood control discharge capacity, local governments should also realize the importance of flood control storage.

For small and medium-sized rivers, spillways can be used to provide the controlled release of flows from a dam or levee. Spillways regulate downstream flows by releasing flood flow in small amounts so that there is enough time for evacuation in the downstream area. After the water level drops to below the critical level, the floodwater can be drained as appropriate so that people in the flooded area can return to their normal life as soon as possible.

Table 6.2 River management approaches by development stage

Understanding	Development		
	The initial development stage, and the industrialization stage	Pollution control	Integrated management and sustainable use
Definition of rivers	Hydrological system Physical system	Hydrological system Physical system	A system with hydrological, ecological, economic and social functions
Spatial extension of rivers	River channel + waters	River channel + waters + riverside space	Waters+riverside +living organisms +communities near the river
Important functions	Flood control, water supply and drainage, fishery, transportation, and hydropower development (A)	A+water quality control (B)	B+biodiversity, landscape diversity, and historical and cultural functions
River management approach	Engineering and economics: focus on controlling rivers	Engineering, economics, and passive pollution control: focus on human intervention	Ecological, economic, social, and cultural aspects of sustainable development: focus on the human-river relationship
Technical water management measures	Use river engineering methods to improve water security and ramp up hydropower utilization (A)	A + improve water management capabilities, prevent water pollution from industrial and domestic sources, and step up river and lake dredging	Ecological restoration, environmental management, closer to nature landscaping, cultural functions and other functions
Flood control measures	Embankment, flood diversion, flood control channels, sluices and pumping station, reservoirs, and flood relief (A)	A + flow diversion system, flood control monitoring and dispatching system, and emergency response (B)	B + rainwater storage, infiltration, floodproofing of buildings, super embankment, underground rainwater storages systems, multi-functional flood detention areas, risk management, etc.

Institutional innovation is crucial to the improvement of flood control systems. Relevant departments should ① scientifically determine the location and design dams and reservoirs; ② use engineering means to control flood flow, make sure the water does not damage or destroy the dam, and minimize the flooded area and the length of flooding; ③ compensate flood losses of residents in polders where floodwater is diverged to; ④ promote inter-departmental cooperation through a combination of administrative tools, policies and incentives and establish a clear link between performance and pay increases.

3. Taking a systematic and proactive approach to management of small and medium-sized rivers on the part of local governments

In fact, the flood control systems targeting large rivers across China has significantly improved. It is the areas around small and medium-sized rivers that are more prone to floods. In order to build flood control and river management capabilities, local governments are calling for holistic planning, phased implementation and removal of the cap (30 million yuan) on flood control investment.

Under the hierarchical river management system, local governments are responsible for managing small and medium-sized rivers within their jurisdiction. However, in recent years, since the central government increased its investment in the management of small and medium-sized rivers, some local governments has been trying to push the responsibility of managing local rivers onto the central government. There are many small and medium-sized rivers in China. On the one hand, the characteristics of flood risk of these rivers vary widely and therefore different rivers required different flood control approaches. On the other hand, the water control needs, targets and investment capability concerning a particular river will also change over time. Considering the diverse flood risk characteristics, the hierarchical structure of China's small and medium-sized river management system should continue to be implemented. Local governments should still assume the leadership role in the management of small and medium-sized rivers within their jurisdiction and work together to create synergies.

The central government should offer necessary support and guidance. The "river chief" system implemented in China mainly focuses on problems such as river pollution and environmental damage. From the perspective of comprehensive water management, it is necessary to promote institutional innovation related to the management of small and medium-sized river basins.

4. Increasing investment in basic research

(1) The Chinese government should amend the *Flood Prevention and Control Law of the People's Republic of China*. The key is to: ① establish a risk management mechanism; ② coordinate related policies; and ③ put in place an operating system under which local governments assume a leadership role in the management of rivers within their jurisdiction and all sectors of the society are encourage to participate.
(2) A reasonable mechanism should be established to compensate flood losses of residents in areas where floodwater is diverged to. A hierarchical compensation

mechanism should be put in place to compensate flood losses of residents in polders around or near small and medium-sized rivers and lakes so that the proactive flood flow divergence method can be efficiently implemented without obstruction by local residents.

(3) A flood insurance management system should be established in flood-prone areas. The introduction of such a management mechanism will help steer the organization of farming activities towards formats that are best fit for the characteristics of the flood risk in the area. In the meantime, how to design insurance to provide protection from extreme weather events is a field that still remains unexplored.

(4) The flood risk management system should be further improved. Flood control planning activities in China are carried out at the river basin or administrative region level. Small and median-sized rivers often span multiple administrative regions and their management requires a combination of the planning mechanism and the market mechanism.

(5) The flood risk management capabilities of front-line agencies should be strengthened. Front-line flood control agencies have the most demanding work but relatively weak capabilities. Executive officials of these agencies often lack awareness of risk management and there are also wide inter-regional divergence in terms of awareness of risk management. In addition to increasing investment and technological input to improve the flood control grey infrastructure, it is also necessary to explore how to improve comprehensive flood risk management and overall planning by water management departments at all levels.

References

1. Ministry of Water Resources. *China invested about 700 billion yuan in water-related projects during 2011–2015*. Retrieved December 25, 2010, from http://news.cntv.cn/20101225/100495.shtml.
2. China's water management reform achieved remarkable results during 2011–2015. Retrieved February 17, 2016, from http://www.ndrc.gov.cn/gzdt/201602/t20160217_774779.html.
3. Hu, J., Wang, Y., et al. (2016). A glance into the Chinese economy in 1998. *The Economic Observer*.
4. The Department of Water Affairs of the Wuhan Government. Report on the Implementation of the Three-Year Plan for the Construction of the Drainage System in the Downtown Area of Wuhan. Retrieved August 10, 2016, from http://www.whwater.gov.cn/water/tzgg/7709.jhtml.
5. Ma, J., Huang, S., et al. (2017). Remote monitoring of surface area fluctuations of lakes in Wuhan from 1973 to 2015. *Journal of Hydraulic Engineering*, 2017(8).
6. The following portion is an excerpt of *Flooding in the Anhui Section of the Yangtze River Basin in 2016: Characteristics, Problems and Countermeasures* by Cheng, X., Liu, H., Huang, S., et al., published on China Flood & Drought Management, 2017(1).

7. Cheng, X. (2009). Supporting development and ensuring water security—The dual functions of the flood and drought management system in the new era. *China Flood & Drought Management*, 2009(4).
8. Song, Q., & Yang, Z. (2002). Reflection on the integrated management of rivers in Chinese cities. *Advances in Water Science, 3*.

Chapter 7
Climate Resilient Cities: Water Security

Yongying Tian

Abstract A well-function urban water security system is central to a climate resilient city. This paper examines problem identification, systematic planning, policy implementation and coordination mechanisms related to water security and offers policy recommendations for the development of a climate resilient urban water security system. Such recommendations include promoting water conservation practices, building sponge cities, and updating urban planning and building standards.

Keywords Climate change · Climate resilient cities · Urban water security systems

7.1 Introduction

The opening ceremony of the Rio Olympic Games depicted catastrophic impacts of global warming, from melting of glaciers in the Arctic and Antarctic to rising sea levels and sinking coastal cities. Climate change is not only an environmental issue but also a major political issue faced by the international community. But ultimately it is a development issue. Climate change is a huge challenge for all mankind at present and for a long time to come, but it also offers a major innovation opportunity to human society.

Mitigation and adaptation as two complementary approaches to combating climate change. Climate mitigation is any action taken to eliminate or reduce risk and

---

Yongying Tian, deputy director and research associate at the Center of Science and Technology & Industrialization Development, the Ministry of Housing and Urban-Rural Development. Tian's research interests include climate resilience of cities, urban ecological restoration, and sponge cities.

Y. Tian (✉)
Center of Science and Technology & Industrialization Development,
The Ministry of Housing and Urban-Rural Development, Beijing, China
e-mail: tyy_tj@163.com

W. Wang (ed.), *Annual Report on China's Response to Climate Change (2017)*,
Research Series on the Chinese Dream and China's Development Path,
https://doi.org/10.1007/978-981-13-9660-1_7

hazards of climate change, mainly by reducing greenhouse gas (GHG) emissions. Climate adaptation refers to adjustment in natural or human systems in response to actual or expected climatic stimuli or their effects, which moderates harm or exploits beneficial opportunities. In ancient China, people lived in caves or used wood to build dwellings to protect themselves from disasters. Compared with mitigation, adaptation focuses more on improve human relationships with the nature. Cities are an important platform for development and spaces in which people work and live. They are agglomerations of population, resources and industries. At present, more than one half of the world's population lives in cities. By 2050, this proportion will rise to two thirds. Cities consume 80% of energy produced worldwide and are major contributors to global greenhouse gas emissions. With high population density and concentration of economic activities, cities are particularly vulnerable to increase in temperature, smog, heavy rain, strong wind, and water shortage caused by climate change. Making cities climate resilient is a matter of vital public interest and has significant implications sustainable development of cities. Green development is one of the five development concepts set out in China's *Thirteen Five-Year Plan*. Climate adaption is an inherent requirement of green development. The "Beautiful China" campaign is part of China's contribution to global ecological security.

7.2 Impact of Climate Change on Water Security

The major water security issues caused by climate change include water shortage, flooding, water environment deterioration, and degradation of water-related ecological service functions.

1. Water shortage. According to the criteria of UN-HABITAT, more than 300 cities in China faces water scarcity, and water supplies in Chinese cities is six billion m^3 below water demands, causing economic losses of about 200 billion yuan. The development of local water resources in most cities are close to or have reached the maximum level, and groundwater in some cities is already over-exploited. According to the *Communiqué on the Environmental Condition in China (2016)*, among the 6,124 groundwater quality monitoring points (GQMP), more than 60% GQMPs reported poor and very poor water quality. Urban water scarcity, caused by the lack of enough water (quantity) and lack of access to safe water (quality), has seriously affected citizens' work and quality of life.
2. Flooding. Rainstorms are very common in China. Some cities are often battered by heavy rainstorms accompanied by strong convective weather phenomena such as thunder, strong winds and hail, causing some rivers to rise and flood cities. Some cities fail to capture and use stormwater runoffs efficiently and are thus frequented by flash floods. For example, on July 21, 2012, Beijing was battered by a heavy rainstorm which resulted in 79 deaths and caused economic

losses estimated at 10 billion yuan. In 2016, heavy rainfalls inundated nearly 100 cities in 26 provinces, including cities in Anhui, Hubei, Hunan, Guizhou, North China, and the Huanghuai Region.

3. Deterioration of water environment. According to the results of a nationwide water survey conducted by the Ministry of Water Resources, 46.5% of the country's rivers are polluted, and their water quality only reaches Grade IV or Grade V; 10.6% of the rivers are seriously polluted (Worse than Grade V) and cannot be used as water resources; more than 90% of urban water bodies are seriously polluted. The article entitled "More Rain Brings More Pollution" on *Science* (2017) points out that global water quality will worsen as climate change brings more rainfall.
4. Degradation of water-related ecological service functions. Due to global warming, evaporation in most parts of China has increased, exacerbating soil erosion. Water environment degradation in North China has worsened. Climate change, combined with extensive urbanization, has led to water environment degradation, dry rivers, disappearance of wetlands and lakes, and loss of ecosystem service functions related to water.

7.3 Climate Resilient Cities

In order to build climate resilient cities and facilitate the implementation of China's national climate adaptation strategy, the National Development and Reform Commission and the Ministry of Housing and Urban-Rural Development jointly issued the *Urban Climate Action Plan* in February 2016, setting out the guiding ideology, basic principles, goals, vision, key tasks of urban climate adaptation action and supportive measures. This is the first time the term "climate resilient cities" was mentioned in a Chinese policy document. In February 2017, the National Development and Reform Commission and the Ministry of Housing and Urban-Rural Development issued the *Notice on the Launch of the Climate Resilient City Pilot Program*, which contained a list of twenty-eight pilot cities including Hohhot City in Inner Mongolia Autonomous Region. However, climate adaptation has not yet been put at the top of China's urban planning and development agenda. There are problems such as a lack of awareness and weak institutional mechanisms.

The selected twenty-eight pilot cities are distributed in Northeast China (2), North China (1), Central China (7), Northwest China (8), East China (5), South China (2), and Southwest China (3). The majority of the pilot cities have conducted preliminary climate vulnerability and risk assessments. The climate risks faced by these cities are primarily heat waves, droughts, floods, strong wind, extreme cold, and typhoons. Some pilot cities have set specific climate adaption goals and corresponding quantitative indicator systems.

As a vast country, China is susceptible to heavy rainstorms, floods, droughts, and other natural disasters. Among the twenty-eight pilot cities, Changde, Yueyang and other wet cities are rich in water resources but face high flood risk and severe water pollution whereas dry cities such as Qingyang and Xining face severe water scarcity. Water problems faced by the pilot cities vary from city to city. The current priority of the pilot program is to adapt urban water systems to climate change. The pilot program aims to improve water security of Chinese cities by promoting the sponge city model, the water-saving city model and scientific urban flood control systems. However, due to lack of data support for climate vulnerability and risk assessment, the top-level design, plan and coordination mechanism of the program are yet to be developed. Currently, climate adaptation actions of the pilot cities are hopelessly disorganized. Therefore, building a well-functioning water management system is crucial to a climate-resilient city and involves scientific problem identification, planning, and policy implementation.

7.4 Policy Recommendations for Water Security Systems in Climate Resilient Cities

Urban water security is a complex issue and should be addressed using a holistic approach with both temporal and spatial dimensions in mind. To improve climate resilience, a city may first identify its water security problems, goals and needs and then work to alleviate its water security problems and related environmental problems in a systematical manner and build its water security capabilities. This is a holistic approach that combines adaption and mitigation.

In view of water challenges faced by Chinese cities, this paper builds on the "hybrid" approach proposed by the EU, which combines grey infrastructure which is construction measures using engineering services, green infrastructure which aims to upgrade ecosystem service functions, and soft measures which refers to policies, plans, programs, and procedures [1], and proposes a framework for the construction of water security systems in climate resilient cities in China (Fig. 7.1).

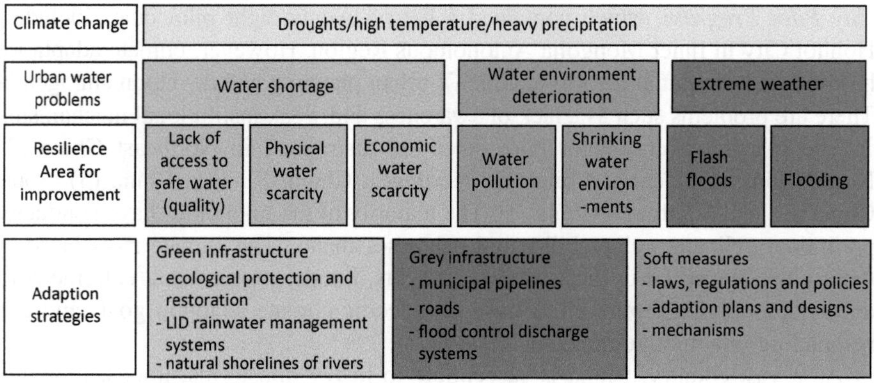

Fig. 7.1 Structure of an urban water security system in the context of climate change

1. Identification of problems

The first assessment report of the United Nations Intergovernmental Panel on Climate Change (IPCC) introduced the climate vulnerability concept. The scope of the IPCC's assessment has been growing. When it comes to urban climate adaptation policies, strategies and plans, developed countries such as the United States and EU countries attach great importance to problem identification and methodology. The IPCC has also developed a framework for the identification and assessment of key vulnerabilities to climate change. Cities are complex systems consisting of natural, economic, and social elements. Manifestations of climate change and cities' vulnerabilities to them affect the potential impacts of climate change on cities. The main goal of urban climate adaption is to improve cities' adaptive capabilities through multi-level governance actions and reduce cities' vulnerabilities to the effects of climate change. Only after we get the facts straight can we make a move. Climate risk and vulnerability assessment is crucial to the development of a scientific top-level design and informed decision-making regarding how to improve the city's climate resilience.

It is necessary to scientifically access the potential impacts of climate change on social and economic development and planning of cities and identify their urgent issues and key vulnerabilities of different districts and groups. In the long run, it is also very important to analyze the vulnerabilities and adaptive capabilities of districts, industries, and communities within cities, establish and improve urban climate monitoring and risk assessment systems, create inter-departmental data sharing mechanisms, and increase data interoperability.

2. Systematic planning

The problem-oriented New York's 2030 Plan (PlaNYC) is developed in accordance with the "identification of challenges/problems—target setting—planning—determination of measures—implementation" path. The plan covering areas of land, water, transportation, energy, air and climate change. It contains a climate change section which includes a commitment to create a strategic planning process to adapt to climate change impacts, develop floodplain management strategies and amend the building code to address the impacts of climate change. The City of London's Climate Change Adaptation Strategy is centered around urban development issues, goals and needs, provides a scientific assessment of climate change impacts, vulnerabilities and risks and set out the objectives, approaches and pathways for the city of London to address flood risks, water scarcity, heat risks, air pollution, and other risks and challenges. In the *APA Policy Guide on Climate Change*, the American Planning Association points out that climate change will require proactive responses across all planning sectors, from environmental protection to land use to transportation to public awareness of risk to decision-making support. As we can see from above, climate adaptation is an integral part of urban planning. As a technical tool, urban planning seeks to support rational urban functions including land use, spatial layout, transportation, and public services. Urban planning is also an important policy tool used by the government to manage work, life and green spaces, guide urban and rural green development, and safeguard public safety and interest.

(1) Top-level design

Pilot cities such as Dalian and Huaibei plan to align economic and social development plans, urban spatial plans and other plans and integrate climate adaptation and climate risk management into urban planning. They are working to raise awareness of climate adaption, strengthen cross-field integration, and design quantitative indicators to measure the effects of climate adaption actions. Their adaption plans and programs are developed based on the results of climate change risk, vulnerability and adaptive capacity assessment, aiming to protect and restore forests, lakes and other ecosystems in cities. The plans and programs identify areas of interest, demarcate protection zones for rivers, lakes and low-lying areas, integrate the protection zones into the cities' overall functional zoning maps and put forward enhanced control measures. Jiujiang's climate adaption program covers planning, development, governance and protection and aims to establish a well-functioning water protection system that best fits the city.

(2) Coordination and implementation

Plans of all relevant sectors, from water security to land use, green spaces, transportation, water, environmental protection, buildings, drainage and flood prevention, should be coordinated. Climate adaption plans should include clear objectives, quantitative indicators and implementation guidelines. When planning urban water systems, land use, and drainage systems, planners should combine green infrastructure and grey infrastructure wisely and develop a holistic plan. Green and above-ground infrastructure should take precedence over grey and underground infrastructure. Quantitative indicators of water-saving city and sponge city models and other indicators related to water security (leakage rates of pipe networks, annual maximum total rainwater runoff, etc.) should be included in overall plans, control programs, and green space, transportation, water system and other specialized plans of cities.

3. Differentiated policies
(1) Water conservation

The city of Zaragoza, Spain has embarked on an ambitious water conservation program with the aim of establishing a 'water saving culture' among businesses, industry and the local population. By mobilizing key stakeholders and residents and reforming the billing system, the city has succeeded in significantly reducing its water consumption. China has also issued a series of policies, including the *Several Opinions of the CPC Central Committee and the State Council on Further Strengthening Urban Planning and Management*, the *Thirteenth Five-Year Plan for National Economic and Social Development*, the *Notice of the State Council on the Promulgation of the Action Plan for Water Pollution Prevention and Control*, to promote water conservation practices. The *Urban Water Conservation Guide* points out that cities should speed up the transformation of the relevant infrastructure, develop implementation plans for water conservation, water source development and water recycling and reuse projects The Code for Green Building Evaluation (GB/T50378) also requires that green buildings must have water conservation programs and contains a set of water conservation guidelines and technical requirements, including requirements related to pipe network leakage, prevention of overpressure, water-saving appliances. In addition to promoting water conservation practices, cities should also attach importance to rainwater harvesting and water reuse.

(2) Sponge cities

Cities around the world have stepped up research and adopted best practices in rainwater management in response to climate change. Programs designed to improve rainwater management include the United States' Low Impact Development (LID), Australia's Water Sensitive Urban Design programs (WSUD), the United Kingdom's Sustainable Drainage Systems (SuDS) and China's sponge city imitative. China's sponge city imitative aims to increase rainwater infiltration and capture and reduce surface runoff by improving the urban underlying surface. It combines green infrastructure and grey infrastructure to improve the security and adaptive capacity of urban water systems and is an important part of the larger climate-resilient city program.

After identifying climate risks and urban problems, policymakers in urban planning should analyze the ecological security pattern of the downtown areas and surrounding areas, identify water related problems, assess the vulnerabilities and adaptive capacity of the downtown area, demarcate areas with ecological service functions, reserve space for future urban development, and improve human relationships with nature. To improve adaptive capacity, cities should make full use of urban spaces, rationally plan land use, construct water security system, develop appropriate objectives, indicators and strategies, offer guidance on the use of different types of land and implementation of projects, and design follow-up procedures.

(3) Adjustment of planning and development standards

In response to heavy rainstorms, heat waves, droughts, typhoons and other extreme weather events, cities should improve and strengthen their flood control, drainage, water supply, rainwater management, and other water systems. Some of China's existing urban planning and development standards are incompatible with the requirements of the climate-resilient city program. For example, the provision that curbs in urban green spaces should be above the road surface is contradictory with the climate-resilient city program's requirement that urban green spaces should allow greater infiltration of rainwater; the provisions in vertical land use planning and park design codes that require water in the peripheral areas to be discharged are contradictory to the climate-resilient city program's requirement that cities should build sponge parks and green spaces such as rain gardens, sunken green spaces, and artificial wetlands to capture and hold rainwater, and allocate space to store rainwater in the peripheral areas.

Table 7.1 New and revised urban planning and development standards in China

New standards	Code for Sponge City Development and Evaluation
Revised standards	Code for Vertical Planning on Urban Development Land (CJJ83-99)
	Code for the Engineering and Planning of Urban Wastewater Systems (GB50318-2000)
	Code for the Planning of Urban Water Systems (GB50513-2009)
	Code for the Planning and Design of Urban Residential Areas (2000) (GB50180-93)
	Technical Specifications for Rainwater Harvesting Systems of Buildings and Residential Areas (GB50400-2006)
	Code for Urban Road Design and Planning (CJJ37-2012)
	Park Design Code (CJJ48-92)
	Urban Green Space Design Code (GB50420-2007)
	Urban Green Space Soil (CJ/T340-2011)
	Outdoor Sewage System Design Code (GB50420-2006)

In order to facilitate the implementation of the sponge city initiative, the Ministry of Housing and Urban-Rural Development announced a plan in October 2015 to develop and revise relevant standards and codes (see Table 7.1).

Furthermore, coastal cities should pay attention to the impacts of sea level changes on urban infrastructure and development, and adjust the planning, design and engineering standards of protective facilities in a timely manner, and amend the flood control standards at river basin and administrative region levels as appropriate.

4. Concerted efforts

A stakeholder engagement program is central to the achievement of climate resilience goals.

At present, the Ministry of Housing and Urban-Rural Development has launched multiple pilot programs related to adaptation to climate change, including the climate resilient city pilot program, the sponge city pilot program, and the urban ecosystem restoration pilot program. China is promoting urban rainwater capture and storage systems under which green infrastructure takes precedence over grey infrastructure. But, in practice, cities face many obstacles in putting such systems in place.

The *Notice on the Launch of the Climate Resilient City Pilot Program* requires that the pilot cities should develop an over-arching plan to guide climate adaption actions. When developing such a plan, urban planners should look at the whole picture, determine appropriate pathways, medium- and long-term adaptation goals, key indicators, key tasks, and supportive measures, and make sure infrastructure, green space management, industrial structure adjustment, risk monitoring and early warning, disaster prevention and mitigation and other plans are aligned with the climate adaption action plan. In the meantime, when it comes to urban water security systems, cities must properly handle the relationships between the interests of individuals and the interest of the city as a whole, short- and long-term benefits, the visible hand of the government and the invisible hand of the market, and technological advancement and economic feasibility, and try to develop models that are easily emulated.

Building adaptive capacity is an integral part of the climate resilient city program. To build adaptive capacity of cities, it is necessary to increase investment in climate research and development, raise the awareness and capabilities of stakeholders (government, businesses, communities, residents, etc.) and put in place an effective stakeholder engagement program. Tangible actions should be taken to solve problems most citizens are concerned with such as flash floods and smog and promote wellness of the general public. It is also important to build science education platforms, develop audiovisual education materials about climate science, raise public awareness about the climate resilient city program and engage the public in the program.

7.5 Conclusions

In the face of new developments in domestic and global climate governance, policymakers in urban planning should look at the whole picture, and incorporate the requirements of the climate resilient city program into urban planning. Climate adaption actions should fit the climatic and geographical characteristics and economic and social conditions of the cities. Under the guidance of the over-arching program, the twenty-eight pilot cities should be encouraged to try new measures. Best practices should be promoted.

Experimental trials are an effective method to promote climate adaptation of cities. Whether the pilot program can produce produced fruitful results will directly affect the development direction of Chinese cities in the future. The pilot cities must accurately grasp the essence of the pilot program and follow through with it, come up with realistic measures that best fit the cities, think more boldly, and try out new decision-making, coordination, information sharing, financing, research and development, capacity building, cooperation and other mechanisms and establish clear accountability. Relevant central government agencies and departments should strengthen supervision, offer guidance and scientifically deploy resources to support the implementation of the pilot program. They should work with the pilot cities to analyze new situations, solve new problems, explore new ideas, discover and promote the latest best practice, and strive to improve human relationships with the nature.

Reference

1. European Environment Agency. (2014). *Urban adaptation to climate change in Europe: Challenges and opportunities for cities*. In M. Zhang, L. Feng, X. Li, et al., Trans. Ma, W., (Eds.), China Environmental Science Press.

Chapter 8
Energy Transition Driven by the Energy Internet

Jijiang He, Yu Wang and Wenying Chen

Abstract To achieve carbon neutrality, a country must first phase out fossil fuels and increase the percentage of renewable energy in its energy systems, including electric power, heating, and transportation systems. Wind and solar power will be the primary energy sources of the future. To solve the volatility of wind and solar power, grids which integrate a high proportion of renewable energy sources must provide sufficient flexibility to ensure energy security. The Energy Internet is a new energy utilization system which offers greater flexibility and increases the share of energy generated from renewable sources. The development of the Energy Internet has significant implications for carbon neutrality and energy transition. By using it wisely, the entire society, including construction, mining, manufacturing and transportation sectors, will be able to replace fossil fuels with renewable sources. China has rolled out policies to support the development the Energy Internet, and launched a wide range of Energy Internet pilot projects.

Keywords Energy internet · Energy transition · Flexibility

Jijiang He is the Director of Energy Policy Research Office, Energy Internet Research Institute, Tsinghua University. He's research interests include Energy Internet and energy policy. Yu Wang is a lecturer at the Institute for Energy, Environment, and Economy, Tsinghua University. Wang's research interests include low-carbon policy. Wenying Chen is a professor at the Institute for Energy, Environment, and Economy, Tsinghua University. Wang's research interests include low carbon policy.

J. He (✉)
Energy Policy Research Office, Energy Internet Research Institute, Tsinghua University, Beijing, China
e-mail: hejijiang@mail.tsinghua.edu.cn

Y. Wang · W. Chen
Institute for Energy, Environment, and Economy, Tsinghua University, Beijing, China
e-mail: wyu04@mails.tsinghua.edu.cn

W. Chen
e-mail: chenwy@tsinghua.edu.cn

W. Wang (ed.), *Annual Report on China's Response to Climate Change (2017)*,
Research Series on the Chinese Dream and China's Development Path,
https://doi.org/10.1007/978-981-13-9660-1_8

8.1 Introduction of Concepts: Energy Transition and Energy Internet

1. Energy transition at the core of climate action

The IPCC Fifth Assessment Report (AR5) points out that "emissions of CO_2 from fossil fuel combustion and industrial processes contributed about 78% of the total GHG emissions increase from 1970 to 2010, with a similar percentage contribution for the increase during the period 2000 to 2010." How to reduce emissions from fossil fuel combustion is the key to global GHG reduction. The Paris Agreement aim to "reach global peaking of greenhouse gas emissions as soon as possible," "undertake rapid reductions thereafter and reach net zero around or shortly after the middle of this century (21st century)". To reach net zero, the unabated use of fossil fuels must cease by 2050 at earliest and 2100 at latest.

Developed countries such as the U.S. and European countries have set both GHG reduction targets and energy transformation targets. In 2008, the European Union set three key targets for the year 2020: 20% of EU energy from renewable sources, 20% improvement in energy efficiency and 20% cut in GHG emissions [1]. For 2030, the EU has a target of 27% renewable energy (in primary energy consumption), with the share of renewable energy in the electricity sector increasing to at least 45%. Germany aims to reduce GHG emissions by 80 to 95% from the level of 1990 and increase the share of renewable energy in its total energy consumption to 80% by 2050 [2]. Denmark and Iceland have planned to end their dependence on fossil fuels by 2050.

Energy transition in some European countries is rapidly advancing. According to a report released by the European Environment Agency in 2016, the EU's greenhouse gas emissions in 2015 decreased by 22% from the level of 1999, and the share of renewable energy in total energy consumption reached 21% in 2013. The EU's 2020 GHG reduction target has been achieved ahead of schedule.

In 2014, renewable energy sources accounted for 85% of Ireland's total primary energy consumption. In the meantime, Iceland is the only country in the world that can claim to obtain 100% of its electricity from renewable sources, primarily hydro power and geothermal power [3]. In 2016, wind power accounted for 42.1% of Denmark's annual electricity consumption, making Denmark the country with the largest share of wind energy in electricity demand. In 2015, the share of renewable energy rose from just 3.4% of Germany's gross electricity consumption in 1990 to 32.5%, [4] exceeding the target it previously set for 2015. The progress in these countries has driven more countries to accelerate energy transition.

According to the Energy Research Institute of the National Development and Reform Commission, the target of 60% renewable energy in China's primary energy consumption by 2050 is feasible. The simulation research of the electric power system in 2050 shows that if renewable energy accounts for 85% of electricity generation, about 60% will come from volatile renewable energy sources [5].

Integrating a high percentage of solar and wind power pose to the grids is a huge challenge. Solar power systems only generate electricity during the day and the greatest amount of solar energy reaches a solar power collector around noon. Wind power also has strong volatility. Integrating a high proportion of wind and solar power poses a huge challenge to the stability of the grids, which becomes a key obstacle to the transition of the grids. This is where the Energy Internet comes in.

2. Energy Internet

The term "Energy Internet" was first mentioned in an article entitled "Building the Energy Internet" published in the British magazine *The Economist* in 2004. Germany began to explore the technicality of the Energy Internet around 2008. It launched the Energy Program which leverages information technologies and telecommunication technologies to create an Energy Internet to solve problems faced by power grids integrated with distributed energy. The concept is made popular in China by the US scholar Jeremy Rifkin through his *The Third Industrial Revolution*. In Rifkin's design, the Energy Internet is a new energy utilization system that integrates renewable energy, telecommunication technology and grids, and is made up by multiple types of energy networks and transportation networks [6].

3. Development of the Energy Internet in Europe

In 2011, Europe launched the Future Internet for Smart Energy (FINSENY) project. FINSENY aims to identify needs of smart distribution grids, analyze smart energy scenarios, and create ICT platforms for the Energy Internet of the future [7].

Germany's exploration in this field is worthy of special attention. In 2008, the German Federal Ministry of Economics and Technology (BMWi) and the Federal Ministry for the Environment, Nature Conservation and Nuclear Safety (BMU) jointly launched the E-Energy Program, aiming to create an Internet of Energy. To meet the potential needs of electric power systems based on distributed energy generation in the future, E-Energy will integrate telecommunication technologies and energy systems and increase the use of wind and solar power. In fact, E-Energy can be understood as Germany's version of the Energy Internet, which is an ICT-based energy system that integrates a high proportion of renewable energy.

The Energy Internet has played an important role into increase the share of renewable energy in electricity consumption in countries such as Germany and Denmark. At noon on June 9, 2014, the share of solar power exceeded 50% of Germany's total electricity consumption. On April 30, 2017, the share of biomass and wind, solar and hydro power accounted for 85% of Germany's total electricity consumption. In Denmark, wind power production is often higher than electricity consumed in the country. Germany and Denmark have provided an example of using the Energy Internet to increase the use of renewable energy. As an effective solution to go renewable, the Energy Internet is gaining traction.

8.2 Energy Internet for the Integration of a High Percentage of Renewable Energy to Grids

1. Energy Internet increasing the flexibility of electric power systems

The Energy Internet uses the Internet to achieve information sharing between different equipment in the energy system, improve the flexibility of the electric power system, ensure dynamic balance between power supply and power demand. It can integrate a high share of renewable energy into grids while ensuring a reliable, stable power supply.

As the cost of wind and solar power rapidly decreases, the installed capacity of wind and solar power is growing fast. However, due to volatility of weather-dependent wind and solar power, integration of a high share or 100% renewable energy requires high flexibility which can be achieved through:

(1) Increasing flexibility of conventional electric power plants. The flexibility of hydro power and pumped storage power plants and coal-fired generating units should be increased as a means to address the volatility of wind and solar power.
(2) Improving the peak shaving capability of natural gas and biomass power generation facilities. The share of natural gas in the electric power system is rising rapidly. Gas-fired power generation facilities, especially small and medium-power gas turbine units, have a good peak shaving capability. Biomass power generation facilities is at a disadvantage compared to large electric power plants in terms of size and cost, but they are often used to shave the peak due to their flexibility.
(3) Developing the transmission infrastructure. To stabilize power system, the transmission infrastructure should be developed and improved to ensure wind and power in a larger area can complement each other.
(4) Connecting the grid and the meteorological network so that grid operators can obtain weather information required to forecast the output of solar and wind power so they can adjust operating procedures in a timely manner.
(5) Improving demand-side management. Interruptible demand of businesses can be integrated through the Internet technology to create large-scale peak shaving capacity, providing flexibility to the grid through peak shifting and load transfer. Internet-connected smart home appliances such as refrigerators, air conditioners, and energy storage devices are a crucial part of demand response management, and participate in the peaking shaving and frequency modulation of the power grid in a distributed manner. In addition, energy flexible heat pumps and refrigerated warehouses also have great potential for balancing purposes.
(6) Developing and using energy storage technology and electric vehicles. Supply- and demand-side energy storage devices can effectively stabilize the output from volatile wind and solar energy. In the meantime, electric vehicles can be

considered as mobile distributed energy storage units and integrated through the Internet to provide the grid with massive demand response capacity.

2. Electric vehicles and the Energy Internet

The current transportation system relies mainly on fossil fuels such as gasoline and diesel. Electric vehicles are an important renewable energy solution for the transportation sector.

Electric vehicles and fuel cell vehicles are the key to the electrification of the transportation system. They can help the transportation sector phase out gasoline and diesel, and at the same time deepen the integration of the transportation system and the power system. As the share of fossil fuels in the electric power system continues to decrease, the electrified transportation system will also phase out all fossil fuels.

Electric vehicle charging facilities can obtain electric power from the grid or directly leverage solar power. The combination of solar energy and electric vehicle charging is the most direct way of which electric vehicles can increase the use of renewable energy [8].

Electric vehicles not only use electricity but also store energy. They are mobile energy storage units. Integrating a large number of electric vehicles can offer tremendous flexibility for power systems. If electric vehicles are charged during peak times, they will put immense pressure on the grid and cause safety hazard. However, if owners of electric vehicles are encouraged to charge during off-peak periods, electric vehicles can offer tremendous flexibility and demand response capacity for the power system. China has set a target of 5 million electric vehicles on the road by 2020. In a decade, the vast majority of new cars on the road in Beijing and the Beijing-Tianjin-Hebei region will be electric cars. When a distributed energy storage system composed of more than one million electric vehicles is integrated with the power system, it can not only greatly reduce the pressure placed by the charging demand of electric vehicles on the power grid but also provide a strong demand response capability [9]. It is estimated that, by 2030, electric vehicles will create hundreds of millions of kilowatts of off-peak demand and flexible energy [10]. The Energy Internet can be used to manage electric vehicles as storage units and as tools to increase demand-side flexibility, thus greatly improving the grid's ability to integrate renewable energy.

Mature Vehicle-to-Grid (V2G) technology will enable electric vehicles act as backup power sources in emergencies. Electric vehicles can participate in peak shaving by returning power back to the grid during peak times. Therefore, electric vehicles are both consumers and producers of energy, i.e., prosumers in the theoretical framework of the Energy Internet. According to the current national standard, the standard power rate of slow charging piles is seven kilowatts. From a technical point of view, such charging piles can be easily transformed to 7 kW integrated charging and discharging facilities.

Provided that there are three million electric vehicles with charging and discharging functions in Beijing, the discharge power will reach 21 million kilowatts, which is almost equivalent to the maximum power load of Beijing in August 2016.

If each vehicle stores 40 kWh electricity, the total amount of electricity stored in three million electric vehicles can power Beijing for two days.

3. Heating systems and the Energy Internet

The heating sector also plays a crucial role in energy transition and must be taken into consideration when developing the Energy Internet.

Energy transition in the heating sector is a process of replaying oil and gas with renewable energy. Space heating consumes more energy than electricity generation, especially in cold regions. In the future, heating systems of buildings, consisting of central heating, community-based boilers, heat pumps, and other components, will increase the use of renewable energy such as solar energy, biomass, and geothermal energy.

Space heating systems can also provide flexibility for the electric power system. Combined heat and power (CHP) systems integrate heat and electricity generation. Conventional cogeneration systems focus primarily on heat demand and electricity is a by-product. The heat demand can be regulated by controlling devices such as switch boilers, heat storage units, and heat storage pipes. The flexibility of the power generation system can be increased through heat demand transfer. In the meantime, the stability of heat supply will also be ensured.

An important advantage of thermal energy over electricity is that it is easier to store. Thermal energy (hot water and space heating) in homes can be easily stored in insulated tanks in a central heating system or a distributed heating network. Such thermal storage systems can provide heat for hours or days at very low cost. The energy loss is also much lower than that of electricity storage systems. Similarly, cold can also be stored for a short period of time using relatively low costing commercial refrigeration systems.

When there is sufficient output of wind and solar power, the system can convert electricity at off-peak rates into thermal energy through electric boilers or electric heat pumps, and store thermal energy in the heat storage devices, thus greatly improving the ability of the heating system to integrate wind and solar power.

4. A mix of energy sources that complement each other

Integration and renewable are two important features of zero-carbon energy systems of the future. First of all, the primary energy source for future energy systems will be non-fossil energy sources. Biomass and solar and wind power will account for a large proportion of total energy consumption.

Electricity generation, heating, cooling and transportation systems will be the main consumers of energy. Currently, the four systems are powered by separate energy systems. In the future, their energy systems will be integrated to form a "smart grid" which consists of thermal pipe networks, natural gas pipe networks, transportation networks, centralized energy networks and distributed energy networks [11]. In the meantime, the sustainability, safety and reliability of the entire energy system will be improved and energy prices will be reduced.

Electric power grids, natural gas networks and heating networks are at the core of the Energy Internet, Electric power grids and natural gas networks will be integrated by leveraging gas turbines, electric hydrogen, synthetic natural gas and other devices and technologies; electric power grids and heating networks are integrated by levering cogeneration units, heat pumps, heat storage units and the like; cogeneration technologies also enable the integration of natural gas networks and heating networks. Electric vehicles enable the integration between smart transportation networks and smart grids.

In the long term, the use of interconvertible gaseous fuels, such as natural gas, biogas or synthetic natural gas (power-to-gas), will deepen the integration between the electricity and gas networks. Power-to-gas is a technology that electrolyzes water into oxygen and hydrogen and then combines hydrogen with carbon dioxide to produce methane. The electricity-to-gas technology can also convert surplus wind and solar power into methane, stores them in gaseous form or transport them through natural gas pipelines. Natural gas mentioned above can be replaced with biogas, which is gases produced from biomass. Biogas can be purified to natural gas quality and then be transported via the natural gas pipeline network. Gaseous methane can be used by centralized or distributed generation cogeneration, and heating systems. It can be stored for long periods of time in the existing gas storage facilities and transported via the existing pipe networks.

The Energy Internet can integrate electric power, thermal, cooling, natural gas systems into coordinated energy networks to consistently meet all types of energy demand. It integrates Internet of Things, appliances in manufacturing, mining, construction, transportation and other sectors, pipe networks, and distributed solar, wind, and geothermal generators into the smart grid and help cities achieve the 100% renewable energy target.

5. Three development stages of the Energy Internet

The development of the Energy Internet can be divided into three stages: (1) integration of different energy networks, (2) integration of communication and energy networks, and (3) commercial operation of Internet technology-enabled energy systems. The first stage is the integration of different energy networks, including electric power, heating, natural gas, and transportation network, which is the foundation for the Energy Internet. At the second stage, the Energy Internet leverages the Internet of Things, big data, cloud computing and other technologies to integrate communication and energy networks, improve the flexibility of energy systems, increase the adoption of wind and solar power, raise energy efficiency and reduce costs of energy systems. At the third stage, new commercial models will be created in the energy sector. On the one hand, the Internet will spawn more creative business models in the energy sector. On the other hand, the Energy Internet can turn rooftop solar panels, electric vehicles, and energy storage units into energy consumers, and create a new energy market, which will help the Energy Internet integrates with other related industries, generating creative energy, technology and information services and new business models.

8.3 Policy Framework for the Energy Internet Taking Shape in China

Most Energy Internet policies in China primarily aim to increase the use of renewable energy and drive energy transition.

In July 2015, the State Council issued the *Guiding Opinions on Promoting "Internet Plus"*, which contains an entire section devoted to "Internet plus Energy." The section sets out the goals of "Internet plus Energy" actions, including "to flatten energy profiles and drive innovation of energy production and consumption models," "to support the development of distributed energy networks and increase the share of renewable energy" and to improve the energy structure. Following that, the National Development and Reform Commission, the National Energy Administration and other ministries and commissions issued a series of policies related to the "Internet Plus Smart Energy", integration of energy systems, and management of micro-grids to support the Energy Internet.

1. Internet Plus Smart Energy

In February 2016, three ministries and commissions under the State Council, including the National Development and Reform Commission, issued the *Guidelines for Promoting the Development of "Internet Plus Smart Energy"*. This policy document plays a crucial role in promoting the development of the energy Internet. It offers an official definition of the energy Internet, set a road map for this sector, and reaffirms the importance of the energy Internet to the energy revolution. The documents define the Energy Internet (i.e., Internet Plus Smart Energy) as "a new energy system that integrates the Internet, energy production, transmission, storage, consumption and energy markets". It is a smart, coordinated system with a flat structure and enables information sharing, open transactions and distributed supply and demand.

The document emphasizes the coordination between different types of energy infrastructure and aims to (1) integrate heating networks natural gas networks, transportation networks and other energy networks into the smart grid; (2) integrate different energy systems; (3) integrate microgrids that support distributed energy trading; and (4) develop infrastructure that supports coordination between different energy systems, including electricity, cooling, heating, gas and hydrogen fuel systems.

The document emphasizes the integration of energy and communication systems and promotes flexible energy trading. It contains provisions related to (1) real-time measurement, information sharing and active control of energy consumption of electric power, heat, refrigeration and other system; (2) Internet-based smart energy trading platforms; and (3) transactions of distributed sources, energy demand, and energy storage capacity.

In June 2016, the National Development and Reform Commission and the National Energy Administration issued the *Notice on the Launch of the "Internet Plus Smart Energy" (Energy Internet) Pilot Projects*, announcing a list of park-based, urban and cross-regional energy Internet pilot projects. Among them, the urban energy Internet demonstration zones will "integrate renewable energy, smart grid, EV and charging/discharging technologies." The government also seeks to promote the development of the completely renewable energy powered pilot zones; furthermore, it also encourages the development of smart cities which leverage information and communication technologies to improve operational efficiency.

2. Integration of energy systems

In 2016, the National Development and Reform Commission and the *National Energy Administration issued the Guidelines for Implementing the Integrated Energy System Pilot Program* and the *Notice on Issues Concerning the Application to Participate in the Integrated Energy System Pilot Program.* These two documents point out that integration of energy systems is an integral part of the Energy Internet and can help increase the adoption of renewable energy and boost energy efficiency.

The pilot program consists of two parts: (1) host terminals of integrated power supply systems, and (2) systems which integrate wind, solar, thermal, and hydro power and energy storage units. The program supports the construction of host terminals of integrated power supply systems, gas-fired combined cooling, heat and power (CCHP) systems, distributed renewable energy systems and smart microgrids. The two documents require that at least 50% of new industrial parks across the county will be equipped with host terminal of integrated power supply systems in 2020.

3. Microgrids

In February 2017, the National Energy Administration issued the *Microgrid Management Measures (Draft)*, which aims to "build microgrids that integrate natural gas supply and wind and solar power generation" to boost energy efficiency and "establish cooling, heating, electric power and other energy markets on the basis of the microgrids." Both goals are aligned with the inherent requirements of the Energy Internet. In July, the National Development and Reform Commission and the National Energy Administration issued the *Trial Measures for Building Grid-Connected Microgrids*, pointing out that grid-connected microgrids can "help achieve a balance between local energy supply and demand through configuration and trading" and "operate in both grid-connected or island mode," which is also aligned with the development direction of the Energy Internet.

4. Power distribution management

On October 8, 2016, the National Development and Reform Commission and the National Energy Administration promulgated the *Power Distribution Management Policy*. This policy provides that distribution network operators can provide power distribution, value-added services related to electricity planning and smart electricity use, power generation, heating, cooling, gas supply and water supply services. It encourages operators to expand their business scope and provide heating, cooling and other energy services, thereby contributing to the development of the Energy Internet within their respective regions.

The policy includes an institutional framework for the development of Energy Internet in the areas covered by 110 and 220 kV substations in industrial parks.

5. Heating supply from renewable energy sources

In April 2017, the National Energy Administration issued the *Opinions on Promoting Renewable Heat (Draft),* encouraging the use of renewable resources to generate heat. It also aims to "coordinate the planning of heat, electricity and other energy systems within one region and establish an integrated heating system."

The document aims to increase local consumption and utilization of clean electricity by promoting renewable heat and integrated green heating systems which combine renewable energy, geothermal and low-temperature heat sources. It also encourages stakeholders to establish supply-side and demand-side response mechanisms and try out and encourage cogeneration plants and regional energy stations to try out short-term heat storage, seasonal heat storage and other heat storage technologies which can provide electric power systems with flexibility, boost electricity and heat generation efficiency and promote the adoption of wind and solar power. The document sheds light on the technical requirements and institutions of the Energy Internet.

6. Progress in energy Internet projects

The lists of four types of pilot projects, i.e., new energy microgrids, new grids, integrated energy systems, and energy Internet projects, were released in the second half of 2016 (see Table 8.1).

Among these four types of pilot projects, the new energy microgrid projects aim to ramp up renewable energy; the new grid projects focus on institutional innovation; the energy system integration projects seek to the integration of different types of energy systems; the energy Internet projects focus on frontier technologies in the energy Internet field. These four types of pilot projects complement each other and reflect the basic principles of the energy Internet.

Table 8.1 Government-approved energy internet pilot projects

Type of pilot projects	Sponsor	Number of approved projects
New energy microgrids	New energy division and electric power division of the national energy administration	28
Integrated energy systems	Planning division of the national energy administration	23
Energy internet	Technology division of the national energy administration	55
New grids (first batch)	Department of economic system reform, national development and reform commission	105

All the twenty-four grid-connected new energy microgrid pilot projects have designed specific penetration rates of renewable energy. The renewable energy penetration rates of all projects are higher than 50%. Many projects aim to achieve more than 100% penetration. The new energy microgrid pilot project in Suzhou, Gansu, plans to achieve 300% penetration, which is the highest among all microgrid pilot projects. The Yanqing New Energy Microgrid Pilot Project is a group of six microgrids located in Beijing Badaling Economic and Technological Development Zone and surrounding areas, covering 4.3 km^2. The project's electricity supply capacity is 25 MW, thermal load 76.4 MW, and space heating capacity 1.08 million km^2. Its renewable energy penetration rate is over 100% and electricity self-sufficiency is 113%.

Several energy Internet pilot projects also aim to ramp up renewable energy. The Chongming Energy Internet Pilot Project aims to achieve 100% renewable energy. Other important projects include Jiaxing Urban Energy Internet Pilot Project (Zhejiang), Shanghai Lingang District Energy Internet Pilot Project, and 1GW Solar, Gas, Hydrogen, Biomass Energy Integration Pilot Project in Jingbian County, and Huzhou Changxing Energy Internet Pilot Project. These projects integrate rooftop PV systems, gas turbines, natural gas-fueled distributed generation, demand-side management, smart transportation, refrigeration centers, and terminal service providers and other energy technologies. They are based on the Internet Plus model, aiming to promote the adoption of distributed generation, electric vehicles, and distributed energy storage technologies, provide demand response capacity and flexibility, increase renewable energy penetration, and build flexible energy trading platforms and integrated energy systems.

China will select a flagship project among these pilot projects to demonstrate how the Internet and energy can be effectively integrated.

7. Case Study: Qinghai ran entirely on clean energy for 168 h non-stop

In 2016, Qinghai Province launched an electric power development plan that aims to completely phase out fossil fuels in the electric power sector by 2050. This is also the first provincial-level long/mid-term electric power development plan in China that sets a high renewable energy penetration target. In June 2017, Qinghai completed a trial to power the province entirely by renewable energy for 168 h in a roll, marking a significant milestone in the development history of the Energy Internet in China.

Over the 168 h from 0:00 on June 17, 2017 to 24:00 on June 23, Qinghai ran entirely on renewable energy such as wind, solar and hydro power, setting a new world record of non-stop renewable electricity supply. This is the first time China attempted to power an entire province or provincial-level administrative region entirely on renewable energy sources. The following is a list of factors contributing to the success of this trial test:

(1) Qinghai boasts high levels of hydropower, solar, and wind energy. Located in the upper reaches of the Yellow River, Qinghai has a large hydroelectric power capacity and its untapped hydroelectric potential reaches 23 million kilowatts.

With huge expanses of desert land which is ideal location for solar panels, Qinghai is the sunniest province in the country. It also boasts high levels of wind energy. According to data from Qinghai Electric Power Company, as of the end of May 2017, the installed capacity of renewable energy in the Qinghai Electric Power Grid was 19.43 million kilowatts, accounting for 82.8% of the total installed capacity of Qinghai Province [12].

(2) The electricity demand in Qinghai is relatively small. In the meantime, it can also enlist the help of neighboring provinces. Smart peak shaving and demand transfer technologies are central to the Energy Internet. From June 17 to 23, the province's average daily electricity consumption was 7.2 million kilowatts, and total electricity consumption was 1.178 billion kilowatt hours. The total renewable electricity generated within Qinghai was 1.009 billion kWh. Qinghai purchased 169 million kWh renewable electricity from other provinces to make up the shortfall. All coal-fired electricity produced within Qinghai during the test period was sold to other provinces [13].

(3) Hybrid solar-hydro projects played a very important role in the success of this trial. During the trial, 78.3% of the electricity supply came from hydroelectric power, and wind and solar power accounted for 21.7% [13]. Hydroelectric power can effectively balance the volatility of solar power. At noon, output from solar energy reaches the highest, and operators may reduce hydroelectric power to ensure stability. In the afternoon, operators should ramp up hydroelectric power output as solar power output will gradually decline. At night, solar energy systems will stop operating. The 1,280,000 kW Longyangxia Hydropower Station and its complementary 850,000 kW photovoltaic project is the largest hybrid solar-hydro project in China. The Longyangxia Hydropower Station has a large reservoir and fast-responding hydropower units, which help smooth out the peaks and valleys in the output curve caused by intermittent solar power and improve the stability of the power system [14].

Qinghai is China's first province that ran entirely on renewable energy for seven consecutive days. The trial has important symbolic meaning for China and demonstrates the massive potential of the Energy Internet in promoting electric power systems which integrate a high percentage of renewable energy. From a technical point of view, Sichuan and Yunnan provinces, which have a high share of renewable energy in total electricity consumption, also has the capability to successfully complete such trials. After increasing peak shaving capacity of coal-fired power systems, it will also be technically feasible for other provinces to increase renewable energy penetration. The success of this trial demonstrates the massive potential of renewable energy and has significant implications for increasing the adoption of renewable energy in China.

Acknowledgements This study is funded by the "Technological Advancements and Climate Change Policies" research program of the Ministry of Science and Technology.

References

1. Gao, H. (2009). New development in EU climate change policy. *Global Science, Technology and Economy Outlook, 2009*(12), 46–50.
2. Wang, Z. (2011). The German Federal Government's Energy Plan for 2050—Environmentally friendly, safe, reliable and economically viable energy supply. *Global Science, Technology and Economy Outlook, 3,* 5–17.
3. Qin, H. (2017). Visible and invisible. *Wind Energy, 2017*(2), 1.
4. Zhang, W. (2016). Germany relies on market transactions and regulations to ramp up wind power consumption. *Wind Energy, 2016*(2), 36.
5. Energy Research Institute of the National Development and Reform Commission. (2015). *China's 2050 renewable energy development scenario and pathway study*. April 2015.
6. Rifkin, J. (2012). *The third industrial revolution*. China: CITIC Publishing House.
7. Tian, S., Yan, W., Zhang, D., et al. (2015). Energy internet technologies and application. *Proceedings of the CSEE, 2015*(14), 3482–3494.
8. He, J. (2016). Electric vehicles are a pillar of the energy internet. *China Power Enterprise Management, 2016*(3).
9. He, J. (2015). China's clean energy solution. *China Power Enterprise Management, 2015*(7), 18–21.
10. Energy Research Institute of the National Development and Reform Commission. (2015). *China's 2050 renewable energy development scenario and pathway study*. April 2015.
11. Dong, C., Zhao, J., Fu, W., et al. (2014). From smart grids to the energy internet: Basic concepts and theoretical frameworks. *Automation of Electric Power Systems, 2014*(15), 1–11.
12. *Qinghai has been powered by clean energy for seven days non-stop*. Retrieved June 20, 2017, from http://www.sgcc.com.cn/xwzx/gsyw/2017/06/340536.shtml.
13. Qinghai has been powered by clean energy for seven days non-stop. *Power & Energy,* 2017 (3), 336.
14. Zhang, W., & Yang, T. (2015). A study of the hydropower and solar power supply systems in longyang valley. *Journal of North China University of Water Resources and Electric Power (Natural Science Edition), 2015*(3), 76–81.

Chapter 9
Issues Concerning the Design of China's National Emissions Trading System

Maosheng Duan, Zhe Deng, Mengyu Li and Dongya Li

Abstract An Emissions Trading System (ETS) is a market-based tool for controlling greenhouse gas emissions and has been used by many countries or regions. Built on the results of previous carbon market pilots, China plans to launch a nationwide ETS in 2017. This paper analyzes the main features of China's National ETS design and the causes of the features, identifies the major issues and challenges that need to be addressed. The National ETS consists of a central-level system and provincial systems. The design not only attaches great importance to the uniformity of trading rules but also provides the provincial authorities a certain degree of autonomy. It sets carbon intensity targets and industrial benchmark based on historical emission rates of industries, issues free emission allowances to corporate legal entities, and includes indirect emissions in the system. The basic statistical unit of the ETS is corporate legal entities. At present, China's National ETS faces the following major problems and challenges: lack of higher-level legislation; inconsistency in data requirements between the monitoring, reporting and verification (MRV) rules and the benchmarking rules, and lack of effective mechanism to link the ETS to other energy and climate policies. China should pass higher-level legislation for the National ETS as soon as possible, develop operational rules to regulate the allocation of emission allowances, MRV, certification of third-party verification agencies, compliance by companies, trading of emission allowances

Maosheng Duan is a research fellow and Ph.D. supervisor at Institute of Nuclear and New Energy Technology, Tsinghua University. Duan's research interests include climate policy. Zhe Deng, Mengyu Li, and Dongya Li are Ph.D. students at Institute of Nuclear and New Energy Technology, Tsinghua University.

M. Duan (✉) · Z. Deng · M. Li · D. Li
Institute of Nuclear and New Energy Technology, Tsinghua University, Beijing, China
e-mail: duanmsh@mail.tsinghua.edu.cn

Z. Deng
e-mail: dengzhe635099261@163.com

M. Li
e-mail: lmytsinghua@163.com

D. Li
e-mail: lidongya14@mails.tsinghua.edu.cn

W. Wang (ed.), *Annual Report on China's Response to Climate Change (2017)*,
Research Series on the Chinese Dream and China's Development Path,
https://doi.org/10.1007/978-981-13-9660-1_9

and other important activities under the ETS, dovetail ETS rules and financial industry supervision and budgeting regulations and develop a mechanism to correlate the ETS and other energy and climate policies.

Keywords Emissions trading system · Benchmarking · Carbon intensity target

9.1 Overarching Design of China's National ETS

1. Legal basis

China's current legislation on emissions trading consists of ministry-level regulations (for example, the *Interim Measures for the Management of Emissions Trading* promulgated by the National Development and Reform Commission (NDRC), hereinafter referred to as the "Interim Measures") and regulations and policies promulgated by local people's congresses and governments of the pilot areas [1]. The *Interim Measures*, as the center piece of the National ETS, outlines the framework of the National ETS and the principles for its key elements.

On the basis of the *Interim Measures*, the NDRC rolled out the *Regulations on Emissions Trading (Draft)* (hereinafter the "Regulations"), which has been submitted to the State Council for approval. The *Regulations* is intended to be promulgated in the form of administrative regulations. On the basis of the *Interim Measures*, the *Regulations* further clarifies the roles and responsibilities of the regulatory authorities, confirms the legality of the emission allowances, provides for the certification of the verification agencies, and imposes penalties on major emitters, verification agencies, and trading agencies for violations.

2. Structure

The National ETS consists of a central-level system and provincial systems. The emissions trading department of the State Council is responsible for developing the top-level design of the National ETS and setting important rules. The provincial emissions trading authorities are responsible for supervising emissions trading within their respective jurisdiction and their rights include determining the list of major emitters, developing and implementing the local allowance allocation plan, reporting on and verifying emissions, and monitor compliance practices of major emitters.

In view of regional differences in economic conditions, total carbon emissions and structure, emission control targets and other aspects, the overarching design of the National ETS also gives the provincial emissions trading authorities a certain degree of autonomy. It allows the provincial emissions trading authorities to increase the industries covered by the system and raise inclusion thresholds within their respective jurisdiction after being approved by the State Council's carbon trading department; to put in place allocation methods and standards that more stringent than the national allowance allocation standards; to sell the remaining allowances if there are any remaining allowances after the free allowances are allocated and use the proceeds therefrom to promote local carbon reduction and relate capacity building.

3. Scope and geographical coverage

In terms of geographical coverage, the National ETS is designed to cover the entire Chinese mainland. As for capped industries and inclusion thresholds, the National ETS currently focuses industries and companies that produce large amounts of emissions and has large emission reduction potential and available data. At present, only industries that have available basic data and produce easy-to-standardize products (such as the electricity industry) are included. In the future, more industries will be included when the system becomes more mature. The inclusion thresholds are legal entities with annual energy consumption of more than 10,000 tons (included) of coal equivalent or annual CO_2 emissions of more than 26,000 tons (included) in any year from 2013 to 2015 [2]. Currently, the National ETS only covers CO_2 emissions.

Considering data availability and feasibility of management, the basic statistical unit of the National ETS is a legal entity rather than a facility. The National ETS not only regulates direct emissions from fuel combustion and industrial activities, but also controls indirect emissions in electricity and thermal consumption.

4. Collective limits and allocation of emissions allowances

Built on prior pilots, the National ETS combines the top-down and bottom-up approaches to determine emissions caps. The top-down approach determines the collective emissions limit of the system and the total emission caps of each industry covered by the system according to the overall emissions control target of the society and the historical emissions of the industries. The bottom-up approach obtains the collective emissions limit of the system by aggregating the total emissions allowances allocated to each industry covered by the system [3].

At the current stage, emission allowances are allocated free of charge. Auctioning of emissions allowances will be introduced at an appropriate time and the proportion of auctioned emissions allowances will gradually increase [4]. According to the preliminary design of the National ETS, emissions allowances are distributed free of charge based on actual production. The allocation process can be divided into initial allocation and post-allocation adjustment. In order to test the rationality of the proposed method and estimate the impact of the proposed method on the capped industries and participating companies, China's National ETS a new method which has not been used by other emissions trading systems—"trial calculation". After the completion of the trial calculation, the State Council's carbon trading department modified and improved the allowance allocation method based on the trial calculation results, and finalized the specific free allowance allocation method and procedure. It determined how to set and update the benchmarks and the share of allowances distributed in the initial allocation process, issued allocation plans and technical guidelines for capped industries and launched nationwide allowances allocation.

5. Monitoring, Reporting and Verification (MRV) System

The NDRC has issued guidelines for the verification and reporting of GHG emissions from twenty-four industries. Among them, ten guidelines have been revised and promulgated in the form of national standards as supporting documents for the National ETS.

To provide data required for allowance allocation, the NDRC has provided a standard reporting template in the *Notice on Launching the National Emissions Trading Market* (hereinafter the "Notice") for the first batch of emitters included in the National ETS. In addition to the information required by the industry guidelines, emitters are also required to provide the relevant key technical information, process information, and production data. The NDRC has also issued reference materials for verification agencies and personnel, and third-party verification agency guidelines [5]. These materials and guidelines are intended to provide local governments with guidance on selection of verification agencies and verification agencies with guidance on how to verify emissions. In order to further standardize local historical data investigation, the state has also established an MRV communication platform where experts will answer questions relating to data investigation.

6. Compliance monitoring mechanism

According to the *Interim Measures*, major emitters shall submit to the provincial emissions trading authority emission allowances snot less than the previous year's confirmed emissions to settle emissions settlement obligation. Major emitters that have not fulfilled their settlement obligations will be given administrative penalties by the provincial carbon trading authorities. In the meantime, the State Council's carbon trading department will keep emissions creditability records on participating companies and link the creditability records to the credit management system. Companies who commit gross violations under the National ETS will be blacklisted and exposed according to law. However, the *Interim Measures* does not provide specific administrative penalties. In light of the lack of specific penalty provisions in the *Interim Measures*, the *Regulations* imposes specific administrative and financial penalties for non-compliance. For emissions in excess of the emissions cap, provincial carbon trading authority will impose a penalty of three to five times the average market price of the allowance one year prior to the settlement deadline and deduct the emissions in excess from the emissions cap for the next allocation period. If the penalty is not paid within the specified time limit, a late fee of 3% of the delinquent penalty will be imposed for each day the penalty is overdue.

7. Other

In addition to the above-mentioned factors (i.e., legal basis, management system, scope and coverage, collective limits and allowances allocation, MRV system, and compliance monitoring mechanism), infrastructure such as the registry and the trading platform is also crucial for the National ETS. The registry is used to record information on the holding, transfer, settlement, and cancellation of emission allowances and It sets up accounts for emissions regulators, major emitters, trading agencies and other market participants, and utilizes a three-tier management structure. A trading platform is also central to the optimization of nationwide emission rights allocation. Nine voluntary emissions reduction trading markets in Beijing, Tianjin, Shanghai, Chongqing, Guangdong, Shenzhen, Hubei, Sichuan and Fujian have been filed with the State Council's carbon trading department. One of them may become the trading platform for the National ETS.

9.2 Understanding the Key Features of China's National ETS

Compared with foreign systems and domestic pilots, China's National ETS is different in its management structure, the setting of the collective limit and the allowance allocation method, and the scope and coverage.

1. Two-tiered (central and provincial) structure

The National ETS consists of a central-level system and provincial systems. At the central level, the emissions trading department of the State Council is responsible for developing the overarching roles of the National ETS. The provincial emissions trading authorities are given the right to tighten control and increase coverage. First of all, the emissions trading department of the State Council is responsible for developing the top-level design of the National ETS to ensure consistency of rules across the country. Inconsistent rules can hinder the efficient operation of the national market and pose obstacles for fair competition. Secondly, since the National ETS is a nationwide scheme designed to achieve the national emissions intensity targets, the primary factor considered in the setting of collective limits and the design of the allowance allocation method is the overall technological competence of each industry in the country. However, province governments also need to rely on the key emitters participating in the National ETS to achieve provincial emissions intensity reduction targets set in their respective 13th Five-Year Plans. For some provinces, it may be difficult to meet the provincial emission reduction targets by just complying with the allowance allocation rules of the National ETS. Therefore, the National ETS allows provincial emissions trading authorities to implement allocation methods more stringent than the national method within their respective jurisdiction.

2. Collective limit and allowance allocation

The National ETS does not set a clear absolute total control target, but aggregates the allowances allocated to each emitter to obtain the collective limit of the national system. The National ETS primarily allocates emissions allowances free of charge by using industrial benchmarks based on historical emission rates. Therefore, in essence, the National ETS sets intensity control targets rather than absolute quantity control targets.

Intensity control targets and industry benchmarking are designed to address the different needs of industries and dovetail the National ETS to industrial policies and other relevant policies.

First of all, the Chinese economy is still rapidly growing which goes hand in hand with increasing GHG emissions, setting absolute total targets may hinder the growth of the Chinese economy. China's National Determined Contribution (NDC) also takes the form of an intensity reduction target [6]. The setting of intensity reduction targets and industrial benchmarks based on actual production not only fit China's development needs but also can facilitate the achievement of its NDC.

Secondly, this design can also solve the uncertainty caused by economic development. As we can see from the existing emissions trading systems in foreign countries using a fixed absolute total target, in the face of unexpected changes in economy, energy prices, and other factors, the systems cannot flexibly respond to changes in allowance demand, resulting in price hikes, declines or fluctuations. Unstable allowance price signals will increase the difficulty in stimulating investments in low-carbon technology or place too much pressure on companies thus affect their competitiveness or even result in carbon leakage.

The results of ETS pilots in China also show that the industry benchmarking method based on actual production can help address the great uncertainty brought by development of industries and coordinate ETS policies and other policies. Therefore, the industry benchmarking method has received wide support from major emitters.

In addition, this allocation method also aims to give greater autonomy to companies in industries subject to strict control. For example, in the power industry, large coal-fired units usually serve as base load power sources, smaller coal-fired units may also serve as backup whereas gas turbine power generation units are generally responsible for peak shaving. Further, power generation of units are not completely determined by the market. The National ETS sets multiple emissions benchmarks for the power industry based on demand, unit capacity and fuel type [7].

3. Scope and coverage

As for the scope and coverage, the National ETS has two distinctive features. First, it includes indirect emissions from purchased electricity and thermal energy. Secondly, its basic statistical unit is a legal entity.

The inclusion of indirect emissions is closely related to China's electricity market regulation and incomplete electricity price transmission. China's power sector is primarily government-controlled. The emissions price signal applied to the supply side cannot be effectively transmitted to the demand side, making it difficult to incentivize consumers to reduce electricity and thermal energy consumption. Although China has rolled out a reform program for the electric power sector, the nationwide problem of incomplete price transmission will continue to exist for a long time. By incorporating indirect emissions, downstream consumers can be effectively motivated to reduce electricity and thermal energy consumption.

The basic statistical unit of the National ETS is a legal person rather than a facility. This is in line with China's statistical system and energy conservation and emission reduction regulatory system. The statistical, industrial and commercial administration, taxation, industry and information technology and other departments of the Chinese government all define their statistical unit or reporting unit as a legal person. Therefore, using "legal person" as the basic statistical unit can guarantee a robust data foundation and allows for cross-checks to ensure parameters selected for the design of the National ETS are reasonable. During the implementation of the National ETS, a consistent statistical unit can also facilitate the coordination between relevant regulatory authorities, and increase the effectiveness of the system by leveraging financial credit, scientific and technological awards, tax incentives and other policies.

9.3 Challenges

The establishment and operation of the National ETS is a complex and systematic project. Although the basic framework of the National ETS system has been established, it still faces a number of massive challenges, including the improvement of legislation and GHG monitoring and reporting systems, alignment with other related systems and energy and climate policies.

1. Improvement of legislation

The current center piece of the National ETS, the *Interim Measures*, is a ministry-level policy and has insufficient influence on participants nationwide. For example, a ministry or commission does not have the authority to establish an administrative licensing system; it is also subject to certain restrictions when imposing administrative penalties; the National ETS requires inter-ministerial cooperation, and ministry-level regulations have limited influence on other ministries or commissions. According to the experience drawn from the prior ETS pilots, it is necessary to establish administrative licensing systems for allowance allocation and payment, certification of emissions verification agencies, and certification of emissions trading agencies to support the National ETS and ensure professional competence of practitioners. Low penalties for noncompliance also do not have sufficient deterrent effects on participants. The formulation of relevant rules for allowance allocation, transactions, MRV, compliance monitoring, and market regulation also requires high-level legislation as the basis. Therefore, the central government needs to promulgate the *Regulations* as soon as possible and issue supporting rules one this basis. The goal is to create a strong legal and regulatory system for emissions trading, and provide institutional support for the establishment and operation of the National ETS.

2. Improvement of GHG monitoring and reporting systems

Although a series of guidelines have been introduced to support the National ETS, these guidelines are not perfect. For example, data collection provisions of these guidelines cannot meet the data demand relating to allowance allocation under the National ETS. New MRV guidelines need to be introduced to ratchet up databases of certain industries to prepare these industries for future inclusion in the National ETS.

Currently, companies are only required to submit production, energy consumption, and GHG emissions data. These data can already meet the data demand of the compliance verification process under the National ETS. However, since the National ETS intends to set industrial benchmarks based on actual production, companies need report technical details so that emission intensity of different processes and technologies can be calculated. During the historical investigation, the NDRC already noticed this issue and asked the emitters to fill out supplementary forms. However, this is not a long-term solution. The verification guidelines should be adapted to the new allowance allocation method as soon as possible.

Data are the key to the determination of the coverage of the ETS system which will determine the contribution of the National ETS to the achievement of the carbon intensity of GDP reduction target. In January 2016, the NDRC stated in the Notice that the first phase of the National ETS will cover eighteen sub-sectors of eight major emitting sectors. However, the *Announcement of the National ETS Allowances Allocation Plan (Draft)* issued in May 2017 only released the drafts of the allowance allocation programs of three sectors due to the lack of data in other sectors. Therefore, setting detailed MRV guidelines to encourage emitters to build data capacity is the prerequisite for future integration of more industries into the National ETS.

3. Coordination with other systems

The National ETS is a new policy and needs to be coordinated with other systems. At present, it seems that the establishment of the National ETS requires special institutional arrangements in finance and government budgeting. The introduction of carbon finance products and the existing regulatory rules in the futures markets are conflicting. From the experience of foreign emission trading systems and domestic ETS pilots, financial derivatives of emission rights such as futures, forwards, pledges and other carbon finance products can effectively attract other investors, increase the size of market, improve market liquidity and efficiency, and help maximize the role of the National ETS in carbon pricing and emissions reduction. They also provide companies with a new way to hedge against long-term risks. However, according to the *Decision of the State Council on Reorganizing Exchanges to Prevent Financial Risks* (G.F. [2011] No. 38) and the *Guidelines of the General Office of the State Council for the Reorganization of Exchanges* (G.B. F. [2012] No. 37), the standardized contracts of emissions rights may not be traded in a centralized manner through collective bidding, continuous bidding, married deal via an electronic platform, anonymous trading, etc., and emissions rights may not be listed and traded in the form of standardized trading units. These regulations, designed to prevent risks, severely hinder the development of ETS, and are contradictory with the trends in the financial sector. Emissions allowances are standardized products and naturally suitable for trading in the form of standardized contracts. Emissions trading authorities need to coordinate with financial authorities to lift unreasonable restrictions on emissions trading while ensuring smooth operation of markets.

As for government budgeting, in order to better incentivize companies and the public to reduce carbon footprints, ETS should use allowance auction revenues and collected penalties to promote low carbon practices. Furthermore, the market regulation under the National ETS also requires timely and flexible financing sources for allowance trading. The EU ETS, the RGGI, and the California Cap-and-Trade Program have set up special funds to manage revenues. However, according to the *Budget Law* and the *Notice of the Ministry of Finance on the Management of Extra-budgetary Funds* (C.Y. [2010] No. 88), all government revenues and expenditures should be included in the government budget. Based on the experiences of prior domestic ETS pilots, if ETS revenues are included in the government budget, ETS revenues may not be used exclusively for the development of the ETS and the funds allocated to incentivize companies to reduce emissions may be insufficient. This problem can be solved by including ETS expenses in the government budget.

4. Alignment with other energy and climate policies

As a market-based policy tool to control GHG emissions, the National ETS is an important attempt to advance institutional reform in the field of GHG reduction. It overlaps with other energy and climate policies that has been or will be rolled out in China, such as the emission intensity reduction assessment system (2016–2020), the renewable energy certificate trading mechanism, and the energy consumption cap and trade system, in regulatory agencies, subject matter, and purposes. Although the synergy created by these policies can promote the low-carbon transformation of China's economy, there is a danger of overkill. These policies will not only increase operation expenses of companies but also put pressure on the government coffer. Therefore, when designing ETS regulations, policymakers should pay attention to coordinating them with other energy and climate policies.

First of all, the National ETS is an important tool for central and local governments to achieve emission intensity reduction targets. Therefore, when designing the allowance allocation method for the National ETS, policymakers should consider both national and local emission intensity reduction targets. Therefore, when designing the allowance allocation method for the National ETS, policymakers should consider both national and local emission intensity reduction targets. Secondly, local emission intensity reduction targets are indicators used by the central government to measure local governments' performance in energy conservation and emissions reduction. After the establishment of the National ETS, whether the allowances purchased from other provinces will be included in the assessment of local emission intensity reduction targets in the buying province will affect provincial governments' enthusiasm for promoting cross-province allowance trading.

A green certificate trading mechanism sets renewable energy quotas for coal-fired generating units and electricity distributors and requires market participants to fulfill renewable energy quota obligations by purchasing green certificates [8]. An energy consumption cap and trade system sets a collective energy consumption control target and an energy consumption cap for each major energy user, and allow the energy consumption allowances to be traded in the market [9]. These two systems set renewable energy quotas and energy consumption caps for market participants and overlap in scope and coverage. They also have similar purposes. If the two systems are rolled out in parallel with the National ETS, policymakers must consider the impact of these systems when setting the collective limit of the National ETS and designing the allowance allocation method, and prevent low emissions price caused by allowance surplus due to the impact of other policies. In addition, in order to reduce the pressure placed by multiple control measures on market companies, companies may be allowed to use green certificates or energy consumption allowances to offset emissions. The *13*th *Five-Year Plan for Renewable Energy Development* also clearly stipulates the green certificate trading mechanism should be aligned to the emissions trading market.

9.4 Outlook and Recommendations

At present, the design of the basic framework of the National ETS has been completed, and the platform construction and capacity building part of the project is also progressing well. Built on the experiences of prior EST pilots, the National ETS has its own distinctive features and takes into consideration both national and provincial needs.

However, it also faces many challenges. For example, the legislation for the system has not been fully fleshed out; the MRV mechanism has failed to meet the data demand of industry benchmarking; further coordination is needed in financial regulation and government budgeting; mechanisms need to be established to link the EST to the emission intensity reduction assessment system (2016–2020), the renewable energy certificate trading mechanism, and the energy consumption cap and trade system.

China should pass higher-level legislation for the National ETS as soon as possible, develop operational rules to regulate the allocation of emission allowances, MRV, certification of third-party verification agencies, compliance by companies, trading of emission allowances and other important activities under the ETS, dovetail ETS rules and financial industry supervision and budgeting regulations and develop a mechanism to correlate the ETS and other energy and climate policies.

The first step is to launch the National ETS. There is still much work to be done. The design of key elements such as auction rules, market adjustment mechanism and offset mechanism is yet to be finalized. These elements are not required for the launch of the National ETS but essential for the future improvement of the system. Following the launch of the National ETS, efforts should be made to gradually include more industries and companies, increase the proportion of paid allowances, and improve the National ETS system to ensure its stability.

References

1. Wang, B. (2015). Development and legislation of emissions trading in China. *Present Day Law Science, 2015*(2), 13.
2. NDRC. *Notice on Launching the National Emissions Trading Market* (Climate Document of National Development and Reform Commission [2016] No. 57). Retrieved January 11, 2016, from http://qhs.ndrc.gov.cn/qjfzjz/201601/t20160122_791850.html.
3. Duan, M., Li, D., & Li, M. (2017). Development of emissions trading markets. In X., Zhang & W., Qi (Ed.), *China low-carbon development report (2017)*. Social Sciences Academic Press, p. 89.
4. NDRC. *Interim measures for the management of emissions trading*. Retrieved December 10, 2014, from http://qhs.ndrc.gov.cn/qjfzjz/201412/t20141212_697046.html.
5. Zeng, X., Li, Y., & Zhang, W. (2016). MRV systems of China's emissions market pilots: practices and inspirations. *Progress on Environmental Economics, 2016*(1), 132.
6. NDRC. *Stepping up climate actions—China's Nationally determined contributions*. Retrieved June 30, 2015, from http://www.ndrc.gov.cn/gzdt/201506/t20150630_710226.html.
7. *Announcement of the national ETS allowances allocation plan (Draft)*. Retrieved May 9, 2017, from http://www.ideacarbon.org/archives/39381.
8. NDRC. *The 13th five-year plan for renewable energy development*. Retrieved December 2016, from http://www.ndrc.gov.cn/zcfb/zcfbtz/201612/W020161216659579206185.pdf.
9. NDRC. *Paid right to use energy and trading pilot program*. Retrieved from July 23, 2016, from http://hzs.ndrc.gov.cn/newzwxx/201609/W020160921341164855785.pdf.

Chapter 10
Low-Carbon Transport: Trends and Prospects

Quansheng Huang

Abstract Low-carbon transport is the transport sector's response to the ecological civilization and green development strategies. This paper discusses latest developments in the transport sector, including restructuring, optimization of energy consumption patterns, development of low-carbon transport systems, low-carbon transport pilots, application of information technology in transport, and international cooperation in this sector, and analyzes the trends and prospects of low-carbon transport.

Keywords Transportation · Low carbon · Practices

Transport is one of the three major contributors to energy consumption as well as one of the three largest sources of carbon emissions. Road and waterway transport accounts for more than 30% of the total consumption of petroleum and petroleum products in China [1]. In 2009, the State Council announced the launch of low-carbon transformation of mining and manufacturing, construction and transport sectors. Since then, a broad effort has been made to promote low-carbon transport and implement the ecological civilization and green development strategies in the transport sector.

Quansheng Huang is a senior engineer and Deputy Director of the Environment and Resources Division, Transport Planning and Research Institute, Ministry of Transport. Huang's research interests include climate change and energy conservation and emissions reduction in transport.

Q. Huang (✉)
Environment and Resources Division, Transport Planning and Research Institute,
Ministry of Transport, Beijing, China
e-mail: hqs68@qq.com

W. Wang (ed.), *Annual Report on China's Response to Climate Change (2017)*,
Research Series on the Chinese Dream and China's Development Path,
https://doi.org/10.1007/978-981-13-9660-1_10

10.1 Recent Developments in Low-Carbon Transport

1. Restructuring of the transport sector

Restructuring is a strategic measure to promote energy conservation and emissions reduction in transport. It is also a complicated and arduous task and affected by factors such as systems, mechanisms, planning and investment, and requires firm determination and pragmatic attitude. To restructure the transport sector for low-carbon development, the competent transport authorities should:

(1) Optimize the structure of the transport sector: They should actively improve the connection between different modes of transport; leverage existing water transport and railway resources to vigorously develop river-sea combined transport, road-rail-water combined transport, and sea-rail combined transport; and increase the proportion of water transport and railway transport in integrated transport. The State Council has released the *13th Five-Year Plan for the Development of Modern Integrated Transport Systems*, which aims to improve the layout of transport infrastructure, promote the construction of modern integrated transport systems, and fully leverage the comparative advantages and combined synergy value of different modes of transport.
(2) Attach importance to public transit: They should build integrated urban passenger transport systems with public transit (bus services and subway) as the mainstay and taxis services and slow transport (walking and biking) as supporting elements, moderate the development of private cars, and increase the rate of the use of public transport. Such systems are essential for green, and low-carbon development of urban transport.
(3) Improve the management models of passenger and cargo transport companies: They should increase the size of road passenger transport companies and improve the organization of logistics activities, and accelerate the development of drop-and-pull transport and multimodal transport as a means to transform the development path of road transport, restructure road transport, and increase the load-to-truck ratio.

By the end of 2016, a total of 209 pilot projects (four lists) had been launched across the country. Among them, 121 projects have received government funding amounting to 810 million yuan. These pilot projects have cut fuel consumption by about 210,000 tons and CO_2 emissions by about 646,000 tons. In 2016, eighteen cabinet-level departments of the State Council, including the Ministry of Transport, jointly issued the *Notice on Supporting the Development of Multimodal Transport*, making institutional arrangements at the national level for multimodal transport. The Ministry of Transport and the National Development and Reform Commission (NDRC) has jointly released the first list of multimodal transport pilot projects, aiming to cultivate a typical transport organization model and develop best practices.

2. Improvement of energy consumption structure in the transport sector

(1) Continue to impose fuel consumption restrictions on road transport vehicles and ships: In 2016, China announced four lists of vehicle models (6,597) and configurations (10,146) that meet fuel consumption requirements and continued to advance international cooperation projects such as Green Freight and China-US Race to Zero Emissions (R2ZE) Challenge. In the second half of 2017, more than twenty Chinese cities submitted applications to participate in the R2ZE Challenge
(2) Increase the adoption of new energy in urban public transport: They should further improve the new energy bus refined oil subsidy policy. In 2016, there were 164,900 new energy buses in the country, accounting for 27.01% of the total number of buses/cable cars in China. In light of the new situation, the Ministry of Transport is assessing the structure of public transport and plans to revise the target. The goal is to increase use of new energy public transport and vehicles, and promote a more sustainable energy consumption pattern in public transport.
(3) Increase the use of liquefied natural gas (LNG) in ships and ports: The first batch of LNG water transport pilot projects have been evaluated and nine projects in the Yangtze River Basin and the Xijiang Basin are included in the second batch of LNG water transport pilot projects.
(4) Promote the use of shore power: Seven shore power projects including Shanghai Port, Ningbo Port and Lianyungang shore power projects have been launched. A shore power subsidy policy has been developed. China is now conducting research for the development of a national shore power grid layout plan.
4. Low-carbon transport pilots

3. Low-carbon transport systems

(1) Improve green and low-carbon transport systems and standards: In May 2016, the Ministry of Transport issued the *Notice of the Ministry of Transport on Promulgating the 13th Five-Year Plan for Low-carbon Transportation (Jiao Gui Hua Fa [2016] No. 94)*. In January 2016, the Ministry of Transport issued the Green Transport Code (2016), which includes six categories of standards (185 provisions), and issued thirteen industry standards such as *Specifications for Hybrid Buses*. Green transport standards provide science-based technical support for the development of green and low-carbon transport and necessary tools and methods for the application of market mechanisms to promote green and low-carbon transport.
(2) Improve the statistical system for monitoring energy consumption in transport: The *Statistical Reporting System for Monitoring Energy Consumption in Transport* has been revised. Beijing, Jiangsu and other municipalities/provinces have established an energy consumption and emissions monitoring platform for the transport sector to support government decision-making, planning, and plan implementation, evaluation and optimization, and low-carbon actions adopted by companies.

(3) Promote the application of low-carbon technologies: The Chinese government has published a list of key low-carbon technologies and products for the transport sector and promoted the application of low-carbon driving, operation and maintenance technologies for vehicles and ships.
(4) Conduct research in green and low-carbon transport: China has carried out the following forward-looking low-carbon transport research projects: "Research for the Development of a Framework of Green and Low-carbon Transport Systems", "Key Factors, Potential and Funding Needs of Energy Conservation and Emissions Reduction Projects in Transport (2016–2020)", "Research for the Development of an Action Plan for the Transport Sector to Contribute the Achievement of China's NDC", "Research for the Development of a Strategy to Include the Transport Sector in China's Emissions Trading System", "Research for the Development of Emissions Accounting Methods and Standards for the Transport Sector", "Research for the Energy Efficiency Forerunner in Transport Program", "Low-carbon Transport Fund Research" and "Applied Research on Energy Management Terms in Transport Contracts". These research projects have played an important role in promoting the development of green and low-carbon transport.

In 2011, the central government decided to allocate funds from the general budget and vehicle purchase tax revenues to support the implementation of the 12th five-year plan for energy conservation and emissions reduction in road and waterway transport. From 2011 to 2016, it invested a total of 4.75 billion yuan in this field. Its investment in 2016 alone amounted to 1.5 billion yuan.

By the end of 2016, the special fund had supported 976 projects and played an important role in promoting the green development of the transport sector and contributed to the realization of China's low-carbon targets and the implementation of polices which aim to "maintain economic growth, promote reform, advance restructuring and benefit citizens." From 2016 to 2018, the central government plans to invest 1.15 billion yuan in three years, allocated from vehicle purchase tax revenues, to support the construction and installation of shore power facilities and equipment on both port and ship sides. In May 2017, the Ministry of Transport completed the assessment of the first batch of shore power projects under the 13th five-year plan for shore power development, and gave monetary awards to fifty-six projects. The total investment of these projects reached about 621.4 million yuan, and the monetary awards amounted to about 206.45 million yuan. These projects reduce fuel use by about 55,000 tons per year. The projects in the ship pollution emission control areas in the Yangtze River Delta, the Pearl River Delta and the Bohai Economic Rim (Beijing-Tianjin-Hebei) received 64.1% of the monetary awards.

The low-carbon transport pilot projects have achieved remarkable results in reducing energy consumption and emissions. It is estimated that the projects supported by the special fund has reduced energy consumption by 2.7428 million tons of coal equivalent and CO_2 emissions by 19.2862 million tons. With the support of the special fund, compared with 2010, energy consumed per unit distance per commercial vehicle has decreased by 6.5%; energy consumed per unit distance per commercial ship has decreased by 10.5%; and energy consumption per unit at ports decreased by 7.5%. The special fund has contributed greatly to the realization of the goal of the *12th Five-Year Plan for Energy Conservation and Emissions Reduction (G.F. [2012] No. 40)* and effectively controlled the increase in energy consumption in transport. The Ministry of Transport has also promoted the construction of green highways and ports. It issued the *Guidelines for Green Road Construction (J.B.G.L. [2016] No. 93)*, aiming to promote the construction of efficient, high quality, environment-friendly highways. It has released three lists of green highway projects across the country. The Ministry of Transport is currently developing a technical guide and an evaluation system for green highway projects. The Green Highway Program of the Ministry of Transport aims to integrate environment-friendly design into road transport, revamp existing highways to make them more eco-friendly, construct green highways corridors, promoting the development of highway carbon sinks and carbon trading, and build a highway environmental management services system, promote the use of green lighting and intelligent control engineering systems in road tunnels, promote the adoption of electronic toll collection (ETC) systems, accelerate the development and large-scale application of clean and new energy in road transport, build low-carbon expressway service areas and toll stations, recycle waste materials generated by road construction, and integrate green practices in the whole process of highway design and construction. As for green ports, a coordinated port air pollutant and GHG control plan has been put in place. The Ministry of Transport has launched port ecological restoration projects, promoted oil and gas recycling at crude oil and refined oil terminals, increased the adoption of energy conservation and environmental protection measures such as ship berthing and shore power, installed green lighting in port areas, promoted the electrification of ports, accelerated the development and application of clean and new energy technologies in port operation, and constructed port energy consumption and environment monitoring and intelligent management systems.

5. Application of IT in the transport sector

China has been promoting the application of information technology in the transport sector, encourage the use of the "Internet Plus" model to improve the operational efficiency of transport systems and harness the environmental benefits of the "Internet+Transport Organization". In the future, it will continue to promote the application of the Internet of Things, the Internet of Vehicles, the Internet of Ships, smart roads, smart ports and public transit systems and push for the integration of smart transport and green transport.

The transport authorities should draw on the experiences of smart bus pilot projects, optimize bus dispatch management, promote the application of the bus service app, accelerate the introduction of a national integrated public transport fare system, and promote the application of expressway ETC systems. As of November 2016, there were 13,572 ETC lanes in 29 provinces across the country, serving 43.45 million users and reducing fuel consumption by 79,000 tons. The smart highway pilot program launched by the Ministry of Transport focuses on promoting vehicle and road coordination and other applications and practices. The "Internet Plus Transport" models such as online car-hailing, carpooling (including electric carpooling) and bicycle sharing are gaining traction in China. According to Mobike, Mobike riders in China have traveled more than 2.5 billion kilometers, reduced carbon emissions by 540,000 tons, equivalent to taking 170,000 cars off the road for a year, and saved 460 million liters of gasoline in less than a year.

6. International cooperation in low-carbon transport

China has actively participated in the negotiations on maritime GHG emission reduction under the framework of the United Nations Framework Convention on Climate Change and the International Maritime Organization (IMO); launched China-US Race to Zero Emissions (R2ZE) Challenge; promoted international cooperation in green freight transport; completed the GEF project "Integrated Transport in China's Urban Agglomerations", including the search project "Reducing Traffic Congestion and Carbon Emissions"and related demonstration projects; and cooperated with Germany in clean fuel development.

10.2 Trends in Low-Carbon Transport

China's transport sector will continue to grow rapidly in 2016-2020. To support the economic growth of the Beijing-Tianjin-Hebei region, the Yangtze River Economic Belt, and the Belt and Road, China needs to advance the supply-side reform of the transport sector. In the context of new urbanization, informationization and motorization, China is moving towards the vision of seamlessly integrated multi-modal passenger and freight transport networks. To achieve this vision, China needs to better incorporate the ecological civilization strategy and promote recycling and low-carbon technologies and practices in the transport sector, and drive the transition to sustainable production and consumption patterns through green transport.

To achieve life-cycle low-carbon transport, China needs to integrate multimodal transport, energy saving and environmental protection initiatives, integrate transport and tourism, promote alternative energy vehicles, integrate smart transport and green transport, promote green and low-carbon transport systems, develop low-carbon market mechanisms, and strengthen international cooperation.

At present, the overall energy consumption and environment monitoring capacity of China's transport sector is still weak. The lack of data increases the difficulty of decision-making and management. The standards system of green transport has not been fully fleshed out. The green transport assessment system is yet to be developed. There is a lack of environmental protection supervision tools. The Chinese government has not issued supporting policies to facilitate the operation of the relevant market mechanisms.

10.3 Prospects of Low-Carbon Transport

1. Better low-carbon transport systems

China should speed up the development of a comprehensive, science-based efficient, green and low-carbon transport system, including key policies, plans, and standards. This is also the most important task in the development of green transport. For example, to strengthen the foundation for such a transport system and improve energy consumption monitoring, the Ministry of Transport has planned to put in place an energy consumption monitoring plan in the transport sector, improve its energy consumption monitoring platform, offer equipment selection, data integration, operation and maintenance guidance for provincial platforms, promote online energy consumption monitoring, and support data-driven decision-making and green and low-carbon practices in the sector.

2. More financing sources for low-carbon transport

During 2011–2015, the central government's low-carbon transport fund played an important role in supporting the development of green and low-carbon transport. However, it should be noted that the fund still cannot meet the financing demand. To create a green transport system that meets the demand of a well-off society by 2020, launch the "10-100-1,000" green transport pilot program and improve the layout and the standards system of the sector, and strengthen related capacity building of the government, massive investments will be required.

China should continue to increase central and local governments' spending on low-carbon transport and leverage market-based tools such as contract-based energy management, green credit, green bonds, green development funds, financial leasing, and emission trading to raise funds.

3. Enhanced role of technology

The "100" in the "10-100-1,000" green transport pilot program refers to one hundred practical technologies for energy conservation and emissions reduction in transport. These technologies pave the way for green and low carbon development of the industry. Technology plays a crucial role in the development of low-carbon transport. First, it can accelerate the restructuring of the sector and facilitate the transition of the sector to a sustainable energy consumption pattern Solar energy, wind energy, natural gas and electric power will be applied in large scale in transport, significantly improving the energy efficiency of transport systems. Second, new materials, new technologies and new processes will be promoted and applied. For example, development of shore power standards and application of the "Internet+Transport" model will significantly improve the operational and regulatory efficiency of the industry. Third, technology can drive the development of strategic emerging industries. For example, the application of rubber asphalt to upgrade used roads and the adoption of online monitoring systems, smart monitoring and dispatch systems, Internet of Things, cloud computing and other technologies will greatly contribute to the development of the transport sector. For transport, with further integration of low-carbon technology and smart transport, the sky is the limit.

4. Raised awareness of low-carbon development

At the 41st collective study meeting of the Political Bureau of the Central Committee, General Secretary Xi Jinping emphasized that China should increase energy efficiency in high energy-consuming industries, promote energy conservation in the transport sector, and encourage green and low-carbon transport. Government officials should be a green ambassador and inspire sustainable practices among companies and the general public. China should develop the "soft power" of green transport and construct an integrated, multimodal, green, low-carbon transport system.

5. Growing international presence

The *2030 Agenda for Sustainable Development*, the *Paris Agreement,* the Belt and Road Initiative and the introduction of the "community of common destiny" concept have shaped the low-carbon future of China's transport sector and forge close ties between countries. To promote green and low-carbon transport, China must continue to strengthen international cooperation, actively participate in international negotiations, improve the green governance system, develop and promote low-carbon technologies and equipment, strengthen communication with international organizations, participate in international green road, port, and hub projects, and step up related capacity building.

6. Significant decline in emission intensity

During 2016–2020, transport infrastructure and service demand will continue to grow rapidly. It is predicted that, by 2020, energy consumption and carbon emissions in the transport sector will increase by 20% from the levels of 2015. The rapid increase in carbon emissions makes carbon intensity reduction in the transport sector more urgent and difficult. Carbon intensity reduction in the transport sector is obviously a complex task that requires systematic planning and long-term commitment. China should strive to reduce CO_2 emissions per unit distance per commercial vehicle by 7.9%, CO_2 emissions per unit distance per commercial ship by 7.1%, CO_2 emissions per unit distance per passenger by 12.5%, and CO_2 emissions per unit of port activity by 7.5% by 2020 from the levels of 2015 [2].

References

1. Notice of the Ministry of Transport on Promulgating the 13th Five-Year Plan for Low-carbon Transportation (J.G.H.F. [2016] No. 94). May 31, 2016.
2. *Notice of the Ministry of Transport on Promulgating the 13th Five-Year Plan for Low-carbon Transportation (Jiao Gui Hua Fa [2016] No. 94).* May 31, 2016.

Chapter 11
Wind Power in China: Current State and Future Outlook

Haiyan Qin and Ying Li

Abstract In recent years, rapid wind power development in China has attracted worldwide attention. China has been ranked first in both cumulative installed wind power capacity and newly installed wind power capacity for several years in a roll (including 2016) and is the largest wind power market in the world. The year 2016 saw further improvement in the policy framework for wind power in China. However, the massive unused wind power capacity and subsidy arrears remain a huge challenge. The prices of electricity from wind farms are still high while the exports of wind turbines as percentage of China's total exports remain relatively low. The wind power sector faces unprecedented challenges from the decline in the benchmark prices for grid-connected wind power. Under the guidance of the 13th Five-Year Plan, China's wind power sector has placed an increasing emphasis on quality than merely quantity. To pave the way to sustainable development of China's wind power sector, it is recommended that Chinese policymakers should innovate and improve the policy frameworks for renewable energy certificates (RECs) trading, grid parity of wind power, reform in the electric power sector, wind power finance and insurance, and global trade in wind power goods and services.

Keywords Wind power · Renewable energy certificates (RECs) · Renewable energy

---

Haiyan Qin is the Secretary General of Chinese Wind Energy Association, China Renewable Energy Society, and Director of the China General Certification Center. Qin's research interests include wind power policy and economics.

H. Qin (✉) · Y. Li
Chinese Wind Energy Association, China Renewable Energy Society, Beijing, China
e-mail: qinhy@cgc.org.cn

Y. Li
e-mail: sdkdfly@163.com

W. Wang (ed.), *Annual Report on China's Response to Climate Change (2017)*,
Research Series on the Chinese Dream and China's Development Path,
https://doi.org/10.1007/978-981-13-9660-1_11

As the consequences of climate change become increasingly obvious, the difficulty in handling the relationship between energy and environment has also increased. Green and low-carbon development has become the mainstream paradigm of the times. There is a growing trend to develop renewable energy which has also become an important tool widely adopted by many developed and developing countries to enhance energy security and tackle climate change Many countries have set out ambitious renewable energy develop visions for 2050. China has also pledged to increase the share of non-fossil energy sources of the total primary energy supply to at least 15% by 2020 and 20% by 2030.

Thanks to the supporting policies, China's wind power technology has advanced, resulting in a continuous decline in wind power generation costs. In the past, wind power was primarily used to supplement energy production. Now, China is fully capable of replacing fossil fuels with wind power. Wind power has become an important part of China's newly installed power generation capacity. So far, China has basically established a comprehensive management and policy system for the wind power sector, and issued regulations and technical specifications covering the entire life cycle of wind power projects, from design to construction, grid connection and operation. It has also streamlined wind power project approval procedures and created a favorable policy environment for the sector.

During 2016–2020, China will continue to stimulate the development of the wind power sector. The *Thirteenth Five-Year Plan for Wind Power Development* sets out a goal of increasing the total installed and grid-connected wind power capacity to 210 million kW by 2020 and points out that China's wind power sector should shift its focus from quantity to quality. The plan provides important strategic guidance on the development of wind power in China.

11.1 Wind Power Development in China

11.1.1 Industry Profile

(1) The wind power market is growing in size

In recent years, thanks to continuous government support, the installed wind power capacity in China keeps ticking upward. China has emerged as the world's largest and fastest growing wind power market. According to *Global Wind Statistics 2016* released by the Global Wind Energy Council (GWEC), the global newly installed wind power capacity was more than 54.6 million kW and the cumulative installed wind power capacity reached 487 million kW in 2016. China's newly installed wind power capacity was 23.37 million kW and cumulative installed power capacity was 169 million kilowatts, accounting for 42.8 and 34.7% of the global cumulative and newly installed wind power capacity, respectively, ranking first in the world [1].

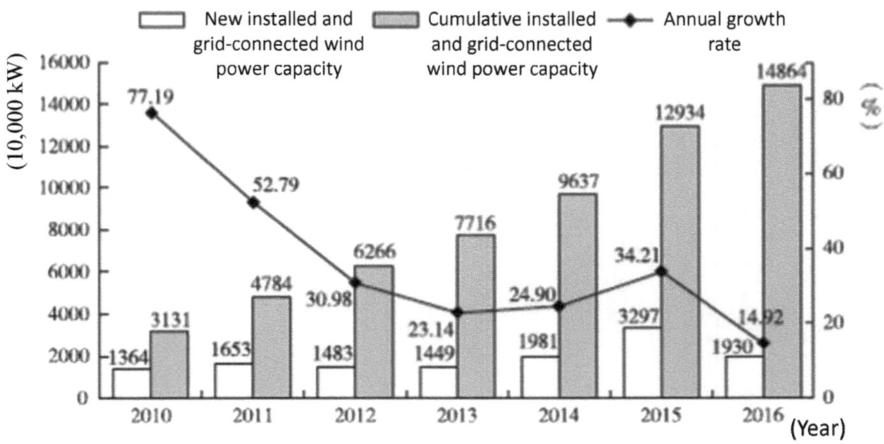

Fig. 11.1 Installed and grid-connected wind power capacity in china, 2010–2016. *Source* National Energy Administration

According to the National Energy Administration, in 2016, China's newly installed and grid-connected wind power capacity reached 19.3 million kW and cumulative grid-connected installed wind power capacity reached 148.64 million kW (see Fig. 11.1) [2].

With the continuous increase of installed and grid-connected wind power capacity, the proportion of wind power in China total installed power capacity has also increased year by year, reaching 9% in 2016 (see Fig. 11.2). Wind power supply keeps ticking up. It reached 241 billion kWh in 2016, accounting for 4% of China's total power supply. Wind energy has become China's largest source of electricity after thermal power and hydropower.

(2) Wind power bases have shifted to the eastern, central, southern regions of the county

In recent years, affected by the excessive wind power capacity in Northeast China, North China, and Northwest China, wind power bases have gradually shifted to the eastern, central, southern regions of the county. According to the Chinese Wind Energy Association (CWEA), China Renewable Energy Society, there are nineteen provinces in Central, Eastern and South China (including Hebei, Shandong, Anhui, Jiangsu, Zhejiang, Fujian, Guangdong, Guangxi, Hainan, Shanxi, Henan, Hubei, Hunan, Jiangxi, Shaanxi, Sichuan, Chongqing, Yunnan and Guizhou). The newly installed wind power capacity in the nineteen provinces as a percentage of China's total newly installed wind power capacity rose from 32.6% in 2010 to 65.1% in 2016 (see Fig. 11.3). The cumulative installed wind power capacity in the nineteen provinces doubled since 2010.

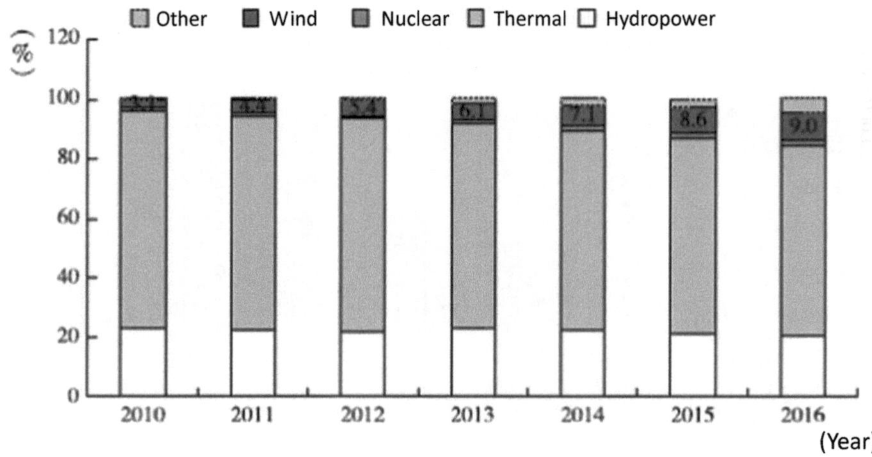

Fig. 11.2 Installed wind power capacity in china as a percentage of total installed power capacity, 2011–2016. *Source* National Energy Administration

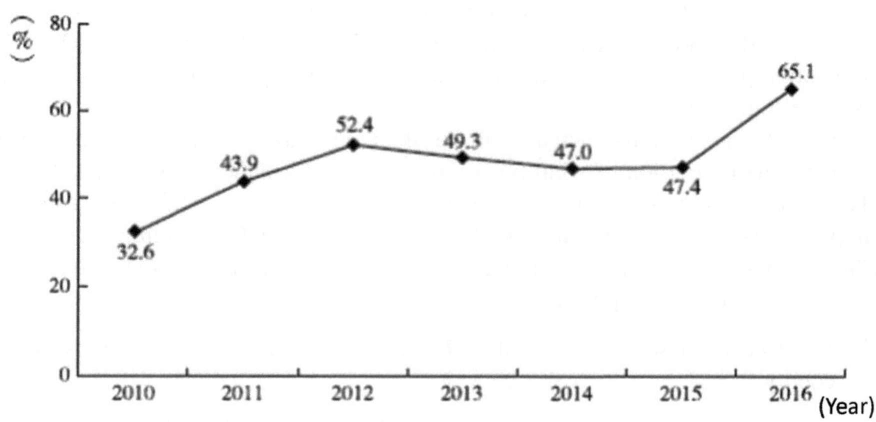

Fig. 11.3 Newly installed wind power capacity in the 19 provinces in central, eastern and south china as a percentage of china's total newly installed wind power capacity. *Source* CWEA, China Renewable Energy Society

In 2016, the newly installed wind power capacity in the nineteen provinces in Central, Eastern and South China reached 152.24 million kW, accounting for 50% of China's total newly installed wind power capacity which stood at 233.70 million kW [3].

(3) Offshore wind power has grown rapidly

In 2016, China's installed offshore wind power capacity reached 590,000 kW, an increase of 64% year-on-year. All new offshore wind power projects are located in

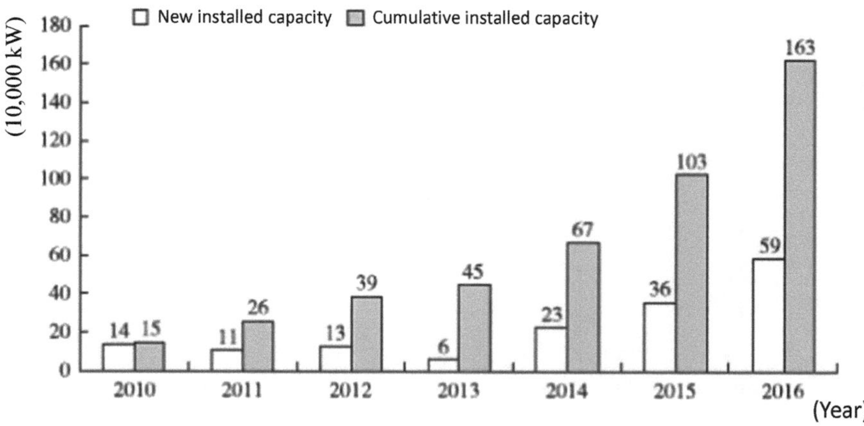

Fig. 11.4 Newly and cumulative installed offshore wind power capacity in china, 2010–2016. *Source* CWEA, China Renewable Energy Society

inshore coastal waters. As of the end of 2016, the cumulative installed offshore wind power capacity in China totaled 1.63 million kW (see Fig. 11.4). The cumulative installed wind power capacity in intertidal zones reached 632,000 kW, accounting for 38.8% of China's total cumulative installed offshore wind power capacity. The cumulative installed wind power capacity in inshore coastal waters reached 995,000 kW, accounting for 61.2% of China's total cumulative installed offshore wind power capacity [3].

As of the end of 2016, the cumulative grid-connected offshore wind power capacity in China reached 1.48 million kilowatts, mainly located in Jiangsu, Shanghai and Fujian. Among them, Jiangsu Province has the largest number of integrated offshore wind power projects, with a total capacity of 1.12 million kW (see Fig. 11.5), accounting for 76% of the country's total grid-connected capacity [4].

(4) The concentration ratio in the wind power market keeps ticking upward

According to the CWEA, in 2016, newly installed wind turbines in China were provided by twenty-five manufacturers. Goldwind ranked first in newly installed capacity which stood at 6.343 million kW, accounting for 27.1% of the Chinese market, followed by Envision, Mingyang Wind Power, United Power and CSIC Haizhuang. As of the end of 2016, there were five Chinese wind turbine manufacturers with cumulative installed capacity exceeding 10 million kW and a combined market share of 55.9%.

Goldwind also ranked first in cumulative installed capacity which stood at 37.48 million kW, accounting for 22.2% of the Chinese market. Chinese suppliers hold eight of the top fifteen spots in FTI Consulting's 2016 global top wind turbine ranking (see Table 11.1).

Statistical analysis of the market share of China's top five and top ten wind turbine suppliers shows that, as the wind power sector becomes more and more

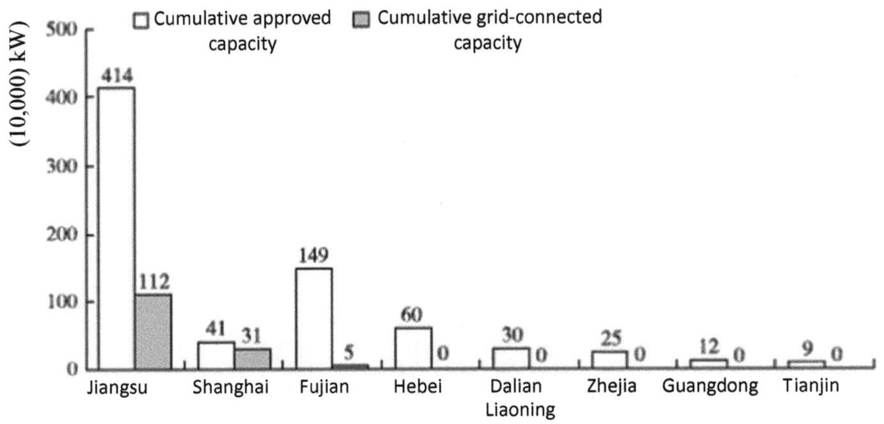

Fig. 11.5 Cumulative grid-connected and approved offshore wind power capacity in major chinese provinces and cities. *Source China Wind Power Report (2016)*

Table 11.1 Top 15 global wind turbine suppliers ranking by market share, 2016

No.	Supplier	Country	Share of Newly Installed Capacity (%)
1	VESTAS	Denmark	15.8
2	GE	U.S.	12.1
3	Goldwind	China	11.7
4	GAMESA	Spain	7.5
5	ENERCON	Germany	6.8
6	SIEMENS	Germany	5.6
7	NORDEX	Germany	4.8
8	United Power	China	3.8
9	Envision	China	3.5
10	Mingyang	China	3.5
11	CSIC Haizhuang	China	3.2
12	Shanghai Electric	China	3.0
13	SENVION	Germany	2.5
14	Dongfang	China	2.2
15	XEMC	China	2.2
	Others		11.8

Source FTI Consulting

commercialized, the concentration ratio of China's wind turbine market is rising. The combined market share of China's top five wind turbine suppliers rose from 54.1% in 2013 to 60.1% in 2016 and that of China's top ten wind turbine suppliers climbed from 77.8% in 2013 to 84.2% in 2016 (Fig. 11.6).

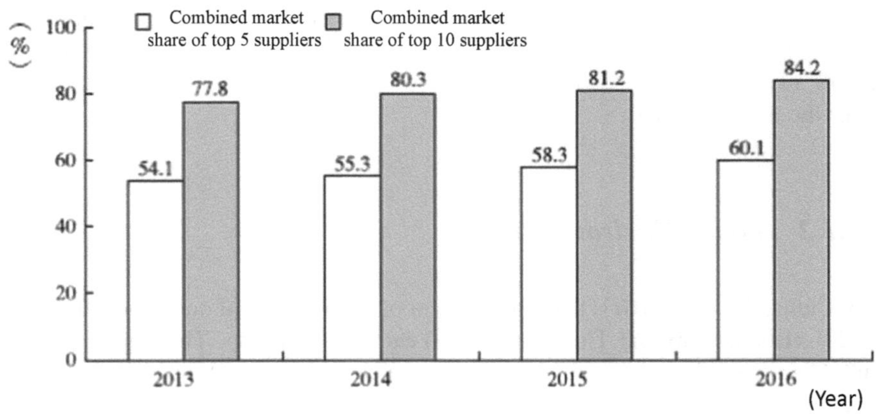

Fig. 11.6 Market share of china's top wind turbine suppliers, 2013–2016. *Source* CWEA, China Renewable Energy Society

(5) China's wind power sector is still dominated by state-owned enterprises (SOEs)

According to the CWEA, more than one hundred Chinese wind turbine suppliers reported newly installed capacity in 2016. Among them, the combined installed capacity of the top ten suppliers reached more than 13 million kW, accounting for 58.8% of the domestic market; the combined cumulative installed capacity of the top ten suppliers was more than 100 million kW, accounting for 69.4% of China's total cumulative installed wind power capacity.

In 2016, SOEs still dominated China's wind power sector and accounted for 77.9% newly installed wind power capacity (Fig. 11.7), which was 0.7% lower than

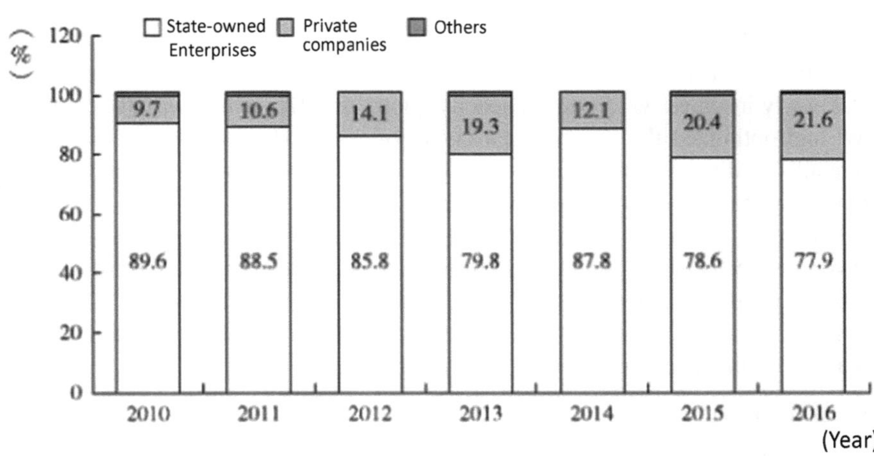

Fig. 11.7 Market share of different types of wind turbine suppliers grouped by ownership type, 2010–2016. *Source* CWEA, China Renewable Energy Society

that in 2015. The newly installed wind power capacity of private companies has kept ticking upward in recent years. In 2016, private companies accounted for 21.6% of China's total newly installed wind power capacity, an increase of 11.9% over the level in 2010.

11.1.2 Policy Environment

For China, the year 2016 is the starting point of a new phase of development (2016–2020) visualized by the Thirteenth Five-Year Plan roadmap. The central government has issued a series of supporting policies and regulations in relation to planning, annual quota management, grid-connection, feed-in tariffs, industry monitoring and investment risk warning. These policies and regulations pave the way for sustainable development of the wind power sector.

(1) Overarching plan

In November 2016, the National Energy Administration (NEA) issued the *13*th *Five-Year Plan for Wind Power Development (G.N.X.N. [2016] No. 314),* setting out the goals, industrial layout and development path of China's wind power sector in the next five years. It is designed as a roadmap for the wind power sector during 2016–2020.

According to the plan, by the end of 2020, the cumulative installed wind power capacity in China will reach 210 million kW, including more than 5 million kW offshore wind power capacity. As for the geographical layout of the sector, the main wind power markets will be shifted from Northeast China, North China, and Northwest China to the eastern, central, southern regions of the county.

(2) Annual quota management

In March 2016, the NEA issued the *Notice on the Release of the 2016 National Wind Power Development Plan (G.N.X.N. [2016] No. 84).* The document set the total newly installed wind power capacity quota for 2016, which was 30.83 million kW, and optimized the geographical layout of the wind power sector. No quotas were allocated to areas with excessive wind power capacity, whereas the quotas for central and eastern regions were increased.

According to the notice, the NEA will no longer release a list of approved wind power projects during 2016–2020. Instead, it will only set out the total newly installed wind power capacity quota and plan the layout of the sector. The document has streamlined the approval process for wind power projects and mobilized local governments and enterprises to develop wind power.

(3) Grid connection

In March 2016, the NEA issued the *Notice on Grid Connection of Wind Power in 2016*, which announced for the first time the suspension of renewable energy project approval in areas with excessive power generation capacity and massive unused wind power capacity. In order to increase the share of non-fossil energy in total primary energy consumption to 15% by 2020, the National Development and Reform Commission (NDRC) issued the *Notice on Promulgating the Measures for Guaranteed Purchase of Electric Power from Renewable Sources (F.G.N.Y. [2016] No. 625)* in March 2016, mandating that the grid operators must purchase output from renewable generators within the planned scope at least up to an allocated number of hours. In May 2016, the NDRC and the NAE jointly issued the *Notice on the Relevant Requirements for Guaranteed Purchase of Wind and Solar Power (F. G.N.Y. [2016] No. 1150)*, setting the minimum number of hours per year of the guaranteed purchase of output from wind and solar power generators in areas with high levels of curtailment and effectively reducing curtailment in these areas.

(4) Investment monitoring and alert

In July 2016, the NEA issued the *Notice on Establishing a Monitoring and Alerting Mechanism to Promote the Sustainable Development of the Wind Power Sector (G. N.X.N. [2016] No. 196)*, setting indicators and methods to measure wind power development and investment risks. The alerting system assigns ratings—red (high risk), orange (medium risk) and green (low risk)—to regions each year. If an area is rated green, investors and local governments can continue to invest in wind power projects at reasonable scale in the area; areas with a red or orange rating will not receive annual newly installed wind power capacity quotas for the year; in areas rated red, local governments are requested to suspend the approval of new wind power projects. By launching such an alerting system, the state can guide investors to areas without investment risks, strengthen the compliance supervision of local governments in wind power development, and ensure rational wind power development across the country.

(5) Tariff management policy

In December 2016, the NDRC issued the *Notice on Adjusting the Feed-in Rates of Solar Power and Onshore Wind Power (F.G.J.G. [2016] No. 2729)* to trim the feed-in tariffs (FITs) of output from onshore wind power generators approved after January 1, 2018. The benchmark FITs were cut by 0.03–0.07 yuan/kWh from the levels of 2016. After adjustment, the FITs of Tier-I, -II, -III and -IV wind resource zones are 0.4 yuan/kWh, 0.45 yuan/kWh, 0.49 yuan/kWh and 0.57 yuan/kWh, respectively. In addition, Yunnan Province has also been upgraded from Tier-IV wind resource zone to Tier-II. The adjustment of the FITs further steers wind power investments to areas with high wind power demand, including Central and Eastern China.

11.2 Challenges

11.2.1 High Levels of Curtailment

In 2016, energy loss due to wind power curtailment reached 49.7 billion kWh (Fig. 11.8), an increase of 46.6% year-on-year. The country's average wind curtailment rate was still high, with Jilin, Xinjiang, and Gansu witnessing curtailment rates of more than 30%.

Curtailment has become the biggest roadblock for the development of China's wind power sector. Take a 50,000 kW onshore wind power project for example. If we set the generation cost per kilowatt at 8,000 yuan and the FIT at 0.50 yuan/kWh (tax included), the project's rate of return after tax is 8.04% when the equivalent full load hours (2,500 h) are achieved. In the case of 10% curtailment, the after-tax rate of return will drop to 6.34%, leading to a sharp decline in the project's revenue. Therefore, high levels of wind curtailment have become a key bottleneck restricting the sustainable development of China's wind power sector.

11.2.2 Outstanding Debts in Renewable Energy Subsidies

Outstanding debts in renewable energy subsidies has become a major hurdle hindering the development of renewable energy. According to the NEA, as of the end of 2016, the accumulated debts generated by renewable energy subsidies were over 60 billion yuan. As China's annual installed renewable energy capacity continues to increase, the rapidly growing subsidy demand combined with the massive

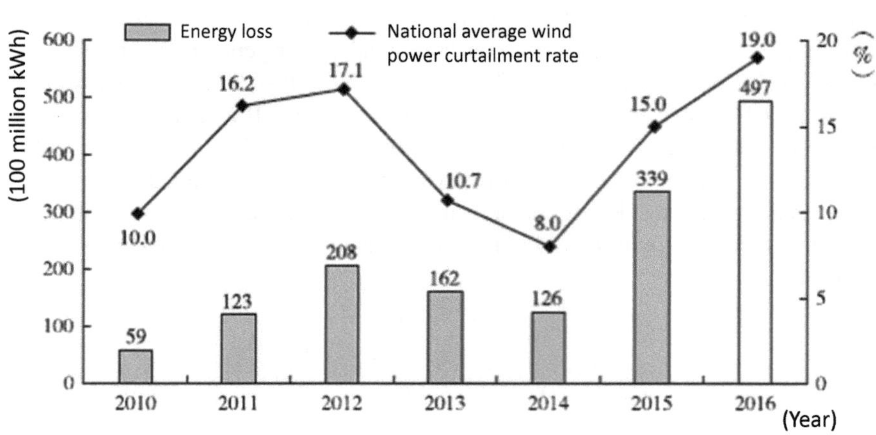

Fig. 11.8 Wind power curtailment rate in china, 2010–2016. *Source* National Energy Administration

outstanding debts results in a widening subsidy shortfall. It is estimated that China's renewable energy subsidy deficit will rise to more than 300 billion yuan by 2020.

Delays in getting government subsidies have caused financial problems in wind farms. With tight cash flow, many wind farms are unable to cover financing cost. Some smaller wind farms are facing the risk of a cash flow crisis. If we set the annual outstanding debts in renewable energy surcharges at 1.7 billion yuan and the interest rate at 4.6% (based on the benchmark rate for one-year loans), the annual increase in financing costs of wind farms will reach about 78 million yuan, equivalent to a decrease of 0.012 yuan/kWh in the FIT. Obviously, the old subsidy system can no longer meet the massive demand generated by growing installed wind power capacity in China.

11.2.3 High Generation Costs

During 2011–2015, the estimated average costs of wind power were about 8,500 yuan/kW, and the final costs was about 7,700 yuan/kW. Wind turbine and installation projects accounted for about 77% of the total costs. According to the CREEI, the decline in wind power costs in 2011–2014 was primarily contributed by equipment costs and financing costs. However, since 2015, the price of wind turbines has basically stabilized at around 4,200 yuan/kW with some areas witnessing a slight increase in wind turbine prices. During 2016–2020, China will shift wind power bases to the eastern, central, southern regions of the county. These regions have complex terrains and are densely populated, leading to an increase in wind power projects' land costs, development difficulty and costs per kilowatt. Even if technological advancement, integrated development and other factors are considered, the wind power development costs in some areas still show an upward trend. In addition, the operating and maintenance costs of wind farms are directly related to the reliability of wind turbines. The lack of unified technical specifications and standards leads to unreliability of wind turbines, which in turn results in frequent accidents, low efficiency and high operating and maintenance costs of wind farms.

11.2.4 Low Export Ratios

In 2016, Goldwind held the top spot in the ranking of Chinese wind turbine suppliers by exported capacity. Goldwind exported 273,500 kW wind turbines to three countries, accounting for only 4.1% of its newly installed capacity in the same year. According to FTI Consulting, among the top five global wind turbine suppliers in 2016, Vestas, GE, Gamesa and Enercon, except for Goldwind, accounted for more than 40% of installed capacity in non-major markets (Table 11.2) [5]. As of the end of 2016, global wind power giant Vestas had installed wind turbines in seventy-six

Table 11.2 Top five global wind turbine suppliers ranking by market share, 2016

Supplier	Major market	Number of major markets	Total installed capacity (1,000 kW)	Installed capacity in major markets	Share of major markets	Share of non-major markets
Vestas	U.S.	34	896	358.96	40.1	59.9
GE	U.S.	19	684.9	376.47	55.0	45.0
Goldwind	China	4	661.6	634.25	95.9	4.1
Gamesa	India	18	426.2	146.59	34.4	65.6
Enercon	Germany	26	383.3	182.92	47.7	52.3

Source FTI Intelligence

countries and regions on six continents. In contrast, China's exported wind power capacity and market coverage remain small.

11.3 Outlook for 2016–2020

11.3.1 Market Size Forecast

(1) Onshore wind power forecast

During 2016–2020, China's onshore wind power growth will gradually slow down, with the government attaching an increasing emphasis on quality rather than merely quantity. However, an appropriate total newly installed capacity quota will be guaranteed. According to the *13th Five-Year Plan for Wind Power Development* released by the NEA, during 2016-2020, the newly installed wind power capacity in China is expected to reach more than 81 million kW, representing an annual increase of about 16 million kW (i.e., 7.4%), which is significantly lower than the average annual growth rate of 23.4% during 2011–2015.

In terms of geographical layout, China will shift wind power development activity from Northeast China, North China, and Northwest China where curtailment rates are high to the eastern, central, southern regions of the county. Given the provincial grid-connected capacity targets set out in the *13th Five-Year Plan for Wind Power Development* and the 2016 grid-connected wind power capacity data released by the NEA, we believe that, during 2016–2020, the growth in the grid-connected capacity in Northeast China, North China, and Northwest China will be limited and Central, Eastern and Southern China will be the main contributors to the newly installed and grid-connected wind power in China. Table 11.3 estimates grid-connected capacity of major provinces in China from 2017 to 2020.

Table 11.3 Estimated grid-connected capacity of major provinces in china, 2017–2020

Province	Cumulative grid-connected capacity in 2016 (10,000 kW)	Cumulative grid-connected capacity by 2020 (10,000 kW)	Newly installed and grid-connected capacity during 2017–2020 (10,000 kW)
Hebei	1188	1800	612
Henan	104	600	496
Yunnan	737	1200	463
Hunan	217	600	383
Sichuan	125	500	375
Shandong	839	1200	361
Guangdong	268	600	332
Shaanxi	249	550	301
Hubei	201	500	299
Guangxi	67	350	283
Guizhou	362	600	238
Jiangxi	108	300	192
Zhejiang	119	300	181
Anhui	177	350	173
Inner Mongolia	2557	2700	143
Qinghai	69	200	131
Shanxi	771	900	129
Gansu	1277	1400	123
Liaoning	695	800	105
Jiangsu	561	650	89
Fujian	214	300	86
Tianjin	29	100	71
Heilongjiang	561	600	39
Beijing	19	50	31
Xinjiang	1776	1800	24
Chongqing	28	50	22
Tibet	1	20	19

Source National Energy Administration

(2) Offshore wind power forecast

According to the *13th Five-Year Plan for Wind Power Development*, during 2016–2020, offshore wind power development activity will concentrate in Jiangsu, Zhejiang, Fujian, and Guangdong. By 2020, the newly installed offshore wind power capacity in the four provinces will reach one million kW; the total newly installed offshore wind power capacity in the China will reached 10 million kW, and the cumulative grid-connected capacity will reach five million kW.

Table 11.4 Estimated newly installed offshore wind power capacity, 2017–2020

No.	Province/ Municipality	Newly installed capacity in 2016 (10,000 kW)	Newly installed capacity target in 2020 (10,000 kW)	Newly installed capacity during 2017–2020 (10,000 kW)
1	Jiangsu	120.59	450	329.41
2	Fujian	7.1	200	192.9
3	Zhejiang	0	100	100
4	Guangdong	0.15	100	99.85
5	Hebei	0	50	50
6	Hainan	0	35	35
7	Tianjin	2.7	20	17.3
8	Liaoning	0.15	10	9.85
9	Shanghai	30.5	40	9.5

Source CWEA, China Renewable Energy Society

Based on the above targets and data provided by the CWEA, we estimated the newly installed offshore wind power capacity in 2017–2020 (Table 11.4).

11.3.2 Policy Environment Forecast

(1) REC trading system

In face of growing wind power curtailment rates and outstanding debts in wind energy subsidies, China is in urgent need of a new renewable energy subsidy system. In January 2017, the NDRC, the Ministry of Finance and the NEA jointly issued the *Notice on Trial Implementation of the Renewable Energy Certificate Approval, Distribution and Voluntary Subscription System (F.G.N.Y. [2017] No. 132)*, announcing the launch of a nationwide REC approval, distribution and voluntary subscription pilot project. An REC is a redeemable certificate issued for every unit of electricity generated from renewable energy sources and can be redeemed. It can be used as an accounting tool or as a transferable financial instrument. The REC trading system is a market-based mechanism designed to subsidize renewable energy power and promote the development of renewable energy. The implementation of the REC trading system can stimulate the growth of the wind power market and help ease the subsidy burden on the Chinese government.

At present, the REC trading system is still in the voluntary subscription stage. Renewable energy generators can choose to receive a fix-rate subsidy or choose to sell the RECs to alleviate the financial pressure caused by subsidy arrears. According to the notice, from 2018 onwards, China will issue mandatory renewable energy quotas. Grid companies must purchase RECs to meet their respective mandatory renewable energy quotas within the prescribed time limit. Companies fail to meet their mandatory quotas will be punished.

If everything goes according to plan, the REC trading system will be gradually fleshed out during 2016–2020. The transition from fixed FITs to REC subscription and a market-based subsidy mechanism is essential for sustainable development of the wind power sector.

(2) Grid parity of wind power

When FITs of wind power are set at current benchmark levels, technological advancement has made wind power development possible in areas where wind resources are difficult to harness. However, in areas with abundant wind resources, the benefits brought by technological advancement have been offset by curtailment, subsidy delays, and snowballing financing costs, which have all contributed to the rising costs of wind power. Curtailment impedes the identification of technical problems of wind turbines and thus hinders technological advancement and improvement.

In May 2017, the General Affairs Department of the NEA issued the *Notice on the Launch of Wind Power Grid Parity Pilot Projects*, requiring local authorities launch the wind power grid parity pilot project application process. Local grids are required to purchase the output from the approved pilot projects at local coal-fired benchmark FITs and not to curtail the pilot projects. In the meantime, RECs will not be issued for purchased output. The pilot projects aim to achieve grid parity through technological advances, market relocation, and reform of the electric power system without the support of other policies, identify factors that affect grid parity (curtailment, unreasonable FITs, poor management, etc.), and develop a feasible grid parity solution for a high wind power penetration scenario. In addition, experiences and boundary conditions of pilot projects can be summed up and promoted to achieve wind power grid parity on a larger scale.

In the scenario visualized by the *13*th *Five-Year Plan for Renewable Energy Development*, by 2020, wind power will achieve grid parity with coal-fired power. The key to achieving this goal is to set boundary conditions and improve the policy framework for grid parity of wind power. Advancing the pilot projects is a good start.

(3) Power sector reforms

Since 2015, related government departments at all levels have made a concerted effort to push for a new round of power sector reforms, seeking to create a well-function market-based power system. The Chinese government plans to deregulate price controls and relax investment restrictions in a progressive manner, diversify investment sources, break the state-owned distribution monopolies' grip on the sector, and build a competitive electricity market. *According to the 13*th *Five-Year Plan for the Power Sector*, China will deepen the power sector reforms, and improve the power market system; create independent and standardized power trading platforms, establish clear ground rules in accordance with fair-market principles, and build a well-functioning electricity market; and continue to deregulate the power sector and create a favorable policy environment for wind power.

(4) Wind power finance and insurance

The major source of finance for wind farms in China is banks and the financing costs are high. In order to reduce the risks related to wind power investments, China must ① adjust its financial policies, promote new financial instruments such as green bonds and supply chain finance, and reduce the financing costs of wind power projects by offering diversified financing sources; and ② design insurance products tailored to meet the financing needs of wind power projects. It should develop wind power equipment and wind farm risk rating standards and release industry risk assessment reports on a regular basis to facilitate the design of the effective insurance solutions for the wind power sector, and issue policies to support the delivery of financial and insurance products and services to meet the needs of wind power projects at all stages of their life cycle.

(5) Exports of wind power goods and services

With the advancement of the Belt and Road Initiative, plugging into the global value chains has become an inevitable trend for China's wind power sector. Although the majority share of the Chinese market remains firmly in the grip of Chinese wind turbine suppliers, Chinese wind turbine OEMs are overshadowed by global giants such as Vestas and Siemens in the global markets and their exported capacity remains small. Chinese wind turbine OEMs must seize every opportunity and leverage the comparative advantage of China in capital and technology to actively expand their global presence. However, the cost of "going out" is relatively high. The central government needs to improve the policy environment to support the "going out" of Chinese wind turbine OEMs and certification of Made-in-China wind turbines under the IECRE system.

11.4 Conclusions and Suggestions

Thanks to strong support from the government, China's wind power sector has grown rapidly and become one of China's strategic emerging industries. In the meantime, China has become the global leader in wind energy. However, with the rapid growth of wind power, the problem of incompatibility between the current power system and large penetrations of renewable energy gradually reveals itself. Wind power curtailment and subsidy arrears have become major roadblocks impeding the sustainable development of wind power in China.

In order to solve these problems and promote the robust development of China's wind power sector during 2016–2020, China should strengthen the policy frameworks for renewable energy certificate (REC) trading, grid parity of wind power, reform in the electric power sector, and wind power finance and insurance. It should ① continue to flesh out the REC trading system and incorporate the mandatory renewable energy quota management element; ② accurately define boundary conditions and improve the policy framework for grid parity of wind power; ③ advance power sector reforms, and strive to solve problems such as high levels of wind power curtailment and subsidy shortages; ④ give full play to the role of the finance and insurance sector in the development of wind power, improve the risk prevention and control capacity of wind power projects, stimulate wind power investments, and reduce the costs of wind power; and ⑤ develop policies to support the "going out" of the wind power sector.

References

1. GWEC. (2017). *Global Wind Statistics 2016.*
2. National Energy Administration. *Grid connection of wind power in 2016*. Retrieved January 26, 2017, from http://www.nea.gov.cn/2017-01/26/c_136014615.htm.
3. CWEA, China Renewable Energy Society. (2017). *Layout of China's wind power sector (2016).*
4. China Renewable Energy Engineering Institute (CREEI). (2017). *China Wind Power Report (2016).*
5. FTI Consulting Inc. (2017). *Global wind market update—Demand & supply 2016.*

Chapter 12
Distributed Renewable Energy in China: Current State and Future Outlook

Ying Zhang

Abstract Development of distributed renewable energy has significant implications for China's energy transition and energy sector cleanup. A distributed renewable energy system can distribute energy directly to end users in its vicinity. It can also be used to deliver combined cooling, heat and power (CCHP) solutions. Besides effectively improving energy efficiency, distributed renewable energy systems also have many other environmental and social benefits. Renewable energy, including solar, wind, hydropower and biomass, have grown rapidly in China, but the grid infrastructure and the grid connection policy could hardly keep up with the growing output from renewable sources. In order to stimulate the development of distributed renewable energy, China should improve the distributed renewable energy policy framework, explore new market-based mechanisms, summarize and promote best practices relating to in situ consumption of output of distributed renewable energy systems, develop industry-wide supporting policies, and promote innovations relating to business models and financing mechanisms for distributed renewable energy.

Keywords Distributed renewable energy · In situ consumption · Energy efficiency

Distributed generation (DR) systems are small-scale energy generation systems installed at scattered locations near end users. DG systems typically uses renewable sources such as solar, wind, hydropower, biomass and geothermal. Development of DG systems has significant implications for green and low-carbon energy transitions. Besides offering environmental benefits and helping alleviate air pollution, flexible DG systems can also help guarantee basic energy supply for remote areas

---

Ying Zhang is a research assistant at the Institute for Urban and Environmental Studies, Chinese Academy of Social Sciences. Zhang's research interests include energy economics, environmental economics, and quantitative economic analysis.

Y. Zhang (✉)
Institute for Urban and Environmental Studies, Chinese Academy of Social Sciences, Xiamen, China
e-mail: zhangying_cass@163.com

W. Wang (ed.), *Annual Report on China's Response to Climate Change (2017)*, Research Series on the Chinese Dream and China's Development Path,
https://doi.org/10.1007/978-981-13-9660-1_12

lacking access to centralized energy supply, help them tackle poverty, stimulate the development of related technologies and emerging industries, and create jobs for local communities. Currently, some areas of China are facing overcapacity in renewable energy. In this context, developing small-scale DG systems and encouraging in situ consumption of output from DG systems will help tackle problems such as wasted solar, wind and hydropower capacity and show immense potential for a sustainable future.

12.1 Current State and Comparative Advantages of Distributed Generation

12.1.1 Current State

Distributed generation is a new model of energy supply developed as opposed to conventional centralized generation. Centralized generation is large-scale generation of electricity at centralized facilities which transfer electricity to a large number of end users through transmission infrastructure. In contrast, DG systems directly serve end users. They leverage small-capacity devices (usually less than 10 MW) located at or near the point of end use to generate and supply electricity, heat, cooling, steam, hot water, etc. to end users on demand, and come with a small or medium-sized integrated energy conversion system.

If we track the history of DG systems back to the very beginning, we will find the earliest form of DG is isolated diesel-based power systems used by small groups of users. In earlier days, most DG projects in China were small coal-fired cogeneration projects. In 2011, the NDRC, the NEA, the Ministry of Finance, and the Ministry of Housing and Urban-Rural Development (MOHURD) jointly issued the *Guidelines for the Development of Distributed Natural Gas-Fueled Generation*, marking the launch of a nationwide initiative to promote distributed energy. Although DG systems have higher energy efficiency and higher environmental benefits than conventional centralized generation, most DG systems built in the past are fossil energy-based. In recent years, advances in energy technology have led to rapid growth of renewable energy-based green DG systems.

There are two approaches to utilizing renewable energy: centralized approach and distributed approach. The principles of centralized utilization of renewable energy are similar to those of conventional centralized generation. Generation systems built in areas with rich renewable sources transport generated energy to load centers through long-distance transmission networks. Distributed renewable energy systems also consist of energy generation and supply systems near the point of end use and primarily supply renewable energy. Distributed renewable energy systems can be employed with combined cooling, heat and power (CCHP) systems and energy storage units to meet the diverse needs of users and achieve tiered energy use [1]. Renewable energy-based DG systems include photovoltaic power generation, solar thermal power generation, solar thermal energy utilization, and small hydropower, wind, biomass, and geothermal energy utilization systems. The combination of production and consumption of renewable energy is achieved through a small power generation system that first meets the needs of local users and then transmits the surplus energy to other users in the vicinity through a smart grid. Compared to conventional generation systems and transmission networks, distributed renewable energy and smart microgrid systems are cleaner, more sustainable and more flexible. They hold great potential to help countries across the world tackle climate change and achieve increasingly stringent energy conservation and emissions reduction targets.

12.1.2 DG Systems and Technologies

DG systems are installed at or near the point of end use to achieve tiered energy use and integration of different types of energy. Distributed power generation and supply or distributed cogeneration are central to DG systems. There are many types of DG systems. For example, by the type of energy sources, DG systems can be divided into DG systems based on non-renewable energy sources, DG systems based on renewable energy sources, and distributed cogeneration systems that use both renewable and non-renewable sources. Distributed non-renewable energy systems can be further divided into DG systems based on diesel, kerosene, natural gas and other energy sources; distributed renewable energy systems can be divided into DG systems based on wind, solar, small hydropower, biomass, geothermal, etc. DG systems also use different engines, including gas turbines, internal combustion engines, steam turbines, Stirling engines, and fuel cells.

Due to the large differences in energy sources and engines used in distributed energy systems, technologies involved are also very diverse and complex, including gas turbine, external combustion engine, energy storage, renewable energy utilization, fuel cell and smart microgrid technologies (Fig. 12.1). Although recent years have witnessed remarkable technological advances, there is still a long way to go. To promote the application of DG systems, it is necessary to increase investment in key technologies, reduce the cost of application, and improve the energy efficiency of related equipment, materials and systems. For example, it is necessary to boost the efficiency of renewable energy use, improve distributed renewable and non-renewable energy systems, and develop more efficient distributed energy storage and smart microgrid technologies.

12.1.3 Comparative Advantages of DG Systems

Compared with conventional centralized generation systems, DG systems have the following unparalleled advantages.

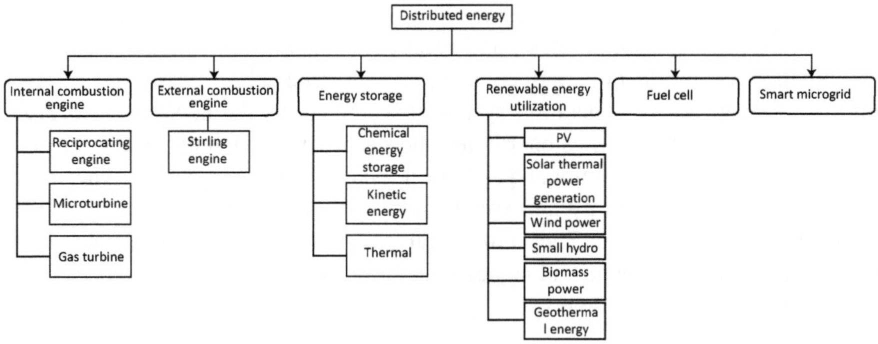

Fig. 12.1 Key technologies related to DG systems

(1) Improved energy efficiency

Compared with conventional centralized generation systems, DG systems are more flexible in terms of scale and location. They can be used to tailor energy supply to demand, achieve optimal energy supply scope and transmission distance and minimize power losses along transmission lines [2] In addition, some distributed energy systems, such as CCHP, can utilize the waste heat from power generation, thus greatly improving energy efficiency.

(2) Improved reliability and stability

In addition to improved energy efficiency, DG systems can provide more stable energy supply to some industries and regions. Stability of power supply is particularly important for industries that require continuous power supply, such as semiconductor manufacturing. In the event of a technical failure, a centralized generation system will be paralyzed and cause huge economic losses. In order to cope with changes in electrical load, centralized generation systems often give up the load of some generation units. Grid-independent DG systems can complement and enhance the stability of large centralized power grids [3]. Developing DG systems to increase the stability of grids is far easier and less costly than revamping existing grids. DG systems can continue to supply power to important users in the event of grid collapse or an emergency, thus ensuring the stability and reliability of power supply. If DG systems and grids are efficiently coordinated, the stability and reliability of power supply will be further improved, and some catastrophic consequences can be effectively avoided [4].

In addition, DG systems can help grids smooth the load curve. In the peak period, DG systems can be used as supplement electricity provided by centralized power grids to alleviate power shortage. In the meantime, small, cost-efficient DG systems with good start-stop performance can be used in combination with the conventional power supply systems to reduce the peak-valley gap of grids throughout the day and night; they can help smooth out daily and seasonal peaks and valleys and thus increase the stability of grids.

(3) Massive environmental benefits

Compared to conventional centralized generation systems, DG systems typically use cleaner energy sources, such as natural gas, which is a low-carbon fossil fuel, and green or renewable energy sources, and thus produce lower air emissions and less solid waste. Most DG systems in China use clean sources such as natural gas, coalbed methane and biogas and can help the country achieve the national energy conservation, emissions reduction and environmental protection targets. Distributed renewable energy systems are eco-friendlier. Large-scale adoption of distributed renewable energy systems can significantly reduce the GHG emissions generated during power generation in a society and effectively alleviate environmental pollution caused by traditional power generation systems using fossil fuels.

(4) Improved cost efficiency

Generally speaking, DG systems enable in situ consumption of energy and thus significantly reduce the costs of transmission infrastructure. Therefore, DG systems can reduce energy costs and bring notable economic benefits to both end users and suppliers. The economic benefits end users receive are reflected in the reduction in the total cost of energy. In the meantime, energy suppliers can also receive some economic benefits by reducing generation costs. In addition, under some DG systems, consumers are also producers (i.e., "Prosumers"). Excess energy produced by these DG systems will be sold to and transmitted through the grid after meeting the needs of Prosumers, bringing Prosumers economic benefits.

As technology continues to evolve, the cost of using renewable energy sources is decreasing. For example, the cost of PV power has been declining since the 1990s. The cost of rooftop PV systems in Germany dropped from 14,000 Euro/kW in 1990 to 1,270 Euro/kW at the end of 2015 [5]. In China, the price of solar cells dropped from 36,000 yuan/kW in 2007 to 4,200 yuan/kW in 2016, and the price of PV systems also dropped from 60,000 yuan/kW to 8,000 yuan/kW [6]. Due to the rapid price decline, distributed renewable energy systems now can compete with traditional centralized generation systems in terms of cost. In some areas implementing strong environmental policies, DG systems can be more cost-effective than centralized fossil fuel power systems.

(5) Social benefits

The flexible and grid-independent operation model enables DG systems to be used in remote areas that are not covered by centralized power grids, helping these areas reduce power supply costs and reduce poverty caused by energy shortage [7].

In addition, the development of distributed energy can also create new business and employment opportunities. For example, it can drive the development of related equipment manufacturing technologies, promote innovation in the machinery industry, form an industrial chain, and benefit capital flows. Distributed energy is expected to become a new engine of economic growth.

(6) Facilitation of in situ consumption of renewable energy

With the slowdown in economic growth, the growth of electricity demand has also gradually slacked off in recent years. In the meantime, in addition to overcapacity in thermal power, the renewable energy sector is growing rapidly and is also facing the problem of overcapacity. Figuring out how to use electricity generated from renewable sources such as wind and solar has become an urgent task for the country. Poor coordination of power grid and power generation projects in China has led to a mismatch between power supply and demand in some regions. The planners of some wind farms and PV projects have failed to consider transmission and demand. As a result, the output of these projects cannot be transmitted to areas with huge demand, leading to wasted capacity. In the past, motivated by high FITs, the number of wind farms and PV projects grew rapidly, causing explosive growth in installed capacity. Furthermore, in China, areas rich in renewable energy resources are mostly located in remote regions such as Gansu, Xinjiang and Inner Mongolia. These areas have relatively small demand for electricity and poor transmission infrastructure, thus facing high levels of wind and solar power curtailment.

Promoting application of DG systems and energy storage technologies in these areas and encouraging in situ consumption and connection to local grids can help reduce the wasted installed renewable energy capacity.

12.2 Distributed Renewable Energy in China: Current State

Most common distributed renewable energy systems in China include distributed PV, wind energy, and small hydro systems.

This section will summarize the development status of distributed renewable energy in China and related policies and development goals.

12.2.1 Distributed PV Systems

Distributed PV systems are grid-independent PV systems located at or near the point of end use, equipped with a heat storage unit or integrated with generation systems based on other energy sources. These systems are primarily installed for self-consumption, and excess electricity produced can be fed back into the grid. They play an important role in balancing power supply and demand in a grid. At present, most of China's solar power projects are large-scale ground-mounted projects, and the proportion of small distributed solar power systems is low. However, the prospects for distributed PV systems look good. Distributed PV

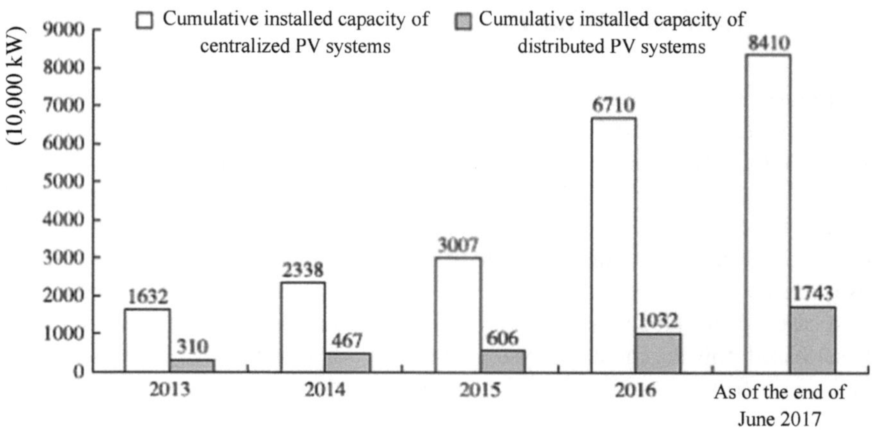

Fig. 12.2 Cumulative installed capacity of centralized and distributed PV systems, 2013-H1 2017. *Source* National Bureau of Statistics

systems offer high flexibility and can be installed in rural, pastoral, mountainous or urban or commercial building closures.

According to the NEA, as of the end of 2016, the new and cumulative installed and PV capacity in China reached 34.54 million kW and 77.42 million kW, respectively, ranking first in the world. The cumulative installed capacity of centralized PV plants was 67.1 million kW, and that of distributed PV systems was 10.32 million kW, accounting for about 13.3% of China's total cumulative installed PV capacity. In 2016, PV systems generated 66.2 billion kWh electricity, accounting for 1% of China's total annual power output. In recent years, investment in distributed PV power generation has grown rapidly in China. In 2016, China's newly installed PV capacity reached 4.26 million kW. In the first half of 2017, the cumulative installed capacity of distributed PV systems reached 17.43 million kW (Fig. 12.2), and the newly installed PV capacity was about three times that in the first half of 2016.

Due to geographical reasons, the type of most common PV systems varies across China. Most large-scale ground-mounted PV projects are located in Northwest and North China, while small-scale and flexible distributed PV systems are mainly distributed in East China. As of the end of June 2017, the cumulative installed capacity of distributed PV systems managed by the State Grid in East China reached 8.47 million kW, accounting for 52% of the total installed and grid-connected capacity of distributed systems managed by the State Grid.

In order to promote the application of distributed PV power generation, China has launched distributed PV pilot projects in economic advanced regions and industrial parks. In 2013 and 2014, China launched thirty distributed PV demonstration zones, the total planned capacity of which reached 33.5 million kW.

Local governments have also invested in public distributed PV systems.

12.2.2 Distributed Wind Power

Distributed wind power systems are distributed power generation systems that use wind turbines to converts wind energy into electricity, with capacity ranging from several kilowatts to hundreds of megawatts (and some experts recommend the capacity of a distributed wind power system should be limited to 30–50 megawatts or even lower). Due to cost and resource constraints, distributed wind power projects are fewer than natural gas and PV projects in China. The profitability of distributed wind power projects is also lower than natural gas and PV projects. In most cases, distributed wind power systems are installed in combination with PV or diesel-based power generation systems to form a hybrid power generation system which primarily use wind and solar, with diesel as a supplementary source. The hybrid systems supply power to target users or loads, and store excess electricity in batteries.

The experience of other countries show that the direct grid connection of small wind turbines has less impact on the grid, which translates into cost efficiency and reliability. China leads the world in wind power equipment manufacturing and small wind turbine manufacturing, so it has a solid foundation for the development of small distributed wind power systems. Compared with PV systems, the installed wind power capacity in China has been growing with some fluctuations. During 2011–2015, the average growth rate of installed wind power capacity was about 32.8%.

As of the end of 2016, the newly installed wind power capacity in China (Taiwan excluded) reached about 23.37 million kW, and the cumulative installed wind power capacity reached 168.73 million kW (Fig. 12.3).

There is also an inter-regional disparity in the development of wind power across China. The northwest region still has the largest number of new wind power

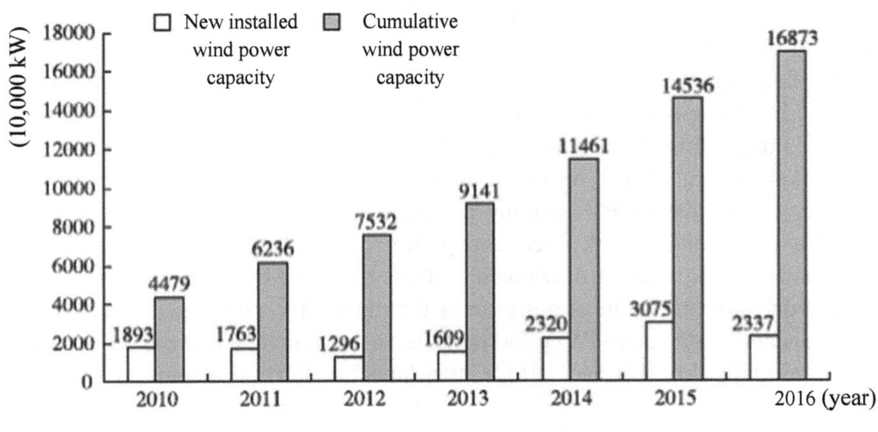

Fig. 12.3 New and cumulative installed wind power capacity in china (Taiwan excluded), 2010–2016. *Source* wind power capacity bulletins of Chinese Wind Energy Association

projects because of its substantial wind power endowment and low population density. In 2016, Northwest China accounted for 26% of China's total newly installed wind power capacity, North China 24%, East China 20%, Southwest China 14%, Central South 13% and Northeast China 3%.

According to the *Twelfth Five-Year Plan for Renewable Energy Development*, it is estimated that, among the planned 100 million kW installed wind power capacity by 2015, distributed wind power will reach 30 million kW. In 2011, the NEA issued the *Guidelines for the Development of Grid-Connected Distributed Wind Power Projects*. The document defines grid-connected distributed wind power project, sets out voltage and scale requirements, and approval procedure, and maps out the vision and direction for the development of distributed wind power in the country. However, compared with distributed solar energy, the growth of distributed wind power is slower. The main reason is that the markets for distributed wind power are primarily in areas with lower wind speed and higher load density. The cost of manufacturing wind turbines for low wind speed is generally higher than that of medium and high wind speed. High cost is a primary factor that impedes the development of distributed wind power in China.

At present, the majority of investors in wind power in China are SOEs. For large SOEs, the higher cost of distributed wind power compared to centralized wind power damps their ardor, so the government should issue policies to encourage private sector investment in the sector. In June 2017, the NEA issued the *Notice on Accelerating the Development of Grid-Connected Distributed Wind Power Projects*, seeking to improve the utilization efficiency of distributed wind energy and optimize the layout of the wind power sector during 2016–2020. The document also suspends the construction of new distributed wind power projects in areas with high levels of wind power curtailment.

12.2.3 Small Hydro

Generally speaking, a small hydro project refers to a hydropower station or installation with a small installed capacity. At present, there is no uniform definition of small hydro projects. In China, hydropower projects with an installed capacity of less than 50 MW are considered as small hydro projects. Hydropower provide a low-emissions alternative to fossil fuels and has significant implications for energy transition. The Chinese government has always attached great importance to the development of hydropower. Small hydro projects are an effective way of utilizing renewable energy in mountainous and rural areas. Public small hydro projects have contributed to electrification of many poor mountainous and rural areas.

By the end of 2014, a total of 47,073 small rural hydro projects had been built nationwide with a total installed capacity of 73.22 million kW and a total annual output of 228.1 billion kWh, accounting for about a quarter of the country's installed hydropower capacity and power supply. At present, there are small hydro projects in thirty-one provinces, and Yunnan and Sichuan have the largest installed capacity in the country. Small hydro projects can be found in 1,535 counties across the country. Most of these counties are located in Sichuan, Yunnan, Hunan, and Guangxi Zhuang Autonomous Region.

In recent years, the Chinese government has placed more emphasis on reducing environment impact of small hydro projects which have grown rapidly across the country. The *Thirteenth Five-Year Plan for Hydropower Development* released by the NEA at the end of 2016 stated: "China must strictly control the development of small and medium-sized river basins and the construction of small and medium-sized hydropower projects. To maintain the ecological health of river basins, basin management agencies should attach importance to mainstream development and tributary protection. The western region is rich in hydropower resources and holds great potential for hydropower. To minimize environmental impacts, relevant authorities in the western region should focus on the development of large rivers, key river sections and major hydropower bases and strictly control the development of small and medium-sized hydropower projects. In principle, no new small and medium hydropower projects should be approved in the eastern and central regions where the density of hydropower projects is already high. During 2016–2020, Sichuan and Yunnan which report massive wasted hydropower capacity should suspend the development of small and medium-sized hydropower projects and hydropower projects with no flood control function, except projects constructed for the poverty alleviation purpose."

12.2.4 Distributed Biomass Power Generation

Biomass is organic material produced by plants in the photosynthesis process, so its sources are diverse and density is low, which is why distributed generation is suitable for biomass energy development. Grid-connected distributed biomass power generation is an important supplement to fossil fuel-based power generation.

Distributed biomass energy sources can be utilized in many ways. For example, people can build small biomass-based power generation stations, use biomass for household cooking and heating, or use biomass as fuel for heating, industrial furnaces or fuel cells. Moreover, distributed biomass energy projects are usually small in scale, low-cost and highly profitable. The prospect for distributed biomass energy in China is good. However, in reality, the development of distributed biomass energy is restricted by factors such as availability of energy sources and changes in policy. The *Twelfth Five-Year Plan for Biomass Energy Development* sets out the targets for the biomass power sector by 2015: generation capacity 13 million kW, annual power generation about 78 billion kWh, annual biofuel supply 22 billion m^3, biogas users 50 million, annual biogas output 19 billion m^3. However, in reality, the number of biogas users was only 43.8 million and the annual power supply from biomass sources was 10.3 million kWh in 2015 (Table 12.1).

Table 12.1 Development of biomass in china as of the end of 2015

Utilization method	Scale of utilization		Annual output		Coal equivalent
	Number	Unit	Number	Unit	10,000 tons per year
1. Biomass power generation	1,030	10,000 kW	520	100 million kWh	1,520
2. Biomass users	4,380	10,000 households	190	100 million m^3	1,320
3. Large biomass systems	10	10,000 systems			
4. Biofuel	800	10,000 tons			400
5. Bioethanol			210	10,000 tons	180
6. Biodiesel			80	10,000 tons	120
Total					3540

[a]The annual output of biogas is the sum of the output of household biogas systems and large biogas projects

Source Notice of the National Energy Administration on the Promulgation of the 13th Five-Year Plan for Biomass Energy Development

12.3 Barriers to the Development of Distributed Renewable Energy

Although distributed renewable energy has grown rapidly, there are still many barriers to the wider adoption of DG systems. The biggest barrier is how to integrate distributed renewable energy systems into a centralized grid. The following are some major challenges faced by the distributed renewable energy sector in China.

12.3.1 High Costs and Unfavorable Business Environment

Technological advances have led a sharp drop in the cost of some renewable energy sources. But distributed renewable energy still cannot compete with conventional centralized energy generation in terms of cost. For example, the development and performance of wind and solar power systems are affected by natural conditions and seasons, so their costs are still higher than centralized fossil fuel-based projects in some areas. PV systems don't work at night. Therefore, if there is no backup power supply or energy storage equipment, it will be difficult for distributed PV systems to become a sustainable energy supply model. Therefore, without supporting policy or government intervention, large-scale adoption of distributed renewable energy seems economically infeasible in the short to medium term. In China, regions such as East China, North China, and Northeast China are suitable for medium-scale industrial and commercial use of distributed PV projects. Only North China and

West China are suitable for large-scale use of distributed PV systems. However, the profitability of the distributed PV projects in North China and West China is also not high enough.

To promote sustainable development of distributed renewable energy, policy-makers should strive to strike a balance between the scale of adoption and costs. But, in practice, it is very difficult to achieve a perfect balance between the two. For example, in Europe, although supporting policies have contributed significantly to the remarkable progress in renewable energy development, consumers still need to bear extra costs for the use of renewable energy. Therefore, in order to reduce the costs for consumers, Spain and Italy have significantly reduced subsidies for renewable energy, which will lead to a slowdown in renewable energy development and have an adverse impact on the related industries.

12.3.2 High Levels of Curtailment

In recent years, some areas are facing high levels of renewable energy curtailment. In 2014, hydropower, wind and solar power curtailment caused power losses up to more than 30 billion kWh in the country. Yunnan and Sichuan alone reported electricity losses of more than 20 billion kWh. The aggregate wind power curtailment reached 12.6 billion kWh. Some areas such as Jiuquan and Dunhuang in Gansu Province and Golmud in Qinghai, wasted huge amount of solar power capacity. The curtailment rate of solar power in some areas exceeded 20% [8]. According to the Renewable Energy Development Report of China, in 2015, the wind power curtailment rate in China was still high. In 2015, the country wasted 33.9 billion kWh wind power, an increase of 21.3 billion kWh year-on-year. Gansu reported a wind power curtailment rate of 39% (8.2 billion kWh wasted); Xinjiang's wind power curtailment rate reached 32% (7 billion kWh wasted); Jilin wasted 2.7 billion kWh wind power and its curtailment rate was 32%; Inner Mongolia wasted 9.1 billion kWh wind power and its curtailment rate was 18%. The levels of wind and solar curtailment in the five northwestern provinces/regions remained high in 2016. The average wind and solar curtailment rates of Gansu, Xinjiang, Ningxia, Shaanxi and Qinghai in 2016 were 33.34 and 19.81%, respectively. High curtailment rates are caused by overcapacity in both conventional fossil fuel-based generation and renewable generation, technological factor and poor supporting infrastructure.

12.3.3 Lack of Legislation and Supporting Policies

Only a few chapters of the *Energy Conservation Law* and the *Renewable Energy Law* mention support for distributed renewable energy. For example, the *Energy Conservation Law* stipulates that the state should encourage the development of cogeneration and the *Renewable Energy Law* has provided a legal basis for grid connection of distributed renewable energy systems. However, there are no specific regulations, technical standards and policies to support the implementation of the legislation, making it impossible to use legal means to guide the development of distributed renewable energy. This has significantly restricted the sustainable development of distributed renewable energy.

Government support is the key to the development of distributed renewable energy. The government should actively promote the development of distributed renewable energy technologies and use policy tools to level the playing field for distributed renewable energy. However, compared with countries where distributed renewable energy is developing rapidly, China's policy framework for distributed renewable energy still has not been fleshed out. Many policies are short-lived, which puts a damper on distributed renewable energy investment and development.

12.3.4 Barriers to Integration of Distributed Renewable Energy Systems into Grids

There are both technical and institutional barriers to grid connection of distributed renewable energy systems. Due to the lack of regulations and technical specifications for grid connection, grid companies can easily refuse to integrate distributed energy generation systems into centralized power grids. Renewable energy power projects are competing with power grid companies for users. Without government intervention through policy tools, grid companies' willingness to connect distributed renewable energy to their grids is low. If we look more deeply into the problem, we will find the essence of this problem is a conflict of interest between power producers and buyers. On the supply side, difficulty in connecting distributed systems to the grid and delay in receiving FITs are among factors that hinder the development of distributed renewal energy technologies and industries.

12.4 Policy Recommendations

In general, affected by natural and institutional factors, most distributed renewable energy projects in China are still in the pilot implementation stage. Although the Chinese government has introduced a series of policies and measures to guide the development of distributed renewable energy, distributed renewable energy is still not mainstream and accounts for a low proportion of China's total installed capacity. Except distributed PV systems, the development of distributed renewable energy is greatly affected by macroeconomic dynamics and policies and the growth rates have fluctuated many times. The growth rates of some distributed renewable energy sources have not reached the expected levels. To address problems and obstacles that hinder the development of distributed renewable energy, this paper puts forward several key policy recommendations for policymakers.

12.4.1 Introducing Effective Supporting Policies for Distributed Renewable Energy

Existing policies and regulations relating to distributed renewable energy are mostly principles and guidelines and are difficult to enforce. More precise legal rules should be developed to address relevant issues. Existing laws and regulations designed to support the development of renewable energy should be revised and updated based on the actual situations. To build a scientific legal system for distributed renewable energy, China should draw on the experience of other countries and make laws and regulations easier to enforce.

At present, there is a lack of targeted policies in relation to development planning, grid connection, price mechanisms, preferential treatment, and operational models of distributed energy, especially distributed renewable energy. Distributed renewable energy and distributed natural gas which is current mainstream are very different in positioning, use conditions, development potential and economic benefits. But most of the existing supporting policies for distributed energy are designed for promoting distributed natural gas. It is therefore necessary to develop policies and regulations for other types of distributed energy.

12.4.2 Encouraging the Development of Effective Market Mechanisms for Distributed Renewable Energy

In order to improve the competitiveness of distributed renewable energy, China needs to introduce new market mechanisms to support the development of distributed renewable energy. For example, an innovative pricing mechanism may be introduced to help the distributed renewable energy sector increase generation efficiency, reduce costs and achieve economies of scale. Currently, there is no "one size fits all" electricity pricing mechanism that applies to all countries. FITs of distributed renewable energy are a new concept and further research is needed. In the early stages of development, the policymakers should appropriately subsidize distributed renewable energy projects to encourage investment in this sector and motivate enterprises to invest in development and research activity. The ultimate goal is to reduce the costs of distributed renewable energy sources so they can compete with conventional electric generating sources in prices. Some more flexible pricing mechanisms can be adopted. For example, the government may link the FITs of distributed renewable energy to the cost of power generation, give higher subsidies in the early stages of development, and make timely adjustments as costs fall.

12.4.3 Exploring and Promoting Best Practices Relating to in Situ Consumption of Output of Distributed Renewable Energy Systems

In order to promote the sustainable development of renewable energy and reduce curtailment rates, best practices must be summarized and promoted. To reduce overcapacity that is not caused by excessive expansion, innovative measures must be taken to plan DG systems in a scientific manner and increase the integration of distributed renewable energy into the grid. At present, centralized systems are still the mainstream in the renewable energy sector in China because there are still a lot of barriers to the direct supply of renewable energy. If the curtailment problem can be solved through institutional innovations, distributed renewable energy will grow rapidly.

To solve the problem of high solar and wind power curtailment rates and encouraging consumption of distributed renewable energy at or near the point of supply, both technological and institutional innovations are needed. On the technological side, China should build smart grids of the Internet of Energy to integrate different energy sources. On the institutional side, China should continue to advance power sector reforms and remove institutional barriers to the full integration of renewable energy; introduce new power generation planning and management methods, allow direct electricity trading between power plants and users, and promote the development of diverse distributed generation business models.

12.4.4 Developing Industry-Wide Supporting Policies

Policymakers should actively promote the development of distributed renewable energy which is of great significance for achieving innovation-driven development, energy conservation, emissions reduction, pollution prevention targets, stimulating domestic demand, creating new engines for economic growth, and striking a balance between development and environmental protection.

To support the development of distributed renewable energy industries, it is necessary to develop stringent criteria for relevant high-tech companies eligible for preferential policies such as income tax reduction/exemption and accelerated depreciation of fixed assets. It is also necessary to plan the development of distributed renewable energy industries more scientifically to put an end to unreasonable expansion of outdated industries.

12.4.5 Boosting Innovations in Business Models and Financing Mechanisms for Distributed Renewable Energy

Distributed renewable energy systems are completely different from conventional centralized generation systems and other DG systems. Therefore, the development of distributed renewable energy requires new business models.

The current financial system is designed to primarily serve the centralized generation sector which is still dominated by large SOEs. The lack of financing sources for distributed projects has become a major roadblock to the development of distributed energy. Some distributed renewable energy projects are heavily dependent on government subsidies. In the event of a decline in the subsidies, prolonged subsidy review or delayed payment of subsides, they will face serious financial problems. In order to solve these problems, the NDRC and the NEA jointly issued the *Notice on Launching a Pilot Program to Promote the Market-Based Electricity Trading Program for Distributed Generation Projects* and the *Opinions on Promoting Engineering Innovations of Gas Turbines* in the first half of 2017 as part of the larger power sector reform program. In addition to consumption by prosumers and purchase by power grid companies, electricity generated by DG projects can be now directly sold to end users. Furthermore, the Chinese government should also put in place a project rating system to facilitate project financing, give full play to the role of the country's multi-tiered capital markets, introduce innovative management methods for financial institutions, and explore new ways to securitize projects.

References

1. Lu, Y. (2016). Development of distributed renewable energy applications and smart microgrids. *Bulletin of Chinese Academy of Sciences, 2*.
2. VTT (Technical Research Centre of Finland Ltd.). (2015). Distributed Energy Systems, DESY. VTT Technology 224. Retrieved from http:www.vtt.fi/inf/pdf/technology/2015/T224.pdf (Utgivare Publisher, Espoo).
3. Yin, Y., & Wang, X. (2008). A comprehensive study of the necessity of developing distributed generation systems. *Industrial Engineering Journal, 1*.
4. Guo, S. (2005). Promising distributed generation. *Power Demand Side Management, 3*.
5. Fraunhofer Institute for Solar Energy System. *Photovoltaics Report 2016*. Retrieved from http: www.ise.fraunhofer.de.
6. Lu, Y. (2016). Development of distributed renewable energy applications and smart microgrids. *Bulletin of Chinese Academy of Sciences, 2*.
7. Schnitzer et al. (2014). *Microgrids for rural electrification, a critical review of best practices based on seven case studies*. United Nations Foundation.
8. Chen, L. *Massive unused hydro, wind and solar power capacity and its causes*. Retrieved March 02, 2016, from https://www.qianzhan.com/analyst/detail/329/160302-0be354e3.html.

Chapter 13
Combating Climate Change, Desertification and Sandstorms: A Collaborative Approach

Chengyi Zhang, Rong Gao, Jun Wu and Zhongxia Yang

Abstract Desertification and dust storms are the result of both human activity and natural causes. Changes in wind speed, precipitation, temperature, and humidity due to climate change can cause desertification and dust storms, and increase the intensity of such phenomena. Human activity such as land development and overgrazing destroy vegetation cover, and cause the occurrence of aggravation of desertification and dust storms as a result; upstream irrigation and urbanization can lead to the seasonal drying up of downstream rivers, lakes and other water bodies and thus become a new or enhanced source of sand. So far, natural sandstorm activity is still the main source of sand and dust input into the atmosphere. The main areas of modern sandstorm activity may become drier in the future due to climate change. As for the subject of land use by humans, it is necessary for us to pay close attention to its long-term effects on the climate and also on its interaction with

---

Chengyi Zhang is a Researcher at the National Climate Center (NCC). His main research interests are in greenhouse gas inventory methodologies, greenhouse gas exchange and flux, and the impact of climate change on ecosystems. Rong Gao is a Senior Engineer at the NCC whose main research interest is in the area of climate-related disaster risk. Jun Wu is Associate Researcher at the Ministry of Environmental Protection Nanjing Institute of Environmental Sciences whose main research interests are in the area of environmental protection and the implementation of, and negotiations on, the Convention on Biological Diversity. Zhongxia Yang is Senior Engineer at the Arxan Meteorological Bureau in Inner Mongolia whose main research interests are in the areas of meteorological observation and meteorological disasters.

C. Zhang (✉) · R. Gao
National Climate Center, China Meteorological Administration, Beijing, China
e-mail: zhangchy@cma.gov.cn

R. Gao
e-mail: gaor@cma.cn

J. Wu
Ministry of Environmental Protection, Nanjing Institute of Environmental Sciences, Nanjing, China
e-mail: wujun@nies.org

Z. Yang
Arxan Meteorological Bureau in Inner Mongolia, Arxan, China
e-mail: 289027280@qq.com

W. Wang (ed.), *Annual Report on China's Response to Climate Change (2017)*, Research Series on the Chinese Dream and China's Development Path,
https://doi.org/10.1007/978-981-13-9660-1_13

various climate elements and the environmental effects caused by such interactions. The deployment of the appropriate technical measures can play a role in alleviating desertification and dust storms.

Keywords Climate change · Desertification · Dust storms · Changes in land use · Impact of climate change

Today, climate change—as characterized by global warming, rising atmospheric greenhouse gas concentrations, and more intense droughts and floods—has become a serious challenge to the sustainable development of human society. At the same time, desertification and sandstorms, which have long plagued the development of human society, continue to threaten the sustainable development of human society. In particular, atmospheric sand threaten to blanket land, homes and roads, and cause a decline in atmospheric visibility, changes in the amount of sunlight received on the ground and air pollution in that sandstorms pass through, in turn leading to problems in the environment and in human society, such as traffic accidents and respiratory diseases in susceptible populations. These problems plague the well-being of mankind today as well as place restrictions on future sustainable development. How does climate change relate to desertification and the occurrence of sandstorms? In particular, does climate change exacerbate desertification and the occurrence of sandstorms, and do climate change and desertification and sandstorms create a positive feedback cycle and thus further worsen the situation? These issues have drawn attention from a wide spectrum of observers, including in academia. In this chapter, we take these questions as the starting point, and analyze the issues involved based on the latest assessments of desertification and sandstorms in the scientific community and the international community, in particular, the results of the Global Assessment of Sand and Dust Storms sponsored by the United Nations Environment Programme (UNEP), the World Meteorological Organization (WMO) and the United Nations Convention to Combat Desertification (UNCCD) published in 2016. The issues include: first, which factors have driven desertification and the occurrence of sandstorms? Second, what is the relationship between climate change and ongoing trends in desertification and sandstorm phenomena? Third, what are the key technical measures that can be taken to prevent and control desertification and to manage sandstorms? In this chapter, we seek to build upon the latest research developments surrounding these issues in human society in order to inspire the academic community and the public to pay more attention to, and deepen their exploration of, the issues at hand so that we may be able to form a consensus, innovate on an active basis, and promote the control of desertification and sandstorm phenomena and as well as the appropriate responses to climate change response and achieve sustainability in land use.

13.1 Recent Studies of the Factors Driving Current Trends in Desertification and Sandstorms

Sandy desertification is a phenomenon of desertification that is characterized by sandstorm activity that leads to the formation or activation or wind erosion or landscapes shaped by said aeolian action [1, 2]. As such, desertification is a main sign of the occurrence or emergence, development or recurrence of the sandstorm activity of the land, with the result being landforms and ecological conditions shaped by such aeolian processes. Sand and dust storms are an atmospheric process and phenomenon wherein sand or dust particles on dry, loose earth surfaces are swept up into the atmosphere by strong wind and travel some distance on the wind before falling back to the earth's surface or onto water [3]. As such, the desertification of the land will inevitably lead to sandstorms, and desertification is often the source of, or one of the sources of, sandstorms. As dust particles are transported along with the airflow, desertification may or may not occur in areas where sandstorms occur (especially in downwind areas). These areas are mainly affected by sandstorms transmitted from the source or areas upwind. Research has shown that desertification and sandstorms are affected by both natural factors and human activity, in particular unreasonable land use and management. In general, the presence of dry, loose particulate matter is the material basis for the formation of desertification and dust storms. The lack of effective surface coverage and strong winds on the surface is the direct driver of desertification and sandstorm formation. Table 13.1 lists the relationships between these factors and desertification and sandstorms are laid out.

We can see from Table 13.1 that factors including strong wind, degree of surface coverage and surface dryness may directly or indirectly affect the occurrence of desertification and sandstorms.

The wind speed or wind erosion wind speed refers to how surface particles are picked up by the wind and moved away or enter the atmosphere when the wind speed reaches a certain value. Clearly, this wind speed is directly related to the characteristics of the surface in question. The number of days and duration of wind speed that meets or exceeds this specific value is directly related to the occurrence of desertification and sandstorms.

Unsustainable levels of human activities such as logging, reclamation, overgrazing, burning and other forms of damage to the vegetation cover will lead to increased or increased sandstorm activity [4]. This is especially obvious in arid and semi-arid regions.

Approximately 32 million km^2 of land around the world are vulnerable to wind erosion, including 17 million km^2 that are highly susceptible [5].

Upstream agricultural irrigation and urban development tend to intercept water flows and thus directly lead to the seasonal drying up of rivers, lakes and other water bodies, thus becoming a new source of sandstorm activity that in turn cause the intensification of desertification and sandstorm phenomena.

Table 13.1 Relationship between various key factors and wind erosion of the soil or sediment

Climate		Soil or sediment		Vegetation cover		Terrain	
Change factor	Impact on wind erosion	Change factor	Impact on wind erosion	Change factor	Impact on wind erosion	Change factor	Impact on wind erosion
Wind speed	Consistent effect	Soil or sediment types	Unclear	Type	Unclear	Surface roughness	Positive or differing relationships
Wind direction	Unclear	Soil or sediment structure	Unclear	Degree of coverage	Negative relationship		
Turbulence	Positive relationship	Organic matter content	Negative relationship	Density	Unclear		
Precipitation level	Negative relationship	Carbonate content	Negative relationship	Distribution	Positive or differing relationships		
Evaporation	Consistent effect	Volumetric weight	Unclear				
Temperature	Positive or differing relationships	Degree of aggregation	Negative relationship				
Air pressure	Consistent effect	Surface water content	Negative relationship				
Freezing and thawing	Positive or differing relationships						

Note Data summarized from UNEP, WMO and UNCCD 2016

The Sahel syndrome has appeared in Latin America, the sub-Sahara region, and arid regions in North Africa and Asia; the Dust Bowl syndrome has also occurred in industrialized nations such as the United States and the Soviet Union.

These occurrences are an indication to human society that the excessive use of natural resources and the unreasonable activities that violate the laws of nature drive sandstorm occurrences and also deal a heavy blow to humanity itself.

13.2 Recent Studies on the Links Between Climate Change, Desertification and Sandstorms

Desertification and sandstorm occurrences are closely related to regional climate conditions, climate fluctuations, and climate change. Climate change leads to changes in hydrothermal conditions with occurrences such as droughts, semi-arid conditions, precipitation and evaporation in semi-humid zones, as well as changes the frequency and intensity of strong wind events. All these have a direct impact on the occurrence of desertification and sandstorms. When the climate changes to one with less rain, the original vegetation cover is degraded and coverage is reduced, and the content of fine organic matter such as soil organic matter and clay decreases year by year. The soil becomes vulnerable to wind erosion, and desertification and sandstorms occur or become more intense. Conversely, when the climate becomes more rainy and humid, plant growth becomes lusher, vegetation cover increases, and grass and soil cover develop in the ecosystem. Soil organic matter and clay particles gradually accumulate, and the frequency and intensity of soil erosion decrease or even goes down to zero. Desertification and sandstorms are alleviated or are reversed.

The areas where modern sandstorms mainly occur may become drier in the future due to climate change. They include: the Mediterranean region in southern Europe and North Africa, the northern Sahara, Central and Western Asia, the southwestern United States, and South Australia [6]. The increase in precipitation in the middle latitudes of the northern hemisphere since the mid-19th century has contributed to the reduction of desertification and sandstorms in the region. In the future, climate change may lead to an increase in precipitation in East Africa, making the region less arid.

With the Sahel region and the Ganges Basin, there is still a great degree of uncertainty with model predictions and we are thus unable to tell if these regions will become more arid or wetter [6].

When we examine the US National Aeronautics and Space Administration's Moderate Resolution Imaging Spectroradiometer (MODIS) data and land use data, we see that annual dust input into the atmosphere totals around 1.223 billion tons to 1.536 billion tons, of which about 25% originates from human activities (mainly agricultural activities) and 75% from natural sources of sand [7]. Hence, we see that natural sources sand are still the primary sources of sandstorm particles in the world. Climate change affects desertification and sandstorms around the world by causing changes in the sources of such particles. In regions where precipitation levels have reduced and led to decreased vegetation cover as a result of climate change, desertification and sandstorm occurrences may be exacerbated [8]; conversely, in areas where the impact of climate change is declining and which are becoming wetter, vegetation is flourishing, and desertification and sandstorms may be alleviated. It should be noted that as the methods, approaches and standards for identifying the sources of windborne sandstorm particles can be very different, and we very much lack detailed information on land use and management around the globe. As such, there is still a great deal of uncertainty in terms of the identification of sources of windborne sandstorm particles, including human sources.

At the same time, it should also be noted that human activity plays a role in promoting desertification and the occurrence of sandstorms through interactions with various climate forcing elements. Studies based on climate models show that the "black storms" that had occurred in the United States in the 1930s was the result of interactions between sea surface temperature (SST) forcing and changes in land use [9]. The feedback effects of dust aerosols and vegetation boundary layer conditions, etc., were integrated into a climate model, and the resulting simulation shows that: land degradation caused by unreasonable human activities had not only contributed to the "black storms" but also magnified the degree of drought in the same period, with a combined effect exacerbating the moderate drought forced by SST to create what as the worst environmental disaster in American history [10].

Thus, with land use and the changes in such use, we should focus not only on the long-term climate effects but also any interactions with climate elements and the environmental effects of such interactions. At the same time, in order to avoid the interaction between land desertification and sandstorms and climate change and the resulting environmental effects that would have a serious negative impact on the regional and even global level, it is still necessary that prevention be conducted on the whole-of-society level.

13.3 Progress in Technological Solutions

Technical measures are key to the prevention and control of desertification and the alleviation of sandstorms. Without such technical measures, it will be difficult for mankind to solve the problems of desertification and sandstorms occurrences, and we may fall into a situation where there is no hope of solution. Different technical measures are required depending on the specific site conditions and protection objectives, which can range from risk management for areas at high risk of desertification to controls over the transportation of sand in areas identified as source areas for sandstorm activity, and the protection of important infrastructure such as roads and buildings from sandstorms.

For farmland or grassland located in semi-arid or semi-humid zones that are at high risk of wind erosion and where no obvious wind erosion and desertification have occurred yet, the primary technical measures would be protection measures to protect the vegetation cover and to ensure the sustainable use of land. Examples include controls over grazing on grassland and technical measures for protection and utilization such as rotational grazing [11, 12]. Other measures that can be taken include no-till or conservation tillage farming, enclosure and reseeding, the protection of forest belts, and agroforestry. These measures can help to protect the earth surface from wind erosion by increasing surface roughness and lowering wind speeds.

In areas that have become a source of windborne sandstorm particles, the movement of sand dunes and semi-fixed dunes in arid, semi-arid and semi-humid areas is often the source of sandstorms due to wind erosion, transporting dust particles into the atmosphere as strong winds blow. In addition, there is also the movement of sand dunes, and sand accumulates or buries infrastructure such as nearby roads and buildings.

In such areas, the primary measures to be taken include the use of mechanical sand barriers, the planting of live sand barriers, and the propagation of planting of plant propagules for the purpose of sand fixation in order to mitigate wind erosion and the wind transport of particulate matter by strong wind currents [13]. Studies have shown that the use of mechanical sand barriers and the planting of living sand barriers, etc., have had an effect in terms of reduced wind speeds, the blocking or "fixing" of windborne sand particles, the changing of the patterns of wind and sand movement and surface erosion, and the protection of objects from wind and sand [14–16]. In recent years, China has worked to afforest the Kubuqi Desert and Mu Us Sandy Land by means of water jetting, a method that has greatly improved the labor productivity of such efforts as well as the plant survival rate [17]. This approach paves a new way forward for efforts to "green up" vast areas of sandy land and to expand the vegetation cover in areas where wind erosion is a problem.

13.4 Conclusion

Due to drought, the occurrence of sandstorms has been impacted by nature. However, human contribution to desertification and sandstorms is also obvious. Moreover, the occurrence of desertification and sandstorms not only transport particulate matter into the atmosphere: to a certain spatial and temporal extent, these phenomena may have a serious impact on human economy and society through interaction with climate forcing factors. The use of various different technical measures for varying land cover and utilization conditions in arid, semi-arid and sub-humid areas can reduce the risk of desertification, expand the scale of vegetation coverage on desertified land, and alleviate the effects of desertification and sandstorms.

For the protection of the homeland of mankind and the achievement of the goal of zero further degradation of land in the world by the year 2030 [18], the use of sustainable land management will certainly become a primary means of countering climate change, of controlling and reversing desertification, and of alleviating sandstorm occurrences [19]. As Xi Jinping pointed out in his congratulatory letter to the 13th Meeting of the Parties to the United Nations Convention to Combat Desertification, desertification is a major global ecological problem that affects the survival and development of mankind [20]. Although mankind has achieved remarkable results in combating desertification, the situation remains grim. The respect for nature, protecting nature, the rational use of land, and efforts to use wisdom to manage desertified land and alleviate sandstorms may be an effective way to synergistically address climate change and the occurrence of desertification and sandstorms.

References

1. Zhu, Z., & Chen, G. (1994). *'Sandy desertification' in China.* Beijing: Science Press.
2. Ma, S. (1998). Desertification. *The study of desertification* In S. Ma, Y. Ma, & H. Yao, et al. (Eds.), Hohhot Inner Mongolia People's Press, pp. 162–173.
3. UNEP, WMO, UNCCD. (2016). *Global assessment of sand and dust storms.* United Nations Environment Programme, Nairobi.
4. Middleton. (2011). Living with dryland geomorphology: The human impact. *Arid Zone Geomorphology: Process, Form and Change in Drylands* In D. S. G. Thomas (Ed.), pp. 571–582.
5. Eswaran, H., Lal, R., & Reich, P. F. (2001). Land degradation: An overview. In E. M. Bridges, I. D. Hannam, L. R. Oldeman, F. W. T. Pening de Vries, S. J. Scherr, & S. Sompatpanit (Eds.), *Responses to Land Degradation* (pp. 20–35). Oxford Press: New Delhi.
6. IPCC. (2013). Summary for Policymakers. *Climate change 2013: The physical science basis. Contribution of working group I to the fifth assessment report of the intergovernmental panel on climate change.* In T. F. Stocker, D. Qin, G. K. Plattner, M. Tignor, S. K. Allen, J. Boschung, A. Nauels, Y. Xia, V. Bex, & P. M. Midgley (Eds.), Cambridge University Press: Cambridge, United Kingdom and New York.
7. Ginoux, P., Prospero, J. M., Gill, T. E., Hsu, N. C., & Zhao, M. (2012). Global-scale attribution of anthropogenic and natural dust sources and their emission rates based on MODIS Deep Blue aerosol products. *Reviews of Geophysics, 50,* 1–36.
8. Gao, X., Wen, L., Liu, H., Liang, C., Liu, D., Zhuo, Y., et al. (2016). An analysis of the factors driving changes in the Hunshandak region based on a logistic regression model. *Journal of Inner Mongolia University (Natural Sciences Edition), 2016*(6), 625–634.
9. Cook, A., Miller, R. L., & Seagera, R. (2009). Amplification of the North American 'Dust Bowl' drought through human-induced land degradation. *Proceedings of the National Academy of Sciences 106.*
10. Lee, J. A., & Gill, T. E. (2016). Multiple causes of wind erosion in the Dust Bowl. *Aeolian Research, 19A,* 15–36.
11. Ren, J., Hou, F., & Xu, G. (2011). The modernization and transformation of grazing management: a lesson that China urgently needs to catch up on. *Prataculturul Science* [*sic.*], 2011 no. 10.
12. Ren, J. (2012). Grazing, the basic way through which the grassland ecosystem exists: also a discussion on the transformation of grazing. *Journal of Natural Resources*, 2012 no. 8.
13. Liu, S., & Wang, T. (2007). A study on the desertification process in Hunshandake. *Journal of Desert Research*, 2007 no. 5.
14. Han, Z., Wang, T., Dong, Z., Zhang, W., & Wang, X. (2004). The main engineering measures and mechanisms of sandstorm prevention and control. *Progress in Geography*, 2004 no. 1.

15. Sun, T., Wang, J., Man, D., Wu, C., Liu, H., Ma, Q., & Zhu, G. (2011). A wind-tunnel simulation study on the sand-fixing effect of sand-fixing shrubs. *Journal of Soil and Water Conservation*, 2011 no. 6.
16. Liang, A., Ma, J., Zhang, J., Ma, Y., & Su, Z. (2016). The Minqin County Desert: an analysis of the granularity of various sand barriers in the oasis[-desert] transition zone. *Journal of Taiyuan Normal University (Natural Sciences Edition)*, 2016 no. 1.
17. Wang, W., Lü, X., Zhang, J., Qiao, R., & Han, Y. (2013). Study on the establishment of the appropriate vegetation density in efforts to afforest the Kubuqi Desert by means of water jetting. *Northern Horticulture*, 2013 no. 23.
18. UN. (2015). *Transforming our world: the 2030 Agenda for Sustainable Development*. Retrieved from http://www.un.org/ga/search/view_doc.asp?symbol=A/RES/70/1&Lang=E20170926.
19. UNCCD. (2017). *Sustainable land management for addressing desertification/ land degradation and drought, climate change mitigation and adaptation*. GE, 2017.
20. Xi Jinping sends letter to congratulate the 13th High-Level Meeting of the Parties to the UN Convention to Combat Desertification. *China Daily*. Retrieved from http://china.chinadaily.com.cn/2017-09/11/content_31856381.htm20170918.

Chapter 14
Extreme Precipitation and Disasters: A Risk Analysis Based on Solar Radiation Management

Yuan Xin, Lili Lv and Feng Kong

Abstract As the threats posed by climate change clearer and greater, issues related to geoengineering have received increasing attention. The potential impact of geoengineering, as well as its associated risks, is central to research in this area. In this chapter, we focus on a key geoengineering technology, solar radiation management, and take disasters caused by extreme precipitation as an example for our study. Here, we estimate and analyze the changes in the frequency, intensity and duration of extreme precipitation events in China under the influence of geoengineering measures between the years 2020 and 2100, and evaluate the spatial pattern of its risk characteristics and of the dynamic changes in such risk. We also share some reflections on the risk management by means of geoengineering in China.

Keywords Solar radiation management · Geoengineering · Extreme precipitation disaster

---

Yuan Xin is Senior Engineer at the China Meteorological Administration Development and Research Center whose main research interests are in the areas of climate change and sustainable development. Lili Lv is Engineer at the China Meteorological Administration Development and Research Center whose main research interest is in risk assessments for meteorological disasters. Feng Kong is Engineer at the China Meteorological Administration Development and Research Center whose main research interests are in the areas of natural disasters and environmental change, and the risks posed by climate change.

Y. Xin (✉) · L. Lv · F. Kong
China Meteorological Administration Development and Research Center, Beijing, China
e-mail: xinyuanforever@163.com

L. Lv
e-mail: lvll@cma.gov.cn

F. Kong
e-mail: kongfeng0824@foxmail.com

W. Wang (ed.), *Annual Report on China's Response to Climate Change (2017)*,
Research Series on the Chinese Dream and China's Development Path,
https://doi.org/10.1007/978-981-13-9660-1_14

14.1 Introduction

Geoengineering is an emergency measure that is used to mitigate and adapt to the adverse conditions of climate change. The goal is to address the rise in temperatures around the world caused by climate change.

There has been much academic discussion on geoengineering since 2006. In particular, the technical means for solar radiation management (SRM) are simple. For instance, stratospheric aerosol injection (SAI) can be carried out by aircraft or airships at a direct economic cost much lower than traditional mitigation and adaptation measures. However, the implementation of SRM is also very risky. This has been one of the core topics in geoengineering research, and there has yet to be sufficient research in the areas concerned. In contrast, China is facing enormous pressures in the area of carbon emissions. At the same time, the need for economic development cannot wait. The pressure on China to further reduce its emissions under the 2 and 1.5 °C temperature control targets of the *Paris Agreement* is likely to increase further. It will be difficult to circumvent the "China question" in international discussions on geoengineering [1]. In this context, it is important for us to explore the impact of geoengineering on the risk of meteorological disasters in China. Disasters caused by extreme precipitation disasters are one of the major meteorological disasters that have an impact on China's economic and social security, while SAL is the most discussed SRM technology. Therefore, in this chapter we focus on an analysis of the risk of extreme-precipitation meteorological disasters in China within the SAL scenario through simulations that estimate the risk of extreme precipitation in various regions of China in both geoengineering and non-geoengineering scenarios between the years 2020 and 2100. Then, we also offer some reflections on the risk management by means of geoengineering in China.

14.2 Basic Approach, Research Method and Data

14.2.1 Basic Approach

Firstly, we use GeoMIP to simulate the changes in extreme precipitation in various Chinese provinces between 2020 and 2100 assuming the implementation of SRM. Second, we conduct a comparative analysis of changes in precipitation in various parts of China in the SRM and non-geoengineering (RCP4.5 medium-range emission) scenarios to obtain the changes in the hazard factors for meteorological disasters in various Chinese regions.

Then, we use historical data on disasters caused by extreme precipitation in China between 2006 and 2015 and the 10-year, 20-year, 50-year, 100-year return periods (labeled as "10a", "20a", "50a", "100a" respectively) to fit the vulnerability curves for extreme-precipitation disasters at various provincial levels in China.

Further, we use Bthe simulation data for the extreme precipitation occurrence factors and the prediction data for entities expected to be affected across China between 2020 and 2100 to obtain the corresponding results of the comparative analysis of extreme-precipitation meteorological disasters. Finally, based on the disaster risk distribution results in the two scenarios and on China's general response to climate change the country's specific needs in the area of meteorological disaster risk prevention, we provide some reflections on the management of geoengineering in China.

14.2.2 Research Method

(1) The basic theoretical model for disaster risk

This study in this chapter is based on theories of disaster risk assessment. We establish a model for disaster risk assessment model to obtain simulation results for the risk picture for disasters caused by extreme precipitation in various Chinese provinces in both the geoengineering and non-geoengineering (RCP4.5) scenarios. According to the principle of disaster risk assessment, it is assumed that in the case of little change in vulnerability, the focus of investigation is on the relationship between the hazard posed by the hazard factor and the exposure of the entities expected to be affected by the disaster in the two scenarios. That is, R = f (H, E). Here, R stands for risk, and is characterized by the spatial and temporal distribution of risk in the two scenarios. H stands for the hazard posed by the hazard factor that is extreme precipitation in both scenarios, while E stands for the exposure of the entities expected to be affected by the disaster. In this chapter, E is mainly represented by population size.

(2) Calculations of precipitation strength

For this study, "heavy precipitation" is defined as a precipitation event in the top fifth percentile, and "extreme precipitation" is defined as a precipitation event in the top percentile. Data sequences with at the top fifth and top percentiles were selected from $0.5° \times 0.5°$ daily precipitation data following statistical downscaling as the samples for "heavy precipitation" and "extreme precipitation". Then we used the Weibull distribution to perform distribution fitting and return-period calculation for each grid sample set.

(3) The fitting and testing of vulnerability curves for extreme precipitation disasters in various provinces

In this chapter, we evaluate the risk of extreme-precipitation disasters in both geoengineering and non-geoengineering (RCP4.5) scenarios by simulating the vulnerability curves of meteorological disasters in various provinces of China.

When building a vulnerability curve, a probabilistic parameter fitting model and a test of the appropriate goodness of fit are used to determine the best probability distribution for each province. The five fitting models used here include: normal distribution (Gaussian), the Weibull distribution, the Generalized Extreme Value Distribution (GEVD), and the Generalized Pareto Distribution (GPD). Finally, the Kolmogorov-Smirnov goodness-of-fit test (K-S test) is used to determine the degree of fit of the vulnerability curve to determine the best probability distribution for the sample observations.

14.2.3 Data

(1) Extreme precipitation as hazard factor

Two types of data are involved in this study.

The first type is the spatial and temporal estimation data for daily precipitation in China in the future obtained from the geoengineering simulation. This data was obtained by using the G4 test of the BNU(R) ESM mode (2.5° × 2.5°) mode in Geometer test is configured for a series of SAL trials between January 1, 2020 and December 31, 2069 (uniformly stated as the year 2070 in this chapter). After that, the G4 test is allowed to run until December 31, 2099 (2100 in this chapter). Precipitation levels following the cessation of geoengineering are reviewed. In short, in this study we used the period between 2020 and 2070 as the simulation period for geoengineering, and the period 2070–2100 as the observation period for the implementation of geoengineering.

Second, the estimated daily precipitation data for the RCP4.5 scenario in various regions of China between 2020 and 2100 is used as comparison. Said data is obtained by entering CMIP5 daily precipitation data (spatial resolution WRF30 km) in the RCP4.5 scenario provided by the Chinese Academy of Sciences for atmospheric physics research into the G4 test in BNU-ESM mode (2.5° × 2.5°).

(2) Population data as a representation of population vulnerability to hazard

In research on meteorological disaster risk, the factors that indicate the exposure of entities likely to be affected by the disaster in question generally include population size, GDP, and building density. Any forecast of China's population, GDP, and surface building density un the period 2020–2100 is in itself a major and complex research project involving many aspects. There are a number of factors at play, which cannot be fully enumerated in this chapter.

In contrast, China's population growth rate is relatively stable and relatively easy to predict. As a preliminary methodological exploration, in this chapter we further simplify the elements that make up the entities that are expected to be affected by the disaster in question and mainly uses data on the Chinese population to represent such entities. Specifically, we use population forecast data obtained by the National Climate Center through the Population-Development-Environmental Analysis (PDE) model [2].

14.3 Historical Data on Extreme Precipitation Disasters in Different Provinces, and Vulnerability Curve Fitting

1. Provincial distribution of disasters caused by extreme precipitation in China according to historical data

The risk model for the population affected by extreme precipitation in each province was constructed using data from the National Climate Center disaster database for the period 2008–2015 on loss incurred due to extreme precipitation (including heavy rain, extremely heavy rain, and extraordinarily heavy rain). It is as follows:

$$Popu = \frac{Affpop_{(i,j)}}{pop_{(i,j)}} * 100{,}000$$

In this equation, Popu stands for the number of persons per 100,000 who are affected by extreme precipitation, *Affpop(i, j)* stands for the number of persons in province j who are affected by extreme precipitation in year i, pop(i, j) stands for the number of persons in province j in the year i, i stands for {2005, 2006,…, 2015}, that is, the ten years between 2005 and 2015. The administrative units here at 31 mainland Chinese provinces, excluding Hong Kong, Macau, and Taiwan. Data on losses incurred in 17,399 extreme precipitation disasters in China between 2008 and 2015 was collected. Using the formula, we have been able to obtain data on population loss due to such disasters in the said period, and thereby the distribution of the affected population in each province. The main conclusions are as follows.

First of all, in the period 2008–2015, the provinces (autonomous regions and municipalities) of the eastern and central regions of China and the western regions of Guangxi, Guizhou, Sichuan, Chongqing, and Shaanxi saw the greatest concentration of persons affected by extreme precipitation. In particular, the provinces of Guangdong, Guangxi, Hunan, Anhui, Hubei, and Sichuan in southeast and central China saw a total of more than 35 million people affected by such disasters. Such a spatial and temporal characteristic has appeared due to the frequent occurrence of extreme precipitation events in these regions during the monsoon season, and due to the population density of these areas.

Second, between 2008 and 2015, the southeastern and southwestern provinces as well as Shaanxi and Gansu were the provinces with the largest number of deaths. There are obvious differences in the distribution characteristics of disaster-caused mortality and the population affected by disaster across regions. Apart from the five provinces of Guangdong, Guangxi, Hunan, Hubei and Guizhou, although many provinces in the eastern coastal and northern China regions were the most affected provinces, these were not the provinces with the most deaths caused by such disasters. On the other hand, the death toll from the provinces such as Shaanxi and Gansu have risen. To understand this situation, we have to consider the intensity of the extreme precipitation hazard factor as well as the degree of vulnerability to said hazard. In the provinces of Shaanxi and Gansu, where the intensity of the hazard factor is relatively low, the mortality number has risen, showing that the vulnerability of the entities affected by the disaster is also an important factor.

14.3.1 Vulnerability Curve Fitting Based on Extreme Precipitation in Chinese History

Based on the historical data on extreme precipitation data in China, formula 4 is converted into a natural logarithmic expression. It is assumed that the population affected by extreme precipitation accords with five kinds of probability models:

Table 14.1 Best-fit probability distribution and parameters for population loss due to heavy rainfall in selected provinces

Province	Best-fit probability distribution	Province	Best-fit probability distribution
Fujian	Gaussian (3.19, 1.71)	Anhui	GEVD (−0.22, 1.66, 4.18)
Guangxi	Gaussian (3.71, 1.68)	Beijing-Tianjin-Hebei[a]	GEVD (−0.32, 1.56, 2.93)
Henan	Gaussian (3.17, 1.42)	Gansu	GEVD (−0.23, 1.53, 2.53)
Hubei	Gaussian (4.22, 1.76)	Guangdong	GEVD (−0.19, 1.51, 2.56)
Hunan	Gaussian (4.21, 1.59)	Guizhou	GEVD (−0.28, 1.61, 2.92)
Jiangxi	Gaussian (4.30, 1.74)	Suzhou + Shanghai[a]	GEVD (−0.34, 1.69, 3.30)
Tibet	Gaussian (3.58, 1.89)	Shandong	GEVD (−0.35, 1.64, 3.12)
Zhejiang	Gaussian (3.88, 1.58)	Shanxi	GEVD (−0.37, 1.57, 2.92)
Xinjiang	Weibull (2.78, 1.56)	Liaoning	GEVD (−0.41, 1.91, 3.57)
Inner Mongolia	Weibull (3.05, 1.77)	Sichuan	GEVD (−0.19, 1.61, 2.68)
Jilin	Weibull (4.11, 2.14)	Yunnan	GEVD (−0.19, 1.35, 2.12)
Hainan	Weibull (7.41, 5.06)	Chongqing	GEVD (−0.39, 1.68, 3.79)
Ningxia	Weibull (3.67, 1.81)	Heilongjiang	GPD (−1.02, 5.43)
Shaanxi	Weibull (4.38, 2.31)	Qinghai	GPD (−0.74, 4.74)

Note Beijing, Tianjin and Hebei have been considered as a single entity ("Beijing-Tianjin-Hebei") as there were insufficient samples in each case. The same has been done for Suzhou and Shanghai ("Suzhou + Shanghai")

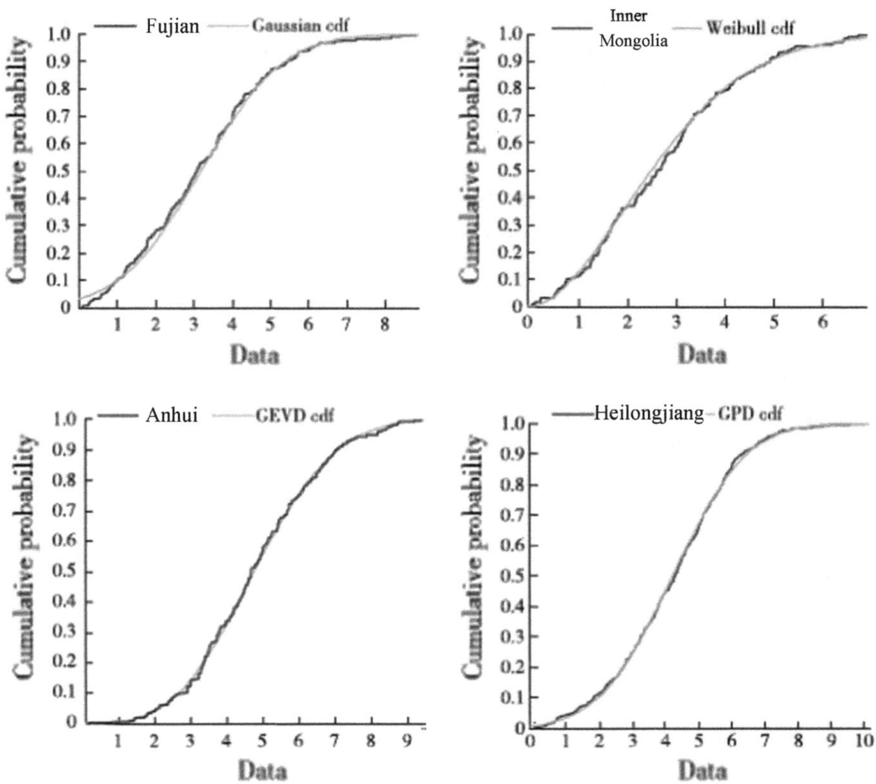

Fig. 14.1 Best-fit vulnerability curve for losses due to extreme-precipitation disasters in four Chinese provinces in accordance with four distribution types

normal distribution, gamma distribution, the Weibull distribution, the Generalized Extreme Value Distribution (GEVD), and the Generalized Pareto Distribution (GPD). Then, we use the K-S test to determine the best-fit probability model for each province (see Table 14.1), that is, the best-fit vulnerability curve.

Figure 14.1 shows the best-fit vulnerability curves for certain provinces. For example, in the case of Fujian Province the best-fitting model is the Gaussian model; for Inner Mongolia, it is the Weibull model; for Anhui, the GEVD model, and for Heilongjiang, the GPD model. The thin lines in Fig. 14.1 indicate the natural logarithmic data for affected populations in various provinces, while the thick lines are the parameter model fitting data. We can see that the vulnerability curves for losses due to extreme-precipitation disasters are well-fitted in four cases (autonomous regions), with the curve fairly close to the historical facts.

Above, we have determined the best-fit vulnerability curve for extreme precipitation disaster losses in various provinces (regions) in China. On this basis, we can then proceed to the assessment of the risk of extreme precipitation disasters in both geoengineering and non-geoengineering (RCP4.5) scenarios, and thus obtain the distribution pattern for meteorological disasters in the SRM scenario.

14.4 Risk of Disaster Due to Extreme Precipitation in Chinese Provinces for the Period 2020–2100 in the Two Scenarios

In this section, based on the best-fit vulnerability curve for extreme-precipitation disaster losses in various provinces (regions) identified in the previous section, we use data for the distribution of extreme precipitation hazards in various regions of China between 2020 and 2100, and data for forecast population size in various provinces (autonomous regions and municipalities) for 2020 to 2100 from by Jiang Tong, et al. (2017) to estimate the risk of extreme precipitation in various provinces in the SAI (geoengineering) scenario in China up to the year 2100. Then, we conduct a comparative analysis using the data for the risk of extreme-precipitation disasters in various provinces in the RCP4.5 scenario to obtain a picture of the risks of implementing geoengineering in China in the 21st century.

In order to more clearly define and demonstrate the risk of extreme-precipitation disasters, in this chapter we classify using two dimensions: time points and intensity of disaster. The two time points used in this chapter are the years 2050 and 2100, and for the measurement of the intensity of extreme-precipitation disasters, various extreme precipitation intensities are classified using the four return periods or grades of 10a, 20a, 50a, and 100a.The analysis and results are as follows.

14.4.1 Affected-Population Risk in Various Provinces in the Year 2050

(1) Affected-population risk in the year 2050 in the non-geoengineering scenario using various return periods for extreme-precipitation disaster

Table 14.2 shows the affected-population risk in various Chinese provinces in the RCP4.5 scenario given four grades of extreme precipitation intensities: 10a, 20a, 50a, and 100a. The results are classified into five risk levels according to the number of persons affected by extreme-precipitation disaster. They are: less than 200,000 persons, 200,000–400,000 persons, 400,000–600,000 persons, 600,000–800,000 persons, and more than 800,000 persons. Hong Kong, Macau and Taiwan are not included in this study as the requisite data is not available.

On the national level, in southeastern, southwestern, northern and northeastern China as well as in Shaanxi, as extreme precipitation intensity increases the size of the population affected by extreme-precipitation disaster also increases. In contrast,

Table 14.2 Affected-population risk within the non-geoengineering scenario in the year 2050 at various extreme precipitation intensity levels

Risk category	Affected provinces (10a)	Affected provinces (20a)	Affected provinces (50a)	Affected provinces (100a)
<200,000 persons	Heilongjiang, Jilin, Inner Mongolia, Beijing-Tianjin-Hebei, Shanxi, Henan, Ningxia, Gansu, Qinghai, Xinjiang, Tibet, Yunnan, Chongqing, Guizhou, Guangxi, Fujian	Heilongjiang, Inner Mongolia, Shanxi, Ningxia, Gansu, Xinjiang, Qinghai, Tibet, Yunnan, Guizhou, Fujian	Heilongjiang, Inner Mongolia, Shanxi, Ningxia, Gansu, Qinghai, Xinjiang, Tibet, Yunnan	Heilongjiang, Qinghai, Tibet
200,000–400,000 persons	Sichuan, Shaanxi, Hubei, Liaoning, Shandong, Suzhou + Shanghai, Zhejiang, Hunan, Jiangxi, Guangdong	Beijing-Tianjin-Hebei, Jilin, Henan, Chongqing, Zhejiang, Guangxi	Chongqing, Guizhou, Fujian	Inner Mongolia, Shanxi, Ningxia, Gansu, Xinjiang, Yunnan
400,000–600,000 persons	Hainan	Liaoning, Shandong, Shaanxi, Suzhou + Shanghai, Sichuan, Jiangxi, Guangdong	Beijing-Tianjin-Hebei, Henan	Beijing-Tianjin-Hebei, Chongqing, Guizhou, Fujian
600,000–800,000 persons	Anhui	Hubei, Hunan	Jilin, Liaoning, Shandong, Fujian, Guangxi	Henan
>800,000 persons	None	Hainan, Anhui	Shaanxi, Hubei, Hunan, Sichuan, Jiangxi, Guangdong, Hainan, Anhui, Suzhou + Shanghai	Liaoning, Jilin, Shandong, Suzhou + Shanghai, Anhui, Zhejiang, Jiangxi, Hubei, Hunan, Shaanxi, Sichuan, Guangdong, Guangxi, Hainan

in the northwestern and western regions, in Tibet, Heilongjiang, and Yunnan, the disaster risk is comparatively lower. The risk of harm from extreme-precipitation disaster is the greatest in Anhui, Shaanxi, Sichuan, Hubei, Hunan, Guangxi, Guangdong, Hainan, Jiangxi, Zhejiang, Jiangsu, Shandong, Jilin, and Liaoning, with more than 600,000 persons at risk at the 50a and 100a levels. Apart from these provinces, Henan, Beijing-Tianjin-Hebei, Guizhou, Chongqing, and Fujian are also at higher risk.

(2) Affected-population risk in the year 2050 within the geoengineering scenario at various levels of extreme precipitation intensity

In Table 14.3, we see the affected-population risk for various provinces in the year 2050 in the SRM (geoengineering) scenario at various levels of extreme precipitation intensity. The pattern of risk reflected in Table 14.3 is basically consistent with the pattern of risk in the RCP4.5 scenario as shown in Table 14.2. The affected-population risk in the coastal areas, the middle and lower reaches of the Yangtze River, the eastern part of northwestern China, northern China and northeastern China rises gradually as the extreme precipitation intensity increases. It is worth noting that compared to the RCP4.5 scenario, Jiangxi has gone up one risk level at the 20a extreme precipitation intensity level while Hainan and Guangxi have moved down at the 20a and 50a risk levels respectively.

For this chapter, in order to obtain a more direct picture of the impact of geoengineering and non-geoengineering on the risk of extreme precipitation in various regions of China in the future, we compare the risk distribution of the populations affected by various precipitation intensity levels in China in the year 2050. The differences are reflected in Table 14.4. The results show that as extreme precipitation intensity levels become higher the risk difference becomes increasingly obvious across various provinces. At the 100a extreme precipitation intensity level, Guangdong, Fujian, Jiangxi, Hubei, Shaanxi, Shanxi, Ningxia, Gansu, Shandong, and Liaoning see the greatest increase in affected-population risk, which also increases in Henan, Chongqing, Guizhou, Beijing-Tianjin-Hebei, Qinghai, and Heilongjiang. On the other hand, the affected-population risk decreases in Xinjiang, Sichuan, Yunnan, Guangxi, Hainan, Zhejiang, Anhui, Jilin, and Inner Mongolia and remains largely the same in both scenarios in Tibet, Hunan, and Jiangsu.

14.4.2 Affected-Population Risk in the Year 2100

(1) Affected-population risk in the year 2100 in the non-geoengineering scenario using various return periods for extreme-precipitation disaster

According to Table 14.5, the extreme-precipitation risk situation across the country in the year 2100 is less severe than in 2050 for all return periods. As extreme precipitation intensity increases, the affected-population risk zone gradually extends from the middle and lower reaches of the Yangtze River to south China, the eastern

Table 14.3 Affected-population risk within the geoengineering scenario in the year 2050 at various extreme precipitation intensity levels

Risk category	Affected provinces (10a)	Affected provinces (20a)	Affected provinces (50a)	Affected provinces (100a)
<200,000 persons	Heilongjiang, Jilin, Inner Mongolia, Beijing-Tianjin-Hebei, Shanxi, Henan, Ningxia, Gansu, Qinghai, Xinjiang, Tibet, Yunnan, Chongqing, Guizhou, Guangxi, Fujian	Heilongjiang, Inner Mongolia, Shanxi, Ningxia, Gansu, Xinjiang, Qinghai, Tibet, Yunnan, Guizhou, Fujian	Heilongjiang, Inner Mongolia, Shanxi, Ningxia, Gansu, Qinghai, Xinjiang, Tibet, Yunnan	Heilongjiang, Qinghai, Tibet
200,000–400,000 persons	Sichuan, Shaanxi, Hubei, Liaoning, Shandong, Suzhou + Shanghai, Zhejiang, Hunan, Jiangxi, Guangdong	Beijing-Tianjin-Hebei, Jilin, Henan, Chongqing, Zhejiang, Guangxi	Chongqing, Guizhou, Fujian	Inner Mongolia, Shanxi, Ningxia, Gansu, Xinjiang, Yunnan
400,000–600,000 persons	Hainan	Liaoning, Shandong, Shaanxi, Suzhou + Shanghai, Sichuan, Guangdong	Beijing-Tianjin-Hebei, Henan, Guangxi	Beijing-Tianjin-Hebei, Chongqing, Guizhou, Fujian
600,000–800,000 persons	Anhui	Hubei, Hunan, Jiangxi, Hainan	Jilin, Liaoning, Shandong, Fujian	Henan
>800,000 persons	None	Anhui	Shaanxi, Hubei, Hunan, Sichuan, Jiangxi, Guangdong, Hainan, Anhui, Suzhou + Shanghai	Liaoning, Jilin, Shandong, Suzhou + Shanghai, Anhui, Zhejiang, Jiangxi, Hubei, Hunan, Shaanxi, Sichuan, Guangdong, Guangxi, Hainan

Table 14.4 Differences in affected-population risk distribution for the geoengineering and non-geoengineering scenarios in the year 2050 at various extreme precipitation intensity levels

Risk category	Affected provinces (10a)	Affected provinces (20a)	Affected provinces (50a)	Affected provinces (100a)
<3,000 persons	Jilin, Guangxi, Hainan	Jilin, Hunan, Guangxi, Hainan	Jilin, Anhui, Guangxi, Yunnan, Hainan	Xinjiang, Sichuan, Yunnan, Guangxi, Anhui, Zhejiang, Hainan, Jilin
−3,000 to −1,500 persons	Hunan	Yunnan, Zhejiang	Xinjiang, Sichuan, Hunan, Zhejiang	Inner Mongolia
−1500 to 0 persons	Inner Mongolia, Xinjiang, Tibet, Yunnan, Sichuan, Chongqing, Guizhou, Guangdong, Zhejiang, Suzhou + Shanghai	Inner Mongolia, Xinjiang, Tibet, Sichuan, Guizhou, Guangdong, Suzhou + Shanghai, Anhui	Inner Mongolia, Tibet, Guizhou	Tibet, Hunan, Suzhou + Shanghai
0–2,500 persons	Heilongjiang, Liaoning, Beijing-Tianjin-Hebei, Shaanxi, Ningxia, Gansu, Qinghai, Henan, Anhui, Fujian	Heilongjiang, Liaoning, Beijing-Tianjin-Hebei, Gansu, Qinghai, Henan, Chongqing	Heilongjiang, Beijing-Tianjin-Hebei, Qinghai, Chongqing, Suzhou + Shanghai,	Heilongjiang, Beijing-Tianjin-Hebei, Qinghai
2,500–5,000 persons	Shanxi, Hubei	Shanxi, Shaanxi, Ningxia, Fujian	Gansu, Henan	Henan, Chongqing, Guizhou, Qinghai
>5,000 persons	Shandong, Jiangxi	Shandong, Jiangxi, Hubei	Liaoning, Shanxi, Guangdong, Ningxia, Shaanxi, Hubei, Jiangxi, Fujian, Guangdong	Liaoning, Shandong, Shanxi, Shaanxi, Ningxia, Gansu, Hubei, Jiangxi, Fujian, Guangdong

Table 14.5 Affected-population risk within the non-geoengineering scenario in the year 2100 at various extreme precipitation intensity levels

Risk category	Affected provinces (10a)	Affected provinces (20a)	Affected provinces (50a)	Affected provinces (100a)
<200,000 persons 200,000–400,000 persons	Heilongjiang, Jilin, Inner Mongolia, Beijing-Tianjin-Hebei, Shanxi, Shaanxi, Henan, Ningxia, Gansu, Qinghai, Xinjiang, Tibet, Yunnan, Chongqing, Guizhou, Guangxi, Guangdong, Fujian, Zhejiang, Shandong, Suzhou + Shanghai, Hubei, Hunan, Jiangxi, Hainan	Heilongjiang, Jilin, Inner Mongolia, Shanxi, Ningxia, Gansu, Xinjiang, Qinghai, Tibet, Yunnan, Guizhou, Chongqing, Fujian, Beijing-Tianjin-Hebei, Henan, Liaoning, Shandong, Jiangsu, Zhejiang, Guangdong, Guangxi, Shaanxi, Sichuan	Heilongjiang, Inner Mongolia, Shanxi, Ningxia, Gansu, Qinghai, Xinjiang, Tibet, Yunnan, Beijing-Tianjin-Hebei, Henan, Chongqing, Guizhou, Fujian	Heilongjiang, Qinghai, Tibet, Shanxi, Yunnan, Gansu, Inner Mongolia, Xinjiang, Ningxia, Chongqing, Guizhou, Fujian
400,000–600,000 persons	Anhui	Hubei, Hunan, Jiangxi	Jilin, Liaoning, Shandong, Suzhou + Shanghai, Zhejiang, Guangxi	Liaoning, Beijing-Tianjin-Hebei, Henan
600,000–800,000 persons	None	Hainan	Sichuan, Shaanxi, Guangdong	Shandong, Suzhou + Shanghai, Zhejiang, Guangxi
>800,000 persons	None	Anhui	Anhui, Hubei, Hunan, Jiangxi, Hainan	Jilin, Shaanxi, Sichuan, Jiangxi, Hubei, Hunan, Anhui, Guangdong, Hainan

coast, the Sichuan Basin, and the eastern part of the western region. Overall, risk is higher along the southeast coast and lower in the northwest. For example, at the 100a extreme precipitation intensity level, the provinces facing the greatest risk are Hainan, Guangdong, Hunan, Jiangxi, Anhui, Hubei, Shaanxi, Sichuan, and Jilin, with an affected-population risk of over 800,000, and Guangxi, Zhejiang, Jiangsu, and Shandong are also expected to see 600,000 to 800,000 persons at risk. The risk of extreme precipitation disasters in Beijing-Tianjin-Hebei, Henan, Liaoning, Chongqing, Guizhou, Fujian, Ningxia, Xinjiang, and Inner Mongolia has also significantly increased, while Heilongjiang, Gansu, Shanxi, Qinghai, Tibet, and Yunnan are at relatively low risk levels.

(2) Affected-population risk in the year 2100 within the geoengineering scenario at various levels of extreme precipitation intensity

According to Table 14.6, the risk grade distribution for the four intensity levels in the 2100 geoengineering scenario is basically consistent with the RCP4.5 scenario. Further, there is no difference in magnitude. This may be related to the model assumption that geoengineering works cease in the year 2070. In such a situation, by the year 2100 the Earth's atmospheric environment would have recovered and the climate impact of geoengineering previously implemented would have basically been eliminated. The backgrounds of extreme precipitation disaster risk in both scenarios have become more consistent, leading to no significant difference in the distribution of disaster risk between the two.

(3) Differences in affected-population risk between the two scenarios in the year 2100

Table 14.7 shows the differences in the risk distribution of populations affected by extreme precipitation in Chinese provinces in the year 2100 at various extreme precipitation intensity levels for both the geoengineering and RCP4.5 scenarios. Although Table 14.6 more or less shows that there is no significant change in the overall risk distribution of meteorological disasters in China in the two scenarios in the year 2100, considering the potential long-term effects of geoengineering on the climate and the differences in local climates there are still some significant differences in the intensity of disaster risk at the provincial level.

When we compare the results of the two scenarios at extreme-precipitation intensity level 100a, we see that the provinces with an increased risk level are Guangdong, Fujian, Jiangxi, Hubei, Shanxi, Shandong, Ningxia, Liaoning, Gansu, Shaanxi, Henan, Qinghai, Heilongjiang, and Beijing-Tianjin-Hebei. The provinces with reduced risk levels include Xinjiang, Sichuan, Yunnan, Guangxi, Hainan, Anhui, Zhejiang, and Jilin, and the provinces with basically the same level of risk are Tibet, Hunan, and Guizhou. The reasons for such a risk distribution in the year 2100 with the two scenarios are different from the reasons for the year 2050. In the year 2100, geoengineering would have ceased for some 30 years and the hazard factors in the two scenarios would have basically converged. In this case, when we examine the reasons for the difference in risk distribution between the provinces, we

Table 14.6 Affected-population risk within the geoengineering scenario in the year 2100 at various extreme precipitation intensity levels

Risk category	Affected provinces (10a)	Affected provinces (20a)	Affected provinces (50a)	Affected provinces (100a)
<200,000 persons	Heilongjiang, Jilin, Inner Mongolia, Beijing-Tianjin-Hebei, Shanxi, Shaanxi, Henan, Ningxia, Gansu, Qinghai, Xinjiang, Tibet, Yunnan, Chongqing, Guizhou, Guangxi, Guangdong, Fujian, Zhejiang	Heilongjiang, Jilin, Inner Mongolia, Shanxi, Ningxia, Gansu, Xinjiang, Qinghai, Tibet, Yunnan, Guizhou, Chongqing, Fujian, Beijing-Tianjin-Hebei, Henan	Heilongjiang, Inner Mongolia, Shanxi, Ningxia, Gansu, Qinghai, Xinjiang, Tibet, Yunnan	Heilongjiang, Qinghai, Tibet, Shanxi, Yunnan, Gansu
200,000–400,000 persons	Shandong, Suzhou + Shanghai, Hubei, Hunan, Jiangxi, Hainan	Liaoning, Shandong, Jiangsu, Zhejiang, Guangdong, Guangxi, Shaanxi, Sichuan	Beijing-Tianjin-Hebei, Henan, Chongqing, Guizhou, Fujian	Inner Mongolia, Xinjiang, Ningxia, Chongqing, Guizhou, Fujian
400,000–600,000 persons	Anhui	Hubei, Hunan, Jiangxi, Hainan	Jilin, Liaoning, Shandong, Suzhou + Shanghai, Zhejiang, Guangxi	Liaoning, Beijing-Tianjin-Hebei, Henan
600,000–800,000 persons	None	None	Sichuan, Shaanxi, Guangdong	Shandong, Suzhou + Shanghai, Zhejiang, Guangxi
>800,000 persons	None	Anhui	Anhui, Hubei, Hunan, Jiangxi, Hainan	Jilin, Shaanxi, Sichuan, Jiangxi, Hubei, Hunan, Anhui, Guangdong, Hainan

Table 14.7 Differences in affected-population risk distribution for the geoengineering and non-geoengineering scenarios in the year 2100 at various extreme precipitation intensity levels

Risk category	Affected provinces (10a)	Affected provinces (20a)	Affected provinces (50a)	Affected provinces (100a)
< 3,000 persons	Jilin, Guangxi, Hainan	Jilin, Guangxi, Hainan	Jilin, Guangxi, Hainan, Yunnan	Anhui, Hainan, Jilin, Yunnan
−3,000 to −1,500 persons	Hunan	Yunnan, Hunan	Sichuan, Hunan, Zhejiang	Xinjiang, Sichuan, Zhejiang
−1,500 to 0 persons	Inner Mongolia, Xinjiang, Tibet, Sichuan, Yunnan, Guizhou, Chongqing, Guangdong, Zhejiang, Suzhou + Shanghai	Inner Mongolia, Xinjiang, Tibet, Sichuan, Guizhou, Suzhou + Shanghai, Anhui	Inner Mongolia, Xinjiang, Tibet, Suzhou + Shanghai	Inner Mongolia, Tibet, Hunan, Suzhou + Shanghai
0–2,500 persons	Heilongjiang, Liaoning, Beijing-Tianjin-Hebei, Shaanxi, Shanxi, Henan, Ningxia, Gansu, Qinghai, Anhui, Fujian	Heilongjiang, Liaoning, Beijing-Tianjin-Hebei, Gansu, Qinghai, Shaanxi, Henan, Chongqing, Guangdong	Heilongjiang, Beijing-Tianjin-Hebei, Gansu, Qinghai, Henan, Chongqing, Guizhou	Heilongjiang, Beijing-Tianjin-Hebei, Qinghai, Chongqing, Guizhou
2,500–5,000 persons	Shandong, Hubei, Jiangxi	Shanxi, Hubei, Ningxia, Fujian	Liaoning, Shanxi, Shaanxi	Henan, Shaanxi, Gansu
> 5,000 persons	None	Shandong, Jiangxi	Shandong, Ningxia, Hubei, Jiangxi, Guangdong, Fujian	Liaoning, Shandong, Shanxi, Ningxia, Hubei, Jiangxi, Fujian, Guangdong

should mainly look at factors pertaining to the affected population, such as the expected changes in the population size of each province.

14.4.3 Average Difference in Affected-Population Risk Between the Two Scenarios for the Period 2020–2100

Above, we have analyzed the pattern of risk for extreme precipitation in various Chinese provinces at the two time points of 2050 and 2100 for both the geoengineering and RCP4.5 scenarios. Although the above analysis provides us with a profile of the impact of geoengineering on meteorological disaster risk, it does not allow us to form an understanding of the overall risk of meteorological disasters caused by geoengineering. As such, we have fitted the affected-population risks for both scenarios and at the four return-period levels for the period 2020–2100. The differences in overall risk between the two scenarios are shown in Fig. 14.2.

As we see in Fig. 14.2, the average risk difference in China's population affected by extreme precipitation events in both geoengineering and non-geoengineering scenarios in the period 2020–2100 bears the following characteristics.

First, overall, the implementation of geoengineering throughout the trial period (i.e., between 2020 and 2100) helps to reduce disaster risk. However, the degree of risk reduction is generally small, and the disaster risk pattern is essentially dependent on the control of the physical environment of Earth's atmosphere.

Second, in the two scenarios, the overall trend of extreme precipitation occurrence risk distribution in China's 10a–100a four-year type is highly consistent. Over time, the risk level rises first and then decreases, and the highest risk level occurs around 2030.

This time point is basically consistent with the current forecasts for global warming and peak levels of greenhouse gas emission reduction [3], indicating that geoengineering can only play a limited role within a limited scope and cannot fundamentally change the overall development pattern of global climate change and its corresponding impact.

Third, in the probability distribution for extreme precipitation risk, the higher the extreme precipitation intensity, the better the curve fit in the geoengineering and non-geoengineering scenarios. For example, at the end of the 100a risk fit curve, the risk fit curves for the two scenarios almost coincide. This result shows that the risk of meteorological disaster depends on the degree of hazard of the hazard factor in the case of a stable affected population.

Fourth, the closer the fit of the curve is to the geoengineering and non-geoengineering scenarios, the closer the two are in year 2100. This indicates that once the implementation of geoengineering ceases the two simulated climatic

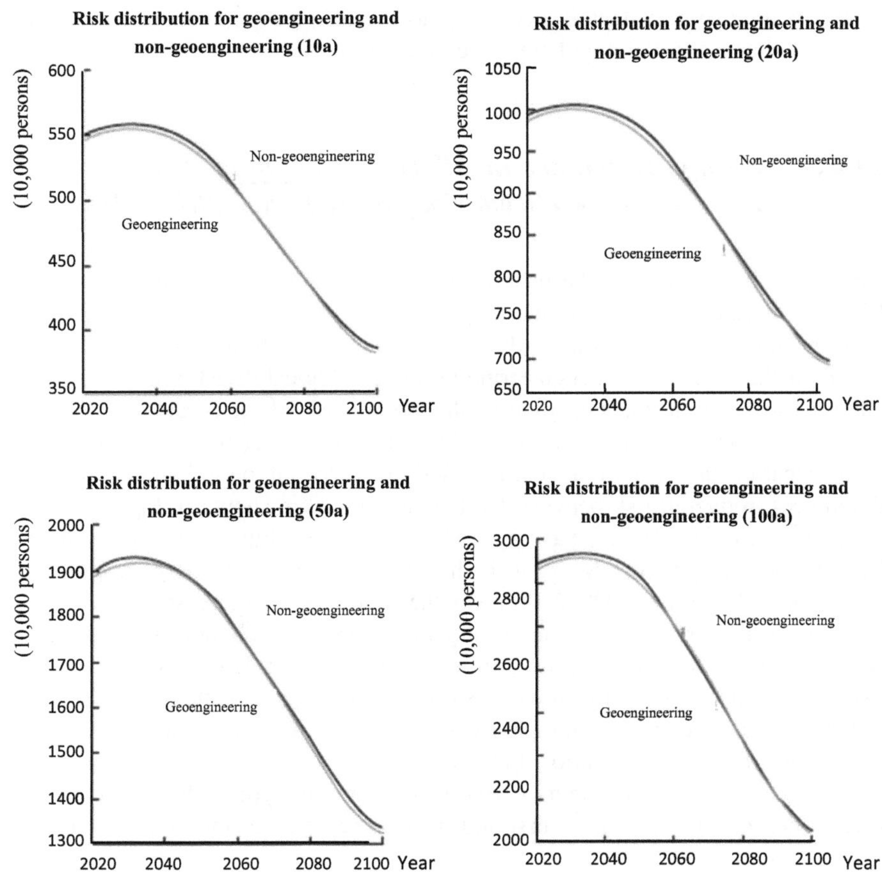

Fig. 14.2 Average risk difference populations affected by extreme precipitation events in China in both the geoengineering and non-geoengineering scenarios, 2020–2100

environment gradually became uniform under the influence of atmospheric circulation and the human disturbance caused by geoengineering was gradually "smoothed" over time. Therefore, the risk level of meteorological disasters in the two scenarios tends to be the same. This also means that at least under the current geoengineering implementation of the GeoMIP model, the "self-recovery capability" of the atmospheric physical environment can still dominate, ensuring that the original meteorological disaster risk pattern is not fundamentally changed. This result also confirms to some extent the 1999 IPCC assessment of the impact of aircraft exhaust on climate change, that is, the impact of human activity on the stratosphere is risky, uncertain, and reversible [4].

14.5 Conclusions and Lessons

Based on the above study conclusions, we can see that that the risk of extreme-precipitation meteorological disasters in China in the geoengineering scenario has two characteristics: first, the implementation of SAI geoengineering between 2020 and 2100 does not change the distribution pattern of China's extreme precipitation disasters within the context of climate change. In fact, it even helps to reduce disaster risk to some extent. Second, the magnitude of disaster risk changes due to the implementation of geoengineering and also depends on the combined effects of hazard factors, hazard exposure, and vulnerability.

The two points above have important implications for China in terms of risk management by means of geoengineering.

First, from the perspective of global climate governance, if geoengineering cannot fundamentally change the atmospheric physical environment and the corresponding risk pattern, or but can have the potential to mitigate the risk of meteorological disasters, then traditional mitigation and adaptation measures cannot be effective in relieving pressures on the world in terms of its response to climate change. In particular, if the 2 and 1.5 °C temperature control targets set out in the *Paris Agreement* are difficult to achieve, will geoengineering become a practical option for some countries? Once geoengineering enters the actual operational phase global climate governance will be further complicated, and China will need to implement the necessary policies and countermeasures.

Second, from the perspective of domestic climate governance and disaster response, there are both common features and spatial heterogeneity in terms of the impact of geoengineering on meteorological disaster risk across China. Overall, the implementation of geoengineering does not worsen the national risk pattern for extreme precipitation according to the simulations. However, the risk distribution at the provincial level has changed to some extent. The main reason for this change are the changes in the affected population in each province, that is, the differences in the ability to prevent and withstand disaster in each province. This tells us that regardless of whether geoengineering is eventually implemented we will continue to have to strengthen and improve disaster prevention capabilities in various places, which has always been the key direction and content of climate governance in China.

In short, the relationship between geoengineering and the risk of meteorological disasters in China is a broad and complex research topic. In this chapter, we have but scratched the surface of the matter. Many elements have been simplified in this study, which will inevitably affect the accuracy of the study results. More and better work is needed in a number of different areas, e.g., a comprehensive analysis of the impact of geoengineering on meteorological disaster risks in various emissions scenarios by specific meteorological disaster type. It is also necessary to run more attribution studies with regard to geoengineering and disaster risk, as these will be great value to disaster risk management. In addition, we should also focus on the issue of the international governance of geoengineering. At present, there is little research in this field, which provides China with plenty of room. It is necessary for us to strengthen research and to intervene as early as possible, so to seize the commanding heights with regard to the rules of geoengineering governance.

Acknowledgements This research was conducted as part of a project titled "A comprehensive impact assessment of geoengineering, and a study of international governance in this area" funded by the National Basic Science Research Program (S/N: 2015CB953603).

References

1. Chen, Y., & Xin, Y. (2017). An analysis of issues in geoengineering and policy recommendations with reference to the 1.5 °C temperature control targets. *Advances in Climate Change Research, 1*, 342.
2. Jiang, T. et al., of the National Climate Center have made use of the PDE model, the IPCC's [Intergovernmental Panel on Climate Change's] Shared Socioeconomic Pathways 1-5, data from the Sixth China census and the latest demographic data from the period 2011-2014 alongside [expected] future changes in China's population structure and climate change policy and policy recommendations to estimate population size and distribution in terms of age, gender and education for 31 mainland Chinese provinces up to the year 2100. In this chapter, we have relied primarily on this data for estimates of China's overall population numbers as well as specific numbers for the 31 mainland provinces [up to the year] 2100.For more details, refer to: Jiang, Tong, Zhao Jing, et al., (2017), Estimates of population changes in China and Chinese provinces in the context of the IPCC Sharing Social and Economic Path, *Advances in Climate Change Research*, 2017 no. 2, pp. 128–137.
3. Third National Assessment Report on Climate Change Editorial Committee. (2015). *3rd National assessment report on climate change* (pp. 13–22). Beijing: Science Press.
4. IPCC. (1999). *Special report on aviation*. Cambridge, UK: Cambridge University Press.

MIX
Papier aus verantwortungsvollen Quellen
Paper from responsible sources
FSC® C105338

If you have any concerns about our products,
you can contact us on
ProductSafety@springernature.com

In case Publisher is established outside the EU,
the EU authorized representative is:
Springer Nature Customer Service Center GmbH
Europaplatz 3, 69115 Heidelberg, Germany

Printed by Libri Plureos GmbH
in Hamburg, Germany